Aquinas's
Ethics

Aquinas's Ethics

Metaphysical Foundations, Moral Theory, and Theological Context

Rebecca Konyndyk DeYoung,
Colleen McCluskey, and Christina Van Dyke

University of Notre Dame Press
Notre Dame, Indiana

Copyright © 2009 by University of Notre Dame
Notre Dame, Indiana 46556
www.undpress.nd.edu
All Rights Reserved

Manufactured in the United States of America

Library of Congress Cataloging-in-Publication Data

DeYoung, Rebecca Konyndyk.
    Aquinas's ethics : metaphysical foundations, moral theory, and
theological context / Rebecca Konyndyk DeYoung, Colleen McCluskey,
and Christina Van Dyke.
        p.   cm.
    Includes bibliographical references and index.
    ISBN-13: 978-0-268-02601-1 (pbk. : alk. paper)
    ISBN-10: 0-268-02601-7 (pbk. : alk. paper)
    1. Thomas, Aquinas, Saint, 1225?–1274.   2. Ethics, Medieval.
I. McCluskey, Colleen, 1957–   II. Dyke, Christina van, 1972–
III. Title.
    B765.T54D475   2009
    241'.042092— dc22

                                                2009006989

∞ *The paper in this book meets the guidelines for permanence and
durability of the Committee on Production Guidelines for Book Longevity
of the Council on Library Resources.*

for Eleonore Stump,

who first inspired this project and whose work on Aquinas

continues to inspire us

contents

Acknowledgments   xi

List of Abbreviations   xv

Introduction   *1*
Aquinas's Connection to Aristotle   3
Happiness as the End of Human Nature and Human Actions   7

PART ONE

HUMAN NATURE

One   The Metaphysics of Human Nature   *13*
           The Hierarchy of Being   14
           Two Ends of the Spectrum: Pure Actuality and Pure Potentiality   18
           Material Substances, Intellects, and Human Beings   20
           Being and Goodness: God, Creatures, and Function   24

Two   Soul and Body   *27*
           Soul   28
           Bodies, Matter, and Human Beings   35
           Souls in Separation from Matter   40
           Human Persons   43

Three   Human Capacities and the Image of God   *46*
        Essence and Capacity   *49*
        The Soul's Capacities in General   *50*
        Specific Capacities of the Rational Soul   *52*
        Intellect and Will   *57*
        Being and Goodness Revisited   *63*

PART TWO

HUMAN ACTIONS

Four   Actions and Ends   *69*
        The Source of Human Action   *70*
        The Ultimate End of Action   *73*
        The Process of Action: Intellect and Will   *78*
        The Process of Action: Passion   *85*

Five   The Moral Appraisal of Actions   *90*
        Good and Bad Actions in General   *90*
        A Closer Look at Bad Actions   *96*
        Sins of Ignorance   *98*
        Sins of Passion   *102*
        Sins of the Will   *104*

Six   Habits and Freedom   *110*
        Habit Formation   *110*
        Freedom of Action   *115*
        Aquinas in the Current Debate   *123*
        The Road Ahead   *124*

PART THREE

HUMAN FLOURISHING

Seven The Virtues   *129*
         What Is a Virtue? *131*
         Kinds of Virtues *137*
         A Closer Look at the Theological Virtues *147*

Eight Law and Grace   *152*
         Law *152*
         Defending an Integrationist Reading of Aquinas's Ethics *159*
         Grace *165*
         Virtue, Law, and Grace as Interior and Exterior Guides to Action *169*

Nine   Theologically Transformed Virtue and Vice   *173*
         The Vice of Sloth *175*
         The Virtue of Courage *181*

         Epilogue   *188*

         Notes *190*

         Index *237*

acknowledgments

This book has been a long time coming. When Rebecca, Colleen, and I first began the conversations that led to our thinking that it would be a great idea for us to sit down and write a book together, we were all (very) junior scholars, and the millennium was just getting underway. It should come as no real surprise, then, that the number of people to whom we owe thanks for their support and encouragement over the course of this project far exceeds the number to whom we can do justice in these acknowledgments. We offer our deepest apologies to all those who deserve more (and better) thanks than we can give them here.

This project went through two distinct phases, each of which was supported by a separate grant: first, a three-year Initiative Grant from the Coalition of Christian Colleges and Universities facilitated our initial conversations on this topic at summer workshops and conferences; second, a two-year grant from the Calvin Center for Christian Scholarship supported our meeting to discuss the manuscript while it was in progress, as well as funding one course-release apiece. As anyone who has collaborated on a long-term project with colleagues at different universities knows, this type of support was absolutely essential for the completion of this book. Our heartfelt thanks to both the CCCU (particularly Harold Heie) and the CCCS — especially to Jim Bratt and Donna Romanowski, whose good-humored flexibility allowed us to rearrange funding timetables and course releases to meet unexpected changes in our schedules.

The CCCU grant culminated in a two-day conference held at Saint Louis University on April 11–12, 2003, which focused on the major themes of our project. The success of the conference encouraged us to stop talking about how Aquinas's ethics needs to be understood in its metaphysical and theological context and to start writing about it instead. We'd like to thank Denis Bradley, Thomas Hibbs, Scott MacDonald, Bob Pasnau, Brian Shanley, Eleonore Stump, and Thomas Williams for their willingness to speak on "our" topic and for their insightful contributions. In addition to CCCU funds, the conference was supported by a variety of sources at Saint Louis University, including the Department of Philosophy, the Wade Memorial Session, the College of Arts and Sciences, the Center for Medieval and Renaissance Studies, and the Manresa Program in Catholic Studies. Ted Vitali, SLU "chair extraordinaire," has been a source of constant enthusiasm for our project since its inception, as well as for our scholarly abilities; he is just one of the many people in our home departments who merit far more gratitude than we can express here. Our thanks, nonetheless, to all the wonderful folks in the philosophy departments at Saint Louis University and Calvin College, especially Eleonore Stump (to whom we owe special thanks for encouraging us to begin this project and for her sustained support during the long process of its completion), John Kavanaugh, Terence Cuneo, Ruth Groenhout, and Del Ratzsch. Additional thanks go to those in other departments who have commented on earlier versions of individual chapters, including Jeff Brower, Scott MacDonald, and John O'Callaghan.

Writing a book with two other people that attempts to present a single argument in a unified voice is a daunting task—and one of the reasons this book has been so long in the making. Each of us read and commented on several versions of the others' chapters, and each of us tried to abide by the others' general rules of writing. Still, the voice of the book as a whole would be far more fractured if it weren't for the hard work and meticulous attention of Gayle Boss, who was the first person (other than us) brave enough to read through the entire manuscript and offer extensive suggestions for copyediting. Comments from the anonymous referees at the University of Notre Dame Press also proved helpful in this respect; we are especially grateful for the substantive suggestions provided by those referees, and we accept full responsibility for any errors that remain in the text.

There is an awkwardness inherent to the "family and friends" acknowledgments section of a coauthored book, which we have decided to handle by taking a completely generic route: our many thanks, then, to all our friends and family members for their love, support, and encouragement. We may not be mentioning you all by name, but our appreciation is no less sincere. You are an integral part of our attempt to live flourishing Christian lives.

Christina Van Dyke

abbreviations

Works by Thomas Aquinas:

DEE   *De ente et essentia* (On Being and Essence)

DPN   *De principiis naturae* (On the Principles of Nature)

DSS   *De substantiis separatis* (On Separated Substances [Angels])

In Sent   *Scriptum super libros Sententiarum* (Commentary on the Sentences)

QDA   *Quaestio disputata de anima* (Disputed Question on the Soul)

QDM   *Quaestiones disputatae de malo* (Disputed Questions on Evil)

QDP   *Quaestiones disputatae de potentia* (Disputed Questions on Power)

QDSC   *Quaestio disputatae de spiritualibus creaturis* (Disputed Questions on Spiritual Creatures [Angels])

QDV   *Quaestiones disputatae de veritate* (Disputed Questions on Truth)

QDVC   *Quaestiones disputatae de virtutibus in communi* (Disputed Questions on the Virtues in General)

SCG   *Summa contra gentiles* (Summary [of Christian Doctrine] Directed against Unbelievers)

ST   *Summa theologiae* (Summary of Theology)

Note on *ST* references: The *Summa theologiae,* the most frequently cited work in these pages, consists of three main parts (I, II, III). Each part contains numbered questions with numbered subsections called articles.

Articles include numbered objections to a thesis, a passage beginning "On the contrary" (in Latin, *sed contra*), a passage beginning "I reply that," and specific numbered replies to the numbered objections. In the reference system employed here, "*ST* Ia.77.4.ad 3" refers to part I (the "a" in Ia is from Latin, *prima*), question 77, article 4, reply to objection 3. Part II of the *Summa theologiae* divides into two large sections, referred to as *ST* IaIIae (section I of Part II; in Latin, *prima secundae*) and *ST* IIaIIae (section II of Part II; in Latin, *secunda secundae*). "*ST* IIaIIae.124.5 reply and ad 2" refers to the passage "I reply that" and the specific reply to objection 2, in section II of Part II, question 124, article 5.

Introduction

St. Thomas Aquinas (1224/25–1274) is a towering figure in the history of philosophy; few scholars can rival either the breadth or the depth of his intellectual pursuits. Above and beyond his independent works (including, most famously, the *Summa theologiae* and the *Summa contra gentiles*), Aquinas also wrote extensive commentaries on most of Aristotle's treatises and on numerous books of the Bible. In addition, he participated actively in the intellectual debates of his day, writing strongly against philosophical and theological doctrines that he thought were erroneous. His scholarly accomplishments have been renowned in philosophical and theological circles for over 750 years.

Aquinas's reputation for brilliance is somewhat dulled, however, by his reputation for tedious prose and meticulous attention to detail. In general, his style of careful argumentation, set in the question-and-answer format that epitomizes high medieval scholarship, is often caricatured as concerned primarily with abstract questions, such as how many angels can dance on the head of a pin.[1] Yet, as we will argue in this book, to think of Aquinas's philosophical project—and, in particular, his ethics—as irrelevant to modern life is to miss its central point. When one takes the time to fit the different pieces of his thought together, one is rewarded with a richly integrated picture of the genuinely happy human life.

Why is it, after all, that two people can live on the same street, work at the same job, and yet one person experiences constant frustration and anxiety in his life while the other flourishes? Is it better to become a marine biologist or a day-care worker? Can anyone justify becoming a professional musician when people are starving throughout the world? How are we to think about the ultimate purpose of our lives—how are we, for example, to balance personal fulfillment with the demands of living in community?

Aquinas's account of human nature and human flourishing turns out to provide a meaningful framework in which to answer pressing life questions. While recognizing that each of us possesses unique talents and shortcomings, he describes a general picture of the flourishing life that proves as provocative, challenging, and attractive today as it first did over seven hundred years ago. Our central goal in this book is to present this rich picture to readers who lack the time or technical expertise to undertake the project themselves.

Aquinas develops his account of the genuinely happy life within a complex metaphysical and theological framework; thus, a large part of our task will be to examine his understanding of what human beings are and how and why they act. With this foundation in place, we'll be able to properly appreciate his conception of the good life human beings are meant to live.

Aquinas's own life underscores his belief that scholarly pursuits can—and perhaps *should*—have practical as well as abstract or contemplative results. When his politically-minded family pressured him to join the highly respected and well-established Benedictine monastic order, Aquinas did not object to the idea of a religious career in and of itself. Instead of choosing the Benedictines, however, he insisted on joining the recently formed Dominican order, a religious order with considerably less prestige and a radical social mission. Founded in 1217 by St. Dominic, a leader with a strong desire to revitalize the church's mission and to rescue it from religious apathy and power-hungry clergy, the Dominican order dedicated itself to a life that combined quiet prayer and contemplation with active Christian service. Like the Franciscans (another recently founded religious order), the Dominicans served as itinerant teachers and preachers, explicitly pursuing intellectual formation *for the sake of* spiritual formation. By joining this order, Aquinas was consciously choosing to integrate the work of his intellectual and spiritual contemplation with an active life of preaching and teaching.

Contemporary readers can see this integration in Aquinas's developed account of human virtue. Instead of focusing purely on a theoretical understanding of the nature of a good moral character, Aquinas also provides practical instruction for living well. When he discusses virtues and vices in the *Summa theologiae,* for example, he addresses not just abstract questions, such as how we should define virtue, but also practical issues, such as how to show gratitude toward someone who does us a favor we are too poor to repay. This dual concern shows up repeatedly in his ethical works and underscores his commitment to putting belief into action.

AQUINAS'S CONNECTION TO ARISTOTLE

The strategy of Aquinas's ethical theory closely mirrors Aristotle's approach in the *Nicomachean Ethics.* Aristotle (384–322 B.C.), whose work profoundly influenced Aquinas's thought, has an explicitly practical aim in his *Ethics*: he wants to explain to people what the true nature of happiness is, so that they can work toward actually living the happy life. According to both Aristotle and Aquinas, every human being desires her or his own happiness, and all human beings do what they do for the sake of becoming happy. Since both see happiness as the end goal of human life and the fulfillment of human nature, they approach ethics as the study of how human beings can best fulfill their nature and obtain happiness. Ethics thus has a practical as well as a theoretical goal. Its dual purpose naturally affects how we should undertake its study. In the same way that the point of going to the doctor with a persistent migraine is not simply to learn more about the migraine but to actively rid oneself of the pain, so the point of reading ethics and thinking about how we should live our lives is to actually live our lives differently—to live them *better.*

Aquinas and Aristotle agree both that the study of ethics should have a practical goal and that the life of happiness is the end goal for human beings. Because they begin with differing metaphysical and theological commitments, however, they diverge when they approach the nature of this ultimate end. Aristotle stresses our status as rational animals and describes the happy life rather broadly as "the life of activity expressing reason well."[2] Aquinas, on the other hand, emphasizes our status as beings created by God; the point of the ethical life for Aquinas is, correspondingly, not just a life of flourishing rationality but, more specifically, a life of intimate union with God. Thus, while Aristotle is highly interested in moral education and character formation, Aquinas sees the deeper purpose of moral education and character formation as preparing us for union with God. Aristotle believes that having the right moral character is necessary for the flourishing human life, and that the right use of reason will show us what counts as the right sort of moral character. Aquinas believes that we are created in God's image, and that we flourish most when our likeness is closest to that image — that is, when we most closely resemble God in the ways appropriate to human beings.

As we demonstrate throughout this book, Aquinas's central project in his ethics is grounded in these metaphysical and theological beliefs. Indeed, one of the most striking features of Aquinas's scholarship is its conscious synthesis of Aristotelian philosophy with his Christian beliefs. He is sometimes said to "baptize Aristotle," but what Aquinas does in his independent works (such as *Summa theologiae*) goes much deeper than sprinkling a few Christian sentiments over a generally pagan system; rather, his theological commitments permeate his philosophical system. By keeping Aquinas's Christian beliefs firmly in mind, we will better understand three central components of his philosophy: the metaphysics of his account of human nature, the theory of action he develops on the basis of that metaphysics, and his ethical theory. With this approach, readers can appreciate the full richness and value of Aquinas's thought.

To demonstrate why we believe a proper understanding of Aquinas's philosophy requires its being seen as part of this larger picture, it is useful to turn to *Summa theologiae* IaIIae, questions 1–5. These five questions, commonly referred to as the treatise on happiness, are a prime example of how Aquinas actively integrates his theological beliefs with an Aristotelian metaphysical and ethical system. Over the course of these questions, Aquinas addresses the opening book of Aristotle's *Nicomachean Ethics,* a book that culminates with Aristotle's famous function argument for human happiness. By examining briefly both the original function argument and Aquinas's treatment of it, we can see how Aquinas simultaneously accepts and transforms Aristotelian claims within a deeply Christian context.

In the *Nicomachean Ethics* 1.7, Aristotle makes a connection between something's nature and its function. He claims that everything has a function or a characteristic activity. The function of a knife, for example, is "to cut." The fact that a knife's function is cutting is hardly accidental to its being a knife; rather, a thing's characteristic activity relates directly to its nature. Broadly speaking, what a thing *is* explains what that thing properly *does*. So, for example, the fact that a knife's essence just is "cutting tool" accounts for the fact that the function of a knife is "to cut."

Human beings, too, have a function, one that is best understood by reference to their nature. According to Aristotle, humans are rational animals. They are animals insofar as they are living, breathing physical creatures, but they differ from all other animals in their ability to cognize — that is, in their rational abilities. This understanding of human nature gives us the key to identifying the human function: since, by nature, an animal lives a life of activity (perceiving with its senses, seeking food, shelter, etc.) and since, by nature, a rational being engages in intellectual cognition, the function of a rational animal must be "a life of activity expressing reason." Thus, the characteristic activity of a human being — the activity that fully captures what it is to be human — is not just activity common to other animals but activity that specifically employs our rational capacities.

Although grounded in Aristotle's metaphysical beliefs, this description of the human function also has deep implications for his ethics. Aristotle holds that a thing's virtue — its excellence — necessarily involves that thing's performing its function *well*. (Aristotle's claim here is a metaphysical one: to say a knife is excellent or virtuous insofar as it cuts well is to say that it is a good knife, not that it is a *morally* good knife.)[3] A thing is excellent precisely when it does a good job in carrying out its characteristic activity. A knife's function is to cut, and so its virtue or excellence consists in its actively cutting well. In the same way, since the human function involves a life of activity expressing reason, human virtue — human excellence — consists in performing that function well. (In this connection, it is important to remember that reasoning itself counts as an action.) Thus, our excellence consists not merely in employing our rational capacities but in employing them *well*.

Aristotle goes on in the *Ethics* to link virtue with human happiness. The highest good, he claims, is happiness. Moreover, the good of a human being is his or her happiness, and what's good *for* a human being is to be good *at* the human function. This might at first seem puzzling, but if one's function follows directly from one's nature, then performing that function actualizes that nature; the better you are at your function, the more you fulfill your nature. Thus, there does seem to be a clear sense in which being good at the human function — living a life of activity expressing reason — is good for you. When you are good at it, you exist fully as the very sort of thing you are. You actualize all of your natural abilities in the best possible way. This radical fulfillment of your nature is happiness, and so, Aristotle concludes, happiness for human beings is itself the life of activity expressing reason well; or, as he also puts it, happiness is the life of activity expressing virtue.[4]

Aquinas fundamentally agrees with Aristotle both that human beings are rational animals and that the human function can be properly understood as living the life of activity expressing reason. He also agrees that human excellence consists in performing that function well. He holds, however, that these claims need to be further understood in the context of our status as created beings. In the prologue to his treatise on happiness, Aquinas states that human beings are created in the image of God. This fact is essential to understanding their nature, he claims, since "human beings are said to be made in the image of God, where 'image' signifies 'intellectual being who possesses both free choice and power over its actions.'" What it means for us to be created in God's image, according to Aquinas, is, first and foremost, that we possess intellect, will, and the resulting ability to act on our own power. This link to the Creator further explains why our function involves both reasoning well and acting on the basis of that reasoning. We have intellects and wills, capacities that allow us to discover what our powers to act are intended *for* and how we are meant to act. In short, we are teleological beings, created by God with a particular function and for a particular purpose.

Although Aquinas agrees with Aristotle's basic metaphysical and ethical claims concerning the human function, excellence, and happiness, then, he goes beyond Aristotle in arguing that what it means for us to live "the life of activity expressing reason well" needs to be understood in the context of our relationship to the Creator. In particular, Aquinas claims that our excellence consists in the activity of knowing and loving God.

Thus, when Aristotle identifies happiness as the highest good and our ultimate end, Aquinas concurs—and then he identifies that highest good with God. Again, when Aristotle argues that the activity of happiness consists in the fullest expression of our rational powers, Aquinas agrees—and then he explains that the fullest expression of our rational powers involves both the cognition of our ultimate end and the proper response to that knowledge. For him, the activity of human happiness consists both in our cognition of God, our ultimate end, and in our appropriate reaction to that ultimate end—namely, love. The activity of human happiness thus maximizes our nature as created rational beings by putting our distinctively human capacities to their best possible use. Since human beings are unique among animals by being created in God's image, by possessing intellect and will, perfect human happiness involves knowing God through our intellects and loving God with our wills.

This brief glance at Aquinas's interpretation of the function argument demonstrates both how his ethical system depends on his theories of human nature and human actions and how Aquinas freely directs Aristotle's basic philosophical precepts toward an explicitly Christian end. It also gives us a basic idea of the flourishing human life as he understands it.

Happiness as the End of Human Nature and Human Actions

Human beings are notorious for failing to flourish, however. In fact, even if we had enormous amounts of time, energy, and money to devote to satisfying our wants and needs, few of us would count as happy on either Aristotle's or Aquinas's standard. Part of the problem, as both scholars would be quick to observe, is our ignorance of what our end actually is. There is much more to the story of human misery, however, and an integrated reading of Aquinas's thought on human nature and action can provide a surprisingly cogent explanation for our unhappiness. In particular, his account of our actions as the end-product of a complex series of interactions between the intellect and the will can help us see more clearly both how we often fall short of fulfilling our own nature and the consequences this has for our moral life. Just as importantly, it can help us understand how Aquinas believes we can become right again—with ourselves, with others, and with God.

To *present our reading of Aquinas's ethics within its original philosophical* and theological context, we have divided this book into three main parts: one addressing his metaphysics, one examining his action theory, and the last showing how Aquinas believes virtue, law, and grace fit together in the flourishing human life of happiness.[5] As we will see, to fully comprehend his ethical theory we need to understand why Aquinas characterizes properly human actions as interactions between intellect and will. To appreciate his descriptions of these interactions, however, we must begin with his account of the nature of human beings as rational animals, created in the image of God.

For this reason the first chapter lays out the metaphysical foundations of Aquinas's account of human nature, focusing on the particular niche that human beings occupy in the continuum between pure actuality (God) and pure potentiality (prime matter). In the second chapter we move to a closer discussion of human nature. We examine how Aquinas's claims that we are composites of matter and form and that we are physical bodies with immaterial intellects presents a picture of human nature in which our physicality is essential to us—in which human beings are living bodies. Finally, in chapter 3 we turn to Aquinas's account of human capacities, since what human beings *are* relates closely to what they can *do.* The most important capacities for our purposes are, of course, intellect and will, and so part 1 of this book concludes with a discussion of those two capacities.

In part 2 (chapters 4–6) we build on this picture of intellect and will by looking at Aquinas's complex and interesting account of human actions. In chapter 4 we consider why we perform any actions at all—that is, we examine the ultimate goal or purpose of our actions. Next we look at what Aquinas thinks we are doing when we perform an action. We can think of this as the mechanics of action: how Aquinas accounts for the fact that human actions are produced in the first place. Understanding the mechanics of action enables us to appreciate what it is to perform good actions and how action goes wrong, which is the focus of chapter 5. Finally, in chapter 6, we consider the freedom of human action. Freedom is an important condition for moral appraisal; ordinarily we do not think that individuals should be held accountable for their actions if it turns out that they did not perform those actions freely. Human freedom also generates certain tensions with other commitments within Aquinas's ethics—the efficacy of grace, for example. Thus, both chapters 5 and 6 set the stage for understanding Aquinas's ethical theory, which is the focus of part 3.

In this last part (chapters 7–9) we examine three integrated elements of Aquinas's moral thought—virtue, law, and grace—in order to understand his conception of human flourishing. First, we address the way virtues perfect the human capacities that are essential to flourishing and show how perfection in virtue unites us with God. Our union with God, for Aquinas, is a relationship modeled on Aristotelian friendship, a relationship based on goodness of character and a shared love of the good. This love, which Aquinas calls charity (*caritas*), is an activity specific to human beings and other persons (such as God and the angels), in that it requires intellect and will.[6] Second, we examine the way that law and grace, rather than standing apart from virtue, are an integral part of this picture of human moral formation. Law and grace show us how and why divine agency is necessary for us to reach our ultimate end, but in a way that leaves room for our freedom. Finally, through a study of a particular virtue and vice, we demonstrate how Aquinas's theological commitments and, in particular, the centrality of the theological virtue of charity shape both the content and purpose of his ethical work.

It is our hope that by the end of this book, readers will understand Aquinas's ethical theory within its original context; furthermore, we hope that our readers will be drawn to share our appreciation for both the usefulness and the appeal of Aquinas's account of the good life.

One further introductory remark is in order: given Aquinas's stature in the history of philosophy and his thorough treatment of topics of perennial interest to professionals as well as nonprofessionals in both philosophy and theology, it should come as no surprise that the examination of the three central areas of his work addressed in this book constitutes an industry in itself. While no one can expect to do full justice to Aquinas's thought without addressing this rich and complex secondary literature, we have made a deliberate decision not to engage that literature directly here. Each of us is conversant with the appropriate literature, and it has influenced our own interpretations of Aquinas's texts in significant ways — ways we have explicitly addressed elsewhere. For the purposes of this work, however, we have chosen to focus on our own explications of Aquinas's views (especially those found in his most famous text, *Summa theologiae*) in order to give the reader an appreciation for the breadth, depth, internal cohesiveness, and ultimate practicality of Aquinas's account. We have avoided the kinds of distractions that would naturally arise in a project that strove both to provide a substantive interpretation of Aquinas's ethical theory — including its complex foundations — and to address the many controversial issues that occur in the secondary literature. Of course, sophisticated readers will realize that our elucidation is not the only alternative; we encourage these readers to pursue further study both of Aquinas's own texts and of the voluminous secondary literature. In fact, if this book leads to such study, we will consider that an equally welcome result of our work here.

Given this approach, we expect that this volume will prove especially useful to those readers who are encountering Aquinas for the first (or perhaps the second) time. Nevertheless, we also hope that experts in this area will find our book interesting and relevant for their own purposes. While our approach leaves open exactly how we respond to interpretive debates in the wider literature, we trust that our offering provides food for thought even for those thoroughly conversant with Aquinas's views.

Human Nature

one

The Metaphysics
of Human Nature

The question of who we are — of what we are — lies at the heart of Aquinas's account of happiness. We must understand what human beings *are* in order to see what they can do, and know what they are *able* to do before we can appreciate how they actually act. Only when we grasp the inner workings of human actions, moreover, can we fully comprehend how and why we *should* act — that is, the best sort of life we can lead.

In this chapter we examine the place of human beings in the universe as a whole. We are rational animals, Aquinas claims, but how are we to understand this? What does it mean to be rational, and what difference does it make that we are *animals* with reasoning capacities? The fact that we are intellective organisms possesses enormous significance for Aquinas's conception of human nature and of human flourishing. According to Aquinas, all of reality is ordered in an elaborate "hierarchy of being" with God at the top. Human beings alone possess both physical bodies and immaterial intellects; in the hierarchy we bridge the gap between material and immaterial creatures. In an important sense, we live in two worlds: the physical world of rocks and trees and the immaterial world of the intellect. Getting clear on human nature thus requires a closer look at the hierarchy of being in order to understand the place occupied by bodies and intellects in the broader context of God's nature and God's relation to creation. As we will see, the structure of the hierarchy of being gives us insight into human beings both on a "species" level—as members of a common species, possessing the same essential nature—and on an individual level, as creatures who actualize this essential nature in different ways and to varying degrees.

THE HIERARCHY OF BEING

Aquinas believes that everything that exists has a place in the universe, and that its place follows directly from that thing's relation to God. In saying this, of course, he does not mean that everything has a particular *location* in the universe. Rather, he means that every existing thing fits in a special way into a larger schema, and that God is responsible for this schema, or hierarchy. In his view, human beings occupy a particularly interesting place in this hierarchy (insofar as we alone possess characteristics of both material *and* immaterial creatures), but every creature has a special relation to God, and every creature has a particular place in the hierarchy. To see what is most interesting about the human case, first we need to focus not on the unique aspects of our nature but rather on how Aquinas frames that nature in the larger context of the hierarchy of being.[1]

It is essential to note that all creatures have their place in the hierarchy from their relation to God, and that all things depend on God both for their coming into existence and for their continuing to exist. According to Aquinas, the creator of the cosmos is not an impersonal force that merely put into motion the process that resulted in our world. Neither is God a personal but disinterested artisan who crafted the universe and then left it to its own devices, like a divine watchmaker or homebuilder. Instead, God is an all-powerful, all-knowing, and completely good Being who remains intimately involved in creation, constantly working for its good. God is the Alpha and the Omega—the beginning and end of everything that is, that was, and that will be. In other words, God is both the first cause of all things that exist and their final end, the very purpose for their existence. Aquinas endorses Augustine's famous sentiment that our hearts are restless until they rest in God: everything receives its nature from God, and everything fulfills its nature only when it comes into right relation with God.

This central belief can be seen in the structure of Aquinas's best-known work, the *Summa theologiae,* in which God is both the beginning and the end of the discussion; God is that which explains the existence, status, and function of everything else.[2] Thus, Aquinas begins Part I of the *Summa* with a discussion of God's nature, moving on to address how created beings such as angels, material substances, and humans all need to be understood as proceeding from God. In Part II Aquinas concentrates on the special case of human beings; he explains how human actions, natural law, virtue, and grace all play a role in the fulfillment of our ultimate end, which is to make our way back to the Creator. Part III (left incomplete at Aquinas's death) addresses that way back to God and focuses on the aspects of God's nature for which we need divine revelation, the work of Christ and the specific practices of the Christian church through which God exercises salvific causality, such as baptism and the Eucharist. As he makes clear throughout the *Summa,* Aquinas believes that human nature can never be fully understood apart from God, and that we will never be content until we realize our place in relation to God and our dependence on God.

Human nature thus needs to be understood, first and foremost, in terms of our place in the general structure of the universe. Aquinas believes that the function of wisdom is to order things.[3] That is, rational beings are naturally disposed to structure the world around them. Beings that reason well, moreover—*wise* beings—do not structure or order things haphazardly; they order things *well.* Thus, it should come as no surprise that God, the supremely rational and perfectly wise Being, would produce a highly structured, complexly ordered universe in which everything has its proper place. It should come as no surprise, either, that humans, who are created in God's image, share this affinity for order, and that we flourish when we order things—including ourselves—well.

Aquinas identifies two central organizing principles for the hierarchy of being: actuality and potentiality. From angels to mushrooms, from tigers to granite, all things fit into a wonderfully complex continuum organized in terms of these two principles. As we will see, the actuality/ potentiality distinction sets God and prime matter as the endpoints of this continuum;[4] Aquinas's characterization of these endpoints also helps us understand human nature more clearly.

It might seem strange at first to think of mushrooms and tigers as falling at different points on a continuum that ranges from pure potentiality to pure actuality. Yet for Aquinas, this is a natural result of the way he thinks of the differences between species. Following Aristotle, he identifies a species as a class of beings who possess the same essential nature. When we "carve reality at the joints"—when we pick out the natural kinds that things fall into—we are picking out species.[5] So, for example, all individual human beings count as members of the same species in virtue of having the same essence, namely, "rational animality." If one imagines the hierarchy of being as a ladder that stretches from God all the way down to pure potentiality, then the rungs of the ladder are made up of natural kinds, or species.[6] Individual things occupy a particular place on the hierarchy only by virtue of their membership in a species. An individual tiger, for instance, shares a rung only with other tigers and not with mushrooms or angels; each species occupies a distinct rung of the ladder of being.

What places one species higher or lower than another on this hierarchy of being is, in short, the extent to which that species more or less closely resembles the fully actual God. According to Aquinas, only God exists necessarily. Neither a mushroom nor a tiger nor an angel could exist apart from God, and so no creature is actual in the sense that God is. Nevertheless, each creature can receive "participated existence" (that is, it can receive existence directly from God) to a certain extent—an extent determined by the natural capacities unique to the species of which it is a member. In Aquinas's words, "Participated existence is limited to the capacity of what participates in it."[7] That is, a species' unique set of capacities limits the extent to which its individual members can participate in God's existence. If tigers are closer to God on the hierarchy than mushrooms, the explanation is that tigers possess a set of capacities that allow them to participate more fully in existence than mushrooms can.

But how are we to understand the claim that a thing's capacities limit its existence?[8] In brief, Aquinas holds that some capacities are of a higher order than others,[9] and that a creature with lower-ordered capacities exists less fully than a creature with higher capacities. Thus, a thing's place in the hierarchy is determined by its possession (or lack) of certain key capacities. The three most relevant sets of capacities, ordered from least to greatest importance, are a familiar trio in the history of philosophy: vegetative or nutritive powers, sensory powers, and intellective powers.

Nutritive powers are the lowest-level capacities of the three; they are powers common to all (physical) living things, and Aquinas claims that it is better to have vegetative life than merely to exist, where he is thinking of "life" primarily in terms of activity.[10] A mushroom's capacity for taking in food, growing, and producing other mushrooms, for instance, places it in the hierarchy above a chunk of granite and a pool of water, neither of which are capable of such directed movement. In general, living things fall higher on the hierarchy than nonliving things. On Aquinas's view it is also better, however, to have sense perception and the corresponding ability to move oneself toward or away from objects of perception than it is merely to have the capacity for growth and nutrition. Thus, a tiger's capacity for smelling the antelope, spotting it moving through the grass, and chasing it down gives it a higher place in the hierarchy than the mushroom. In general, the tiger is able to engage with and respond to the world around it more fully than the mushroom can; in this sense, it exists more fully.

Aquinas holds, moreover, that the creatures capable of engaging with the world *most* fully are intellective beings, since intellective creatures can know and love the beings around them in ways similar, in relevant respects, to God's knowledge and love. For this reason, it is better to have the capacity for intellective thought than simply to have the capacity for sense perception and/or growth and nutrition.[11] According to Aquinas, in fact, intellective cognition is so far superior to nutrition and sense perception that only lower-level intellects — only human beings, as it turns out — even need the other two sets of capacities in order to function. Intellective capacities entail a greater degree of similarity to God and, therefore, a higher degree of actuality; thus, intellective beings belong higher up on the hierarchy than non-intellective beings.[12]

This general point about the structure of the hierarchy of being becomes clearer, perhaps, if we recognize the natural relation Aquinas sees between actuality and perfection. In Latin the word *perfectio,* commonly

translated as "perfection," also means finished, complete—and fully actual. In Aquinas's words, "Anything whatever is perfect to the extent to
which it is in actuality."[13] The more in actuality a thing is, then, the more
perfect it is. When we apply this connection between actuality and perfection to the hierarchy of being, we see that the claim that the continuum progresses in degrees from the most actual (and least potential)
being to the most potential (and least actual) being is also the claim that
the continuum progresses from the most perfect (the most actual) being
to the least perfect (the least actual) being. As Aquinas puts it, things "differ in their degree of perfection, depending on their distance from potentiality and their closeness to pure act."[14] Insofar as a thing possesses
higher-order capacities, it is more perfect than a creature that possesses
only lower-order capacities; higher-order capacities by nature include
everything that is desirable about the lower-order capacities. Thus, on
this view, a creature that possesses sensory capacities always also possesses
vegetative capacities, and an animal that possesses rational capacities also
possesses vegetative and sensory powers. The further up the hierarchy,
moreover, the closer things get to having all the desirable lower-order
capacities contained in one universal and comprehensive higher-order
capacity.

Two Ends of the Spectrum: Pure Actuality and Pure Potentiality

The being that possesses all perfections in one simple act of being
constitutes the culmination of the hierarchy. This being is, of course, God.
God is the "top" of the continuum, and, as we have already seen, his nature as pure actuality provides the ultimate explanation for where everything else in the cosmos falls.

Having now discussed the general organizing principles for the
hierarchy—potentiality and actuality—we can turn to a more detailed
discussion of the main divisions within the hierarchy, beginning with
an examination of its endpoints: pure actuality and pure potentiality. As
we will see, Aquinas's description of the continuum as ranging from the
perfectly actualized God to purely potential prime matter gives us fur-

ther insight into his claim that human beings are composites of rational souls joined to matter.

According to Aquinas, "God is actuality itself."[15] God is the one wholly actual, fully existing being; given Aquinas's equation of perfection with actuality, God is therefore also the one wholly perfect being.[16] Furthermore, God is not only *a* perfect being—a being whose essence is completely actualized existence—God himself *is* perfect being. As the famous medieval dictum goes, God is the only being whose essence is identical with its existence or "act of being" (its *esse*).[17] The fact that God is pure actuality entails that there is no way God could be that he is not already; there is, strictly speaking, no potentiality of any kind present in God.[18] Further, because higher-order capacities or perfections contain everything good or valuable in lower-order capacities, God as Absolutely Perfect Being contains every possible perfection in a completely unified and actual way.[19] God's being is, thus, according to Aquinas, absolutely simple.[20]

Everything apart from God, however, is composite, meaning that every created thing contains some combination of potentiality and actuality, right down to the point of complete potentiality—namely, what Aquinas refers to as "prime matter." The possibility that there is something that is by nature completely *unactualized* presents a certain puzzle, however. The hierarchy of being is, as its name implies, a ranking of *beings,* a ranking of existing things. Yet the very fact that prime matter is pure potentiality seems to entail that it cannot exist, for an individual existing thing is nothing other than "a being in actuality."[21] As Aquinas himself says, prime matter "cannot exist in actuality, since existing in actuality does not occur apart from a form; [instead] it exists only in potentiality."[22]

What, then, is prime matter? In actuality, it is nothing. Yet it still occupies the far end of the hierarchy of being—not as a being in its own right, but as an important idea or conceptual tool.[23] The point on a continuum of being furthest from a purely actual God is matter *considered* completely apart from any sort of form or actuality, not matter *existing* completely apart from any sort of form, for that would be impossible.[24] This also creates a neat symmetry between the endpoints of the hierarchy of being, since it entails that neither end of the continuum is a creature, properly speaking. God is the Creator and source of everything else's existence, not a created being himself, and prime matter is not a being at all, strictly speaking.

MATERIAL SUBSTANCES, INTELLECTS, AND HUMAN BEINGS

Every created being—from angels to tigers to granite—falls somewhere between pure actuality and pure potentiality on the hierarchy of being. As Aquinas puts it: "In beings, there are grades of actuality and potentiality. One being, prime matter, exists in potentiality only. Another being, God, exists in complete actuality. All other intermediate beings exist both in actuality and in potentiality."[25] Indeed, the place of every creature on the hierarchy can be understood in relation to those two endpoints. The more actualized a being is, the closer it is to God and the further away it is from prime matter—in fact, the further away it is from matter altogether.

The reason for this metaphysical distance, of course, is that Aquinas holds that matter is, by its very nature, potentiality. That is why pure *potentiality* is prime *matter;* it is matter in its rawest form. The less actual and the less perfect something is, the closer it is to prime matter, and the more likely it is to be itself material. On the other hand, the more actual and the more perfect something is, the closer it is to the immaterial God, and the more likely it is to be immaterial. Given the endpoints of the hierarchy, it should come as no surprise that the two main classes into which Aquinas divides creatures are immaterial and material. A brief discussion of these two central divisions will illuminate the peculiar case of human beings, who (as composites of immaterial souls and material bodies) fall right on the dividing line between them.

Material Beings

Aquinas draws a direct connection between intellective capacities and actuality; God—pure actuality—is also perfectly intellective.[26] Intellective capacities are thus found only in the beings toward the top of the hierarchy, whereas non-intellective substances (such as tigers, mushrooms, and minerals) are ranked in increasingly close proximity to prime matter depending on the sorts of capacities they possess. Mushrooms rank above minerals, as we saw, because they are living things with vegetative capacities; according to Aquinas, the closer to prime matter something is, the fewer capacities it possesses and the less that thing can "do."

Since matter is, by definition, potentiality, it is not surprising that Aquinas also characterizes the break between intellective and non-intellective creatures as the break between immaterial and material beings.[27] All creatures have essences distinct from their being, insofar as they could fail to exist, and so there is a sense in which all creatures possess potentiality. Physical substances, however, possess not only this general sort of potentiality but also an additional sort, in virtue of their being composed of matter as well as form. That is, all creatures—immaterial and material—have *forms* that have potentiality for *being* (*esse*), but only material creatures also possess *matter* that exists in potentiality for *form*. Physical beings thus have a sort of "double" potentiality.[28] The form of a tiger actualizes the matter that potentially constitutes the tiger; it accounts for the organism's physical structure and biological processes, among other things. At the same time, for an individual tiger to come into existence, God must actualize the essence of "tiger" that exists in potentiality for being.

In addition, the fewer capacities a being possesses, the less actual it is—or, as Aquinas sometimes puts it, the "more immersed in matter" it is. As we saw above, a mushroom falls below a tiger on the hierarchy of being because it possesses only vegetative capacities and not sensory capacities as well. Granite, on the other hand, is less actual than the mushroom, in that it possesses only existence and not also vegetative capacities. On Aquinas's view, moreover, a thing's species-nature is what accounts for the fundamental capacities it possesses. To be a mushroom, a being does not need a sense of sight or smell—but it does need growth and nutrition. To be a tiger, a being does not need to be capable of working multiplication tables—but it does need to be able to smell its prey and chase after it. Furthermore, as we will see in chapter 2, because a material substance's nature is closely linked to its form, its form is what places it in a particular category (or subcategory) on the hierarchy of being.

Intellects

Matter cannot exist without form, according to Aquinas. Certain *forms,* however, can exist apart from *matter.*[29] These forms belong to immaterial substances, also called "separated" or "intellectual" substances— beings that "exist on a level which is far above all matter and all material things."[30] In particular, these "separated" substances are more actual insofar as they possess higher-order capacities, such as intellect and will, that allow them to engage with the creation in a way that mirrors the Creator more closely than other creatures. Indeed, immaterial substances occupy the top rungs of the hierarchy of being—the rungs closest to God. They occupy distinct rungs, however, according to the level of their intellective capacities. In fact, as it turns out, Aquinas's distinction between being and essence allows for a clear hierarchy within the category of intellectual substances that provides insight into what it means for human beings to be both intellective and physical organisms.

The key to understanding the differences between immaterial substances is the relation between essence and form. According to Aquinas, essences are what we capture in a good definition. "Having three sides" is a bad definition of a triangle; a horse stable, for example, can have three sides without being a triangle. "Having three angles equal to 180 degrees," on the other hand, is a successful definition of a triangle because it captures what is characteristic of and essential to all triangles. To capture the true essence of a physical object, Aquinas claims, a definition must refer to both its matter and its form. We can't properly describe a tiger or a mushroom, for example, without referring to its physicality—its matter. Each immaterial being's distinct essence or nature is, however, identical to its form; we can completely capture the nature of an individual angel by making reference only to its form.[31]

Immaterial beings are thus less complex in a certain way than physical creatures. At the same time, however, angels are not completely simple; Aquinas's hierarchy contains only one completely simple being: God. God's essence is identical to God's very being; God exists necessarily. The same cannot be said of other immaterial beings, who depend on God for their being. Since their existence is not necessary, the essences of intellective substances do not themselves include reference to existence. Thus, although not composed of form and matter, immaterial beings are, nevertheless, composed of essence and existence (*essentia* and *esse*).[32]

What distinguishes one immaterial substance from another, then? Quite simply, it comes down to differences between their essences, which Aquinas explains in terms of different levels or degrees of intellective capacities. Material creatures with the same general set of capacities can differ from each other, after all, with respect to the degree to which they possess those capacities. Thus, although both eagles and moles possess the basic capacity for sight, eagles possess this capacity to a higher degree. The mole with the very best possible mole-eyesight, for instance, will still not be able to see as well as an average eagle, for eagles simply possess the capacity for sight to a higher degree than moles. In the same way, immaterial creatures differ from each other with respect to the degree to which they possess the basic intellective capacities.

In short, then, one angel differs from another with respect to its intellectual powers: angels possess intellective capacities to different degrees. God understands both God's own nature and the whole of creation in one eternal act of intellection. The closer an intellective being is to God, the closer it is to this level of simplicity; as Aquinas puts it, the higher angels understand more things using fewer principles.[33] For example, although a lower-level intellect might need to cognize a number of different shapes—triangles, squares, pentagons, and so on—in order to grasp the concept of shape, a higher-level intellect understands the concept of shape immediately and, at the same time, grasps how this concept can be applied in the case of any particular shape possible. A higher-level intellect could also understand the concept of virtue, for instance, without first needing to work through the similarities between justice, piety, and courage.

The relevance of this for our purposes is simply that, according to Aquinas, human beings have the very lowest level of intellect possible. We are the "slow students" of the intellective world; we require so many examples and so much repetition—we possess intellective capacities to such a low degree—that God joins human intellects to sense-perceptive bodies so that they can gather the numerous experiences we need just to grasp abstract concepts like "justice" and "triangle."

Human Beings

Although Aquinas clearly delineates categories on the hierarchy of being (immaterial vs. material beings; sensory vs. nutritive beings), not all creatures fall neatly into a particular category. Rather, as one grade of the hierarchy blends into another, there exist borderline cases. Aquinas calls this the "marvelous connection of things," pointing out that "it is always found that the lowest in the higher genus touches the highest in the lower species."[34] So, for example, a Venus flytrap demonstrates the connection between plants and animals; although it contains primarily plant-like characteristics, it also possesses animal-like qualities, such as sensing its prey and moving of its own accord to trap it. Following Aristotle, Aquinas references such a case when he comments that "nature proceeds through degrees (*gradus*) from plants to animals through certain [beings] which are between animals and plants."[35]

As actuality lessens and potentiality increases on the hierarchy of being, there also exists a borderline case between the central categories of immaterial and material beings: namely, us.[36] As we will discuss in more detail in chapters 2 and 3, human beings possess the very best sort of body and the very lowest sort of intellect—an intellect that serves as the substantial form for an organic body, a rational soul informing matter.

Being and Goodness: God, Creatures, and Function

Before we turn to a discussion of Aquinas's account of human nature and how it grounds his action theory and virtue ethics, however, we must understand one final aspect of his general metaphysics in order to grasp his more specific claims about human nature and human behavior— namely, Aquinas's adherence to the famous medieval doctrine that being is identical with goodness.

According to Aquinas, "being and goodness are the same in reality; they differ only conceptually."[37] Sometimes called the Convertibility Thesis because it takes the properties of being and goodness as genuinely interchangeable, this position holds that everything is good (1) insofar as it exists and (2) to the extent to which it actualizes the capacities unique to a member of its natural kind.

The first point is just that existence is a basic good. God, the completely existing being, is completely good, and everything that exists both comes from him and is good insofar as it comes from him. Nothing in creation has an origin other than God, and so nothing can be bad simply insofar as it exists.

Actually existing things can be bad, however, and not merely in a moral sense. Knives can be blunt, mushrooms can wither and die without producing spores, and tigers can be born without back legs, and Aquinas believes that there is a sense in which these things are "bad" knives, mushrooms, and tigers. He argues for this on the grounds that things are good not merely by dint of existing, but also to the extent to which they exist as fully actualized members of their natural kinds. Thus, the claim that everything that exists is good to the extent to which it exists cannot be taken as a claim complete in itself. Rather, everything that exists is good to the extent to which it exists *and fulfills its nature.* A thing's nature is its essence, and its essence accounts for its function — its characteristic activity. Thus, a knife that cuts a loaf of bread smoothly into firm, even slices is good to the extent to which it exists and performs its function (i.e., cutting) well. Similarly, a bread knife that crumbles a loaf of pumpernickel into broken, misshapen hunks is a bad knife; it is a knife that fails to fulfill its nature. The same is true of mushrooms that wither without producing spores and tigers that cannot run; they are unable to perform their functions well.[38] On Aquinas's view, they are good to the extent to which they exist as mushrooms and tigers, but they are bad insofar as they fail to actualize the natural capacities that follow directly from their essences.

This general point has special force for rational agents. Unlike knives, mushrooms, and tigers, human beings (and angels) have a certain amount of control over how, or even whether, to actualize their capacities. Although human beings can be "bad" in the general sense of being unable to actualize certain capacities fully (because of hearing loss, cataracts, or congenital birth defects, for example), they can also *choose* not to actualize certain capacities. They can, for example, choose not to think carefully about the consequences of their actions, or to acknowledge their relationship to their Creator. This sort of badness is where both action theory and ethics enter the picture. Being moral is, for Aquinas, a matter of properly actualizing the capacities we have *by nature* and can control, and free will is what allows us to choose how we are going to actualize and direct those capacities.

It is significant that, once again, Aquinas makes this point in terms of potentiality and actuality. An individual being's goodness—be that individual an angel, animal, vegetable, or mineral—depends on the extent to which it actualizes the capacities it has as a member of a particular species. An individual human is good precisely insofar as she or he exists as a fully actualized rational animal.[39] We say, for example, that an acorn has the capacity to grow into an oak tree, although it is currently less than an inch tall, and that a newly hatched spider has the capacity to spin a web, although it has never done so. If I have the capacity to learn organic chemistry, I am capable of learning it, but I do not yet actually have that knowledge.[40] I exist in potentiality with respect to that knowledge. On the other hand, when I finally master organic chemistry, when the spider spins a web for the first time, and when the acorn has grown into a massive oak tree, we say that those capacities have been actualized—we have moved from existing in potentiality with respect to that knowledge, skill, size, and so forth, to actually possessing it. In Aquinas's terms, we "exist in actuality" at that point in a way in which we previously existed merely in potentiality. It is precisely *this* sort of potentiality that comes into play in discussions of the moral life.

Before we are in a position to examine the moral life in detail, however, we need to know more about human nature. What does it mean for human beings to be composites of matter and form? Are we simply immaterial souls attached to physical bodies, or is the relationship between soul and body more intimate than this? How, on a practical level, do we exercise our rational capacities at all? How is human action possible? And how does Aquinas's deeply integrated account of human nature reveal the way our place on the hierarchy of being presents us with a unique set of challenges in attaining a flourishing human life?

two

Soul and Body

In the last chapter we presented an overview of Aquinas's meta-
physics. We focused on the hierarchy of being and the distinction between
actuality and potentiality, not just because it proves central to understanding how Aquinas thinks generally about the connection between God and
creatures, but also because it gives us special insight into how he thinks
of human beings and their nature. A species' unique combination of potentiality and actuality locates that species on the hierarchy between pure
actuality—God—and pure potentiality—prime matter. It would seem
natural, then, for the concept of humans as unique combinations of actuality and potentiality to play a central role in Aquinas's account of our
nature—and it does. We constitute the bridge between material and immaterial beings because we possess both the actuality inherent to intellective beings and the potentiality characteristic of material creatures.

Fully understanding Aquinas's account of human nature, however,
requires seeing humans not just generally as composites of actuality and
potentiality, poised between the intellectual and physical realms, but more
particularly as composites of matter and form. We turn in this chapter
to a closer examination of what are sometimes called our "metaphysical
parts": form and matter, which are often equated with soul and body.[1]

Aquinas holds that the rational soul is the form (more specifically,
the substantial form) of the physical human being. This does not mean,
however, that the human body is reducible simply to matter. As we will

see, Aquinas believes that there is one and only one substantial form per individual substance. The living human body is, therefore, in a very important sense identical to the particular human being. Thus, Aquinas consciously sets up his account of human nature in opposition to a more traditional form of substance dualism, according to which soul and body are both separable and complete in their own right. Aquinas's account of human beings is also his account of human *persons.* This underscores the extent to which he sees our intellectual and physical nature as integrated and further demonstrates our connection to God, whom Aquinas describes as the paradigm case of a person. We are created in God's image, and one of the central ways in which humans mirror God is by being ourselves persons, complete with intellects and wills.

The connection between human beings, persons, intellects, and wills has significance that stretches beyond our mere metaphysical makeup, however; it reaches all the way to our moral status. As we saw in chapter 1, the extent to which something actualizes its natural potentialities determines its excellence or goodness as a member of that species. After getting clearer in this chapter about Aquinas's general understanding of human nature, in chapter 3 we will examine the specific way in which he claims that human capacities and the human function relate to our being and our goodness.

For the connection between what human beings *are* and what they *do,* it is necessary to examine more closely certain capacities integral to decision-making and the flourishing moral life—in particular, the rational capacities of both the intellect and the will (Aquinas refers to the latter as the "rational appetite"). Aquinas agrees with Aristotle that the function of a rational animal is "the life of activity expressing reason well." He also holds, however, that human beings are created in God's image. This fact grounds every interesting and important further fact about us and is key to Aquinas's action theory and ethical theory.

SOUL

As discussed in chapter 1, humans fall at the exact point on the continuum where the class of intellectual substances intersects with the class of material substances—where intellectual substances end and physical bodies begin.[2] Possessing characteristics of both material and immaterial beings, we cannot properly be classified as either, a point made clear in the structure of the *Summa theologiae*'s discussion of creatures. Aquinas orders his treatise on creation by beginning with "purely spiritual" creatures (that is, immaterial substances such as angels), moving on to "purely corporeal" creatures (material substances such as tigers and granite), and saving for last the complicated case of the creature "composed of corporeal and spiritual parts, which is the human being."[3]

Human beings are the only substances that possess both intellects and matter: no other intellective substance has a physical body; no other material substance has an intellect. This claim raises two initial questions for Aquinas's account. First, for what reason would something intellective—something that, as we have seen, is inherently superior to material substances—be joined to a physical body? Second, how *could* an intellective substance be joined to a physical body? In his answers to these two questions, Aquinas lays the groundwork for an integrated account of human nature according to which the human body is not a mere accessory to the human being but is, in an important sense, that human being.

Let us begin with the question of fittingness. Aquinas claims more than once that it is appropriate for the class of immaterial substances to intersect with the class of material substances in this peculiar way because it completes the hierarchy of being. Given the continuum of creatures from God to prime matter, Aquinas believes that it is natural for there to be beings at the intersections of different classes.[4] Yet this seems problematic, for Aquinas also holds that intellects are inherently superior to material things. The union of intellect with matter appears unnecessary or even disadvantageous to the intellect, tying it down, as it would seem, with something lower than itself. How, then, can it be fitting for human, *intellective* souls to be joined to matter?[5] It seems as though union with matter can result in nothing good for the soul.

Indeed, many philosophers in the Western tradition have developed accounts of human nature according to which the union of soul with body seems curiously unmotivated. In general, the soul's link to the body puts the soul at a disadvantage; at best the body is irrelevant to the soul's intellective pursuits, and at worst it actively interferes with the soul's search for knowledge. For example, in his *Meditations on First Philosophy,* René Descartes (1596–1650) appears to treat the body as largely unnecessary for mental activity. By the end of the first meditation, Descartes claims to doubt the existence of his own body—yet he doesn't see this as problematic for his continuing search for philosophical certainty. In fact, he states toward the end of the second meditation that "even bodies are not strictly perceived by the senses or the faculty of imagination but *by the intellect alone,* and this perception derives not from their being touched or seen but from their being understood."[6] Here Descartes appears to claim that the sense data received from our physical bodies are not the cause of our knowledge—even our knowledge of physical objects; instead, only intellective perception leads to knowledge.

Plato (428–347 B.C.) goes even further down this path than Descartes. He often portrays the body as an obstacle to acquiring the knowledge that our souls long to possess; on his account of human nature, our desire and bodily need for things like sleep, food, and drink distract us from contemplation, and physical pains and pleasures cloud our thinking. In the *Phaedo* Plato goes so far as to call the body an evil, claiming that "as long as we have a body and our soul is fused with such an evil we shall never adequately attain [the truth]."[7] This attitude toward the body is closely linked with the view advocated throughout the *Phaedo* that the goal of philosophy is to purify the mind and to separate the soul as much as possible from the body.[8]

Many scholars in Aquinas's day favored this sort of position as well.[9] Robert Grosseteste (ca. 1168–1253), for example, attributes our difficulties in attaining knowledge to our bodies: "Because the purity of the [mind's] eye is clouded and weighed down by the corrupt body, all the powers of the rational soul in human beings are occupied from birth by the weight of the body so that they cannot act, and so are in a certain way sleepy."[10] The body "weighs down" the rational soul, preventing it from cognizing effectively. This tradition emphasizes the nobility of the mind or the rational soul, but in so doing it undercuts the reason for the soul's being joined to a body.

Aquinas's description of human beings as a "higher" intellect joined with a "lower" body might seem to indicate that he shares this attitude toward the union of body and soul. Far from it. Rather, one of the most interesting, attractive, and philosophically problematic elements of Aquinas's philosophy is the crucial role he gives the body in human cognition. Union with matter does not actively interfere with rational thought; in fact, in the normal course of things, it is actually *necessary* for it.[11] On Aquinas's account of human nature, embodiment is a great good, a state not to be endured or bemoaned but rather embraced.

To understand his position, we need to look more closely at the nature of the rational soul. As chapter 1 made clear, Aquinas is careful to point out that the rational soul is the very lowest kind of intellect on the hierarchy of being. The human intellect is so weak that, unlike other intellects, it would be unable to acquire knowledge if it existed on its own.[12] As we also saw in chapter 1, Aquinas holds that higher intelligences need fewer principles of cognition to understand universal truths, whereas lower intellects require a greater number of principles to understand the same truths, a fact he frequently illustrates by talking about students. The smarter someone is, he says, the more she can understand, given just a few basic principles; if a student is slower, she will need both a number of examples and a clear laying out of each individual step along the way.[13] So, for example, after listening to an initial lecture, a really sharp student understands not only the basic properties of a triangle, but also the consequences these properties have for further mathematical truths and for solving geometric problems. A slower student, on the other hand, might need someone to explain to her in more detail what the basic properties of a triangle are. She might also need examples of several different triangles and demonstrations of how the angles of each add up to 180 degrees, and she might also need someone to lay out step by step how she can use this information to solve geometric problems.

In the realm of intellects, the rational soul is a "slow student." Human souls are so full of potentiality that they require all the examples they can get from observation of the material world just to reach the lower-level principles of cognition, and they need those lower-level principles in order to reach the higher truths. In the general course of things, a human being has to go through a complex process that begins with sense perception in order to grasp, for example, what an animal is.[14] First, the human being needs to physically perceive various animals, such as cats, dogs, and hamsters. With time, the intellect uses this sense data to form abstract concepts of "dog," "cat," and "hamster." The human being then can use those lower-level abstract concepts as "proximate principles" of cognition in forming the higher-level concept "animal," for example, as she thinks about the ways in which dogs, cats, and hamsters are similar.[15]

Thus, on Aquinas's account, the human body actually helps the soul carry out its proper activity (intellective cognition) by providing it with information gathered through sense perception—information the intellect uses in abstracting to universal truths. Bodies are united to rational souls to facilitate the souls' functioning. Human intellects need help cognizing, and that help is what the body is designed to provide.[16] It is not a curse or an inconvenience for human souls to be joined to bodies; it is quite literally a gift from God, providing the assistance rational souls need in order to actualize their intellective capacities. This examination of the body's role in intellection answers the first question we raised earlier about the relation between body and soul. Human intellects are joined to matter because that is, quite simply, the best way for them to function as they are meant to function.

The answer to the second question—namely, how an intellect *could* be joined to a body—highlights another point of divergence between Aquinas and philosophers such as Plato and Descartes, who denigrate or downplay the role of the body in cognition. Such philosophers also tend to hold that body and soul are two distinct substances, a position commonly referred to as substance dualism. To characterize it rather simplistically, substance dualism is the position that both body and soul are things in their own right, capable of existing independently. Thus, the human soul could exist as a complete thing apart from the body, and the body could exist apart from the soul.

Aquinas holds not only that the soul can exist apart from the body but that it actually does so, for a time, after death and prior to the bodily resurrection.[17] Nevertheless, he consciously rejects a strongly dualistic conception of human nature. Instead, Aquinas wants to present an account of human nature in which the composition of body and soul makes philosophical sense and body and soul constitute an integral unity. His belief in the essential unity of the human being underpins much of his account of the relation between body and soul. In particular, it is a large part of his motivation for adopting a broadly Aristotelian metaphysics, according to which the rational soul is the substantial form of the human body.[18] On Aquinas's account, the human being is a completely unified, individual substance, composed of matter and form, and *not* one substance somehow composed of two further substances.

Although the soul can subsist apart from matter after death, the rational soul is neither identical to the human being nor a substance in its own right (where being a substance involves being a member of a particular species).[19] Rather, as Aquinas puts it, the rational soul is only "*part of what is complete in species,*" namely, the human being. It is not itself a member of the human species—a human being—and so the soul itself "is not complete in species *per se,*" and neither is the body.[20] Instead, possessing both soul *and* body is required for membership in the human species. The disembodied human soul subsists in a highly unnatural state, and it doesn't count as a human being.[21]

Aquinas gives two main reasons for denying that the soul is a substance. First, if the soul is itself a complete thing—a substance—in its own right, it would not seem to require union with the body in any interesting or important sense.[22] If the soul can exist naturally apart from the body and can carry out its proper activity in separation from matter, it seems downright *inappropriate* for it to be joined to a material body, since material things are inferior to immaterial things. More importantly, if both the body and the soul are independent substances, it is hard to see how the human being could be essentially *one* thing.[23] Rather, the human being would seem to be nothing more than a loose composite of two distinct substances, not one complete being. Identifying the soul, the body, or both as a complete substance makes the unity of the composite human being seem extremely weak, if not accidental.[24]

Aquinas rejects this highly dualistic conception of human nature, arguing instead that the rational soul is the substantial form of the human being. As he remarks toward the beginning of his fullest discussion of human nature, in *Summa theologiae* Ia.75–89: "[T]he intellectual soul, as regards its existence, is united to the body as its form."[25] For our purposes, this claim has two crucial implications. First, since Aquinas describes form as what actualizes matter and makes it a particular, existing thing, his claim that the human soul is a form means that the rational soul, *qua* substantial form, actualizes matter and accounts for the existence of a living human being. There can be no human being—no body, nothing distinctively human—in the absence of the rational soul, for "the soul makes the organic body itself to be."[26] Matter on its own is in potentiality to be anything whatsoever; the rational soul (the substantial form of the human being) is what organizes and structures matter into a living, organic human substance with species-specific biological processes and functions. Thus, in the case of a particular individual, David, David's substantial form—his rational soul—is what accounts for him having a liver that purifies his blood, hands with opposable thumbs, and a brain that supports the activity of abstract cognition.

Second, as we saw in chapter 1, the rational soul is a form different both from all other intellects and from the forms of all other material substances (such as tigers and mushrooms). Intellects are also forms, but only the human intellect is joined to matter. At the same time, the rational soul is different from all other material forms because its proper activity— the thing it does by its very nature—is intellective cognition, which involves transcending matter in abstract thought.[27] When David thinks about beauty in and of itself or about God's existence, his intellect "goes beyond" matter. In these cases, the objects of his thought are not physical objects, and Aquinas argues that this entails that the rational soul's proper activity—intellective cognition—is independent of matter. Following Aristotle, Aquinas claims that this activity implies that the rational soul itself is independent from the body in an important sense. As an intellective form, it stands in contrast to wholly material forms, whose existence depends on matter and which do not have a proper act that transcends matter.

This claim about the soul's intellective operation not requiring the body does not conflict, however, with Aquinas's belief that the body is needed for human cognition. Aquinas's theory of human cognition is extremely complex; for our purposes, what is important is the basic way in which the body assists the intellect's cognition. In brief, the physical senses provide us with sensory information—colors, sounds, smells— that the inner sense in turn converts to "phantasms"—a certain sort of mental picture or representation of a physical object. The intellect can then abstract universal concepts, or "intelligible species," from these phantasms, as when we abstract from all the particular features of individual cats to form the universal concept of "cat"—a concept that does not itself involve any particular color, shape, or sound. The intellect's proper operation involves the contemplation of these abstract, universal, intelligible concepts. This sort of contemplation *can* occur apart from matter, as it does in the case of angels and God, but in the case of human beings the intellect requires the sense data it receives from the body to reach this stage of operation.[28]

Aquinas actually grounds his case for the immortality of the soul on the belief that abstract cognition transcends matter. He claims that the intellectual nature of David's soul sets it apart from the forms of other bodies in such a way that, unlike material forms, which perish when the material creature perishes, the rational soul can continue to exist in separation from matter. Before turning to the separation of the soul from the body, however, it is worth examining more closely the connection Aquinas draws between soul and form and between body and matter. As we will see, the soul/body relation differs from the form/matter relation in an important way that both underscores the deeply unified nature of human beings on Aquinas's account and raises a potential problem for the case of disembodied souls.

BODIES, MATTER, AND HUMAN BEINGS

Aquinas frequently compares the soul of a human body to form, and the body to matter. In *Summa contra gentiles,* for instance, Aquinas writes: "Living things . . . are composed of matter and form. Moreover, they are composed of a body and a soul, which makes them actually living things. Thus, one of these [i.e., the body and the soul] must be the form, and the other matter. . . . [And] the soul is the form."[29] We are familiar by now with the idea of the soul as form; new here is the explicit identification of the body with matter. This is, indeed, how the human body is often thought of—a lump of stuff or collection of physical particles, structured or shaped in a certain way by the soul/substantial form. In both this passage and many others, Aquinas draws a neat parallel between soul and form, and between body and matter.[30]

This is not the only, or even the primary, way in which Aquinas speaks of bodies, however. Earlier in *Summa contra gentiles,* for example, he claims that "everything composed of matter and form is a body."[31] This completely general claim — that all bodies are composites of matter and form — is nothing new. Any existing physical object involves both matter (for physicality) and form (for existence as a thing of a certain sort). Focusing on the body as *itself* a composite of matter and form yields a rather different picture from thinking of the body simply as matter, however. In particular, it entails that the human body, too, is a composite of matter and substantial form, rather than being simply matter.

In itself, this might seem a puzzling but not particularly interesting contradiction to the connection Aquinas draws in other places between the body and matter. These two ways of talking about the human body, however, demonstrate something very important about Aquinas's general account of human nature — namely, the extent to which he both emphasizes the role of the soul and integrates the body into what it means to be human.

When Aquinas talks about the body as matter, he generally intends to emphasize the soul's explanatory role in his account of human nature. The body, understood as a physical lump of stuff, is secondary in importance to the soul both with respect to what a human being is and what a human being does. Being human essentially involves rationality; not surprisingly, the *rational* soul accounts for our rational capacities. In this sense, the soul, not matter, also explains our ability to perform other sorts of human activities — eating, sleeping, thinking, and so on. Aquinas does not talk about the body purely in terms of matter, however. We can speak of and understand bodies in different ways, he says, and the sense of body as a composite of matter and form underscores Aquinas's commitment to a deeply integrated concept of human nature.

To understand better the different senses of "body," it helps to note three different ways in which Aquinas speaks of *matter.* First, as in chapter 1, matter in and of itself — prime matter — is pure potentiality, nothing at all apart from form.[32] When he speaks of existing bodies, then, Aquinas is referring to the matter belonging to an individual member of a particular species and already structured by the form of that species. Existing bodies can be thought of as involving two different senses of matter: on the one hand, the collection of individual physical bits of stuff (or elements) that constitute the body and that fluctuate over time, and on the other hand, ensouled matter—the whole organism, composed of functioning parts and organs—which remains the same over time.[33] The body of a human, a tiger, or a mushroom can thus be thought of either in terms of the particles of stuff that constitute it and which come and go (for example, when food is digested or when we sweat), or in terms of an integrated whole—the organism that breathes, sneezes, and grows.

These two senses of matter in turn help resolve our conflicting intuitions that our bodies both change significantly over time and remain the same throughout our lives. After all, none of the physical bits of stuff that constitute David at age ten are the same bits that constituted him at birth; thus, it seems plausible to say that David has a different body now than he did then. On the other hand, since David's birth, *something* has carried out the same biological processes and functions; something now has the scar he got when he ran into a slide as a toddler. Thus, it also seems plausible to claim that there is a sense in which the human body remains the same throughout life, despite the constant change in the "quantity of elements" which constitute that body.

On Aquinas's schema, which of those claims is true depends entirely on whether we think of the body in terms of "compositional" or "functional" matter. Although we are more familiar with the conception of the body as a heap of "stuff" or a collection of compositional matter, the sense of "body" as functional matter also proves philosophically important. Aquinas attributes sameness of organic body to continuity of substantial form: David's body now is the same body it was six years ago because it possesses the same rational soul; it is matter united into an organic, functional whole by substantial form. The body, in this functional sense, is a product of the union of form and matter. Therefore, understood in this way, the human body is not merely one *part* of the human being; rather, the body *is* the human being.

The rather radical-sounding claim that the human body is the human being follows from another of Aquinas's rather radical-sounding claims — namely, that all corporeal substances are composites of matter and exactly *one* substantial form.[34] This doctrine, usually referred to as the "unicity of substantial form," means that each substance has one and only one substantial form — a form that accounts for *everything* involved in some-thing's being an existing, individual member of a particular species.[35] So, for example, Aquinas would deny that a dog possesses one substantial form, "body," which accounts for the dog's occupying a particular location in space/time, another substantial form, "animal," which accounts for its sense perception and locomotion, and yet another form, "dog," which ac-counts for its having a wet nose, wagging tail, and four paws. Instead, Aquinas holds that one and the same substantial form accounts for a thing's being a dog *and* an animal *and* a body *and* a substance.[36]

Aquinas often characterizes the unicity of substantial form in terms familiar to us from the earlier discussion of lower-level and higher-level capacities; he claims that the same form accounts for a substance's pos-sessing both lower-level capacities, such as nutrition, and higher-level ca-pacities, such as sensation and rationality. As we saw in chapter 1, a plant such as an oak tree possesses what Aquinas calls a "nutritive" or "vege-tative" soul, insofar as it possesses the capacity to take in nourishment and grow. A dog, however, possesses not only the capacity for growth but also the capacity for sense perception. Some of Aquinas's contemporaries claimed that this meant that the dog possesses both a nutritive soul *and* a higher-level "sensory" or "animal" soul. In contrast, Aquinas claims that the dog does not possess two numerically distinct souls, one of which ac-counts for nutrition and the other of which accounts for sense perception. Instead, he argues that the dog's sensory and nutritive souls are the same in number — that is, they are numerically identical. What explains the dog's capacity for growth (that is, the substantial form "dog") is exactly the same as what explains its capacity for sense perception (that is, the substantial form "dog").[37]

In the case of humans, then, the rational soul (i.e., the substantial form "human being") accounts not just for David's being a thinking thing but also for his hearing and seeing, his growing, and even his three-dimensionality. In short, the unicity of substantial form entails that the human body is a composite of matter and exactly one substantial form, "human being." As Fernand Van Steenberghen observes, "It is not to the *body* but to *prime matter* that the soul is united as substantial form."[38] The body is itself the living composite of matter and the one substantial form "human being."[39] If both the human being and the human body, however, are properly described as composites of matter and the substantial form "human being," then on the functional sense of body, the human body *is* the human being. Thus, although Aquinas does speak at times of human beings as composites of soul and body, it seems just as accurate—if not more so—to speak of them as living bodies composed of soul and matter.

Indeed, Aquinas himself speaks of the rational soul as part of the human *body* in at least one passage, where it seems fairly clear that he is thinking of the human body as the composite of form and matter. In his commentary on Paul's famous passage on the resurrection, Aquinas writes: "Since *the soul is part of the human body,* it is not the whole human being, and I am not my soul."[40] Although this sounds odd at first glance, strictly speaking, the rational soul *is* one part of the human body. It is the substantial form that organizes and vivifies matter in a way that results in a living human body—that is, a living human being.[41] When "body" is understood as ensouled matter—as a living organism rather than as a lump of "stuff" or collection of elements—then Aquinas can truly claim that a human being *is,* rather than *has,* a human body.

On this understanding, we are not composed of two separate (and separable) elements, body and soul. Rather, we are composites of soul *and matter.* In stark contrast to Descartes's claim that "I am really distinct from my body, and can exist without it,"[42] Aquinas claims that "I am not my soul," and that we cannot survive the separation of soul from body.

This proves crucial not just for Aquinas's general metaphysics of human nature but also for his theory of human actions. Although the soul properly receives the emphasis for its role in actualizing matter and explaining the existence of a living human being, Aquinas claims that it is the matter-form composite that is properly said to act, not the soul alone: "The action of anything composed of matter and form belongs not to the form alone, nor to the matter alone, but to the composite."[43] *All* the operations or activities of the human soul naturally involve the body, up to and including intellective cognition.

This is easy to see in the case of nutrition, for example. While the human substantial form might account for our ability to take in food and water and grow, the activities of eating, digesting, and growing require a body. The same goes for sensation; we require a body to exercise our human capacities for hearing, smelling, tasting, touching, and seeing.[44] Moreover, Aquinas attributes even most *intellective* operations to the soul/matter composite, not just to the rational soul. "It can be said that the soul understands . . . but it is said more properly that the human being understands through the soul."[45] Although the intellect is immaterial, as are all intellects, it nevertheless requires access to powers such as imagination and sensation, which themselves require physical organs.[46] In general, as Aquinas puts it, "It is necessary that [the soul] receives intelligible species from external things through the mediation of the sensory powers, which cannot carry out their proper operations apart from bodily organs."[47] In the normal course of things, human cognition requires that the body supply the intellect not merely with raw sense data but also with the mental images (phantasms) it needs to contemplate intelligible species—the universal objects of abstract thought.

Souls in Separation from Matter

By this point, careful readers will have noticed what seems to be a serious difficulty for Aquinas. So far we have focused on Aquinas's general claims about body and soul, and we have argued that the intimate connection he draws between form and matter commits him to a radically integrated account of human nature—an account which contrasts sharply with that of traditional substance dualists such as Plato and Descartes. One major component of Aquinas's theory, however, involves the *separation* of form from matter at death. Aquinas holds that the rational soul survives the death of the physical body and exists disembodied until the bodily resurrection, at which point it is reunited with matter. This seems problematic on two accounts. First, how can the soul survive death? Second, how can it carry out its proper activity—cognition—in separation from matter if the body is necessary for cognition?

The second problem is actually the easier to answer; it also provides the key to solving the first problem. Although Aquinas claims that the body is intimately involved in the process of human cognition, he draws a careful distinction between what is necessary to *support* an activity and what is required to *perform* the activity. Unlike nutrition and sensation, which require the body for carrying out their proper activities, the intellect does not require matter for the actual act of cognition. The act of nutrition requires there to be a body to digest the food, and the act of perception requires there to be a body to smell the coffee, but, on Aquinas's account, intellective cognition is an "organless" activity. The human *brain* is not what thinks—the immaterial *intellect* is. Or, more properly speaking, the human being thinks by means of her intellect. After all, if intellective activity by its very nature required union with a body, God and the angels would be unable to cognize.

The soul does need the body to support its activity, however; it needs the body in order to have something to think *about*. Union with matter provides the soul with the means for acquiring the proper objects of intellection—intelligible species, or abstract universal concepts.[48] As we have seen, human intellects need matter to assist them in acquiring intelligible species because they are the very weakest sort of intellect.[49] Thus, Aquinas believes not that the body is central to the act of intellection itself, but that the body is naturally involved in human cognition for the aid of the human intellect. In separation from matter, human souls can cognize, but again only with assistance; Aquinas claims that they can receive the intelligible species necessary for cognition from either God or other immaterial substances.

The ability of the rational soul to cognize in separation from matter is also what grounds Aquinas's argument that it survives the death of the body. According to Aristotelian principles that Aquinas accepts, if a soul cannot operate on its own, it cannot exist on its own.[50] Thus, for the soul to survive separation from matter, its proper activity (intellective cognition) must be possible in separation from matter, and, as we have just seen, Aquinas believes that it is. Aquinas holds, then, that the intellective nature of the human soul grounds our souls' continued existence in separation from matter at death and prior to the bodily resurrection. Because our souls are capable of cognizing apart from matter—receiving the assistance they need, in that case, from immaterial substances—they are capable of existing apart from matter.[51]

It is important to see, however, that this is not just a slightly modified version of substance dualism that emphasizes union with the body only during earthly life and drops its importance at death. Although Aquinas argues that our souls must be able to persist in separation from matter, he also wants to stress that our souls do *not* continue to exist apart from matter indefinitely. It is so unnatural for the soul to exist apart from matter that it requires unusual measures, a sort of divine intervention, for the soul to perform its proper action and cognize in separation from the body.

In fact, when Aquinas discusses the Christian doctrine that God resurrects human beings as not just spiritual but physical creatures, he appeals to philosophical as well as scriptural principles.[52] Central to his defense of the bodily resurrection is the claim that it goes against the human soul's very nature to exist apart from matter.[53] In a discussion of the bodily resurrection, for example, Aquinas argues that the soul is "naturally united to a body, for [a soul] is, according to its essence, the form of a body. For this reason, it is against the nature of the soul to exist without the body. Nothing that is contrary to nature can exist perpetually, however. Therefore, the soul will not exist perpetually without the body. So, since the soul remains perpetually, it must be joined again to the body, which is what it means to be resurrected. Thus, the immortality of souls seems to require a future resurrection of bodies."[54]

Here we see how Aquinas reconciles his belief that the soul is, by its very nature, immortal with his claim that the rational soul is the substantial form of the human being, and thus is naturally joined to a body.[55] Since the very nature of the rational soul involves structuring, organizing, and vivifying a human body, a soul separated from a body cannot do what it is meant by nature to do. Although the soul's nature does not require its being joined to the body *at all times,* it is unnatural (in the strict sense of "natural") for it to be separated from matter; Aquinas's point here is that this state of affairs cannot continue without end. Since the human soul is immortal, however, it *would* remain in that unnatural state perpetually unless it were reunited with matter, and so it is clear, if we accept the premises of the argument, that the soul must be joined to a body again at some point.

In another argument, Aquinas stresses this point even more strongly: "The soul separated from the body is in a way imperfect, like every part existing apart from its whole: for the soul is naturally *part* of human nature."[56] A perpetual separation of soul from body would mean that complete happiness could never be achieved; complete happiness involves the satisfaction of all natural desires, and the separated soul *naturally* inclines toward reunion with its body. The attaining of the end goal of human nature thus requires both soul *and* body, for, as Aquinas writes: "The soul of Abraham is not Abraham himself, properly speaking, but is *part* of him; and so for all the others."[57] What would be wrong about the perpetual existence of a rational soul apart from the body is that one *part* of the human being—for example, David's soul—would persist forever, while the *whole* human being—David—would be lost. Aquinas's account of human nature virtually demands a doctrine of bodily resurrection, then, for human participation in the afterlife.[58]

Human Persons

So far we have been talking almost exclusively of human beings. Although this terminology accurately reflects Aquinas's usage, it seems to distance him from contemporary discussions that focus almost exclusively on *persons* as possessing primary metaphysical and moral interest. This concern is misguided, however, for, on Aquinas's account, claims about human beings apply equally to human persons and vice versa. This proves important for two main reasons. First, it reemphasizes Aquinas's commitment to the deeply integrated nature of soul and body; second, it establishes an important sense in which human beings are created in God's image, for God is the paradigm person.

In fact, Aquinas's discussion of persons is motivated primarily by his interest in the relation of persons in the Trinity. Following Boethius, Aquinas defines "person" as "an individual substance with a rational nature."[59] God, of course, best fits this definition. As Aquinas states, "Person signifies that which is most perfect in the whole of nature, namely, a sub-sisting being with a rational nature."[60] God is, of all things, the most per-fect; as complete actuality, he exemplifies subsistent existence, and as omniscient, he exemplifies rationality.

Human beings also meet the definition of "person" (although in a less perfect way). We are individual substances, and we have a rational nature. It is important to ask, however, whether Aquinas believes that human be-ings are identical to human persons, for many philosophers believe that the identity conditions for human beings and persons differ. In particu-lar, they often hold that intentional states (desires, beliefs, etc.) and the ca-pacity for first-person reference (such as "I am feeling cold right now") are essential to something's being a person but not to something's being a human being.

This intuition is motivated largely by the case of persistent vegeta-tive states — cases where organic life appears to persist in the absence of the person. Lynne Rudder Baker, a proponent of this position, sets up the situation in the following way: "Suppose that a human organism that goes into a persistent vegetative state caused by the death of the cerebral neurons has no hope of recovery. Although it is still a living organism, it is incapable of suffering or of any awareness whatever, and never will be. It is a being that does not, and never will be able to, care about itself or about anything else."[61] In this case, many people hold that there's reason to deny that human *persons* are living human bodies, even if human *be-ings* are living human bodies.

There is some reason for thinking that Aquinas would agree with this position. Although he believes that human beings are, strictly speak-ing, identical to living bodies, he does want to draw at least a conceptual distinction between being a physical body and being rational—which, for Aquinas, involves the capacity for first-person reference and inten-tional states. Although the substantial form "human being" is at the same time what accounts for Jane's being a living organism (i.e., having organs that function in a certain way necessary for preserving life) and what ac-counts for her ability to intellectively cognize, Jane's existence as an or-ganic body and as an intellectual creature can still be considered in sepa-ration from each other, when, for instance, we concentrate solely on Jane's rationality and ignore her animality.[62] This conceptual distinction might lead one to believe that a horrible injury that puts Jane in a nonreversible vegetative state might be a case where a human organism would exist without being a person.

Aquinas, however, explicitly rules out this possibility when he claims that in the case of human beings, "person" refers to the human substance as a whole—to flesh and bones as well as to rationality.[63] For Aquinas, the human *person* is a composite of matter and form, just as the human *being* is. Even if the living organism in the vegetative state can no longer actualize her rational capacities, Aquinas would argue that that organism is a human person exactly as long as it is a human being. Jane could not meet the definition of human being ("rational animal") without also meeting the definition of person ("individual substance with a rational nature"). Human persons just *are* human beings, flesh and blood creatures with rational capacities.[64] Aquinas's commitment to an integrated account of human nature thus affects his conception of human persons as well as his conception of human beings; human persons *are* living physical substances.

This account of the human person also establishes a close connection between human beings and God. What it means for us to be created in the image of God, according to Aquinas, is primarily for us to be individual substances with a rational nature—that is, for us to be individual creatures who possess both intellects and wills, as God himself possesses intellect and will. In the next chapter we turn to a detailed discussion of human capacities. Our capacities for such things as rational thought and volition are precisely the aspects of our nature that allow us to strive for greater union with God.

three

Human Capacities and
the Image of God

*A*quinas's *basic account of human nature, as we have seen, looks* strongly Aristotelian. Like Aristotle, Aquinas holds that human beings are rational animals. He describes human beings as composites of form and matter, as intellective organic bodies. Also like Aristotle, he believes that the human function can properly be understood as "the life of activity expressing reason." The primary goal of human life is happiness, and the way to attain happiness is to perform the human function *well*. A good human being—a happy human being—is one who lives a flourishing life, using reason to guide her decisions and to act well.

For Aquinas, however, we are more than just composites of matter and form; we are children of God, created in his image. This fact is central to our nature, on his account, in our status as rational animals. It is impossible to appreciate Aquinas's account of human nature fully without understanding the relation of human beings to God, and it is impossible fully to understand that relation without seeing that it works on both a metaphysical and a personal level.

So far in this book we have focused on the metaphysical relation of God to human beings. In chapter 1, for instance, we saw how human beings fit into the general hierarchy of being, poised between immaterial and material creatures; in chapter 2 we saw how our intellective and physical aspects are parts of a radically unified composite. In both chapters we concentrated on Aquinas's conception of God as pure actuality, since this conception proves key to understanding both our place in the hierarchy of being and the concepts of matter and form.

In this chapter, we focus on the necessary conditions for our *personal* relation to God. The fact that God is the paradigm person and that we are created in God's image has important ramifications for understanding both our nature and the sort of life human beings are meant to lead. We are not ready yet to delve into Aquinas's detailed account of the actual loving relationships that human beings can have with God; that falls in the realm of the ethical and will be discussed in the chapters in part 3. Rather, here we will focus on the aspects of human nature that make an intimate relationship with God possible in the first place — the basic components of human psychology, which Aquinas develops in his discussion of the soul's capacities.

As we mentioned in the introduction, Aquinas reinterprets Aristotle's description of the human function in light of his belief that we are made in God's image. Aristotle speaks of our final goal, happiness, as "the life of activity expressing reason well," leaving open the question of what, exactly, constitutes reasoning well. Happiness is, in general Aristotelian terms, the flourishing human life. It is a life that exemplifies excellent practical and theoretical reasoning; it is also a life that ends at death.[1]

Aquinas agrees that the goal of human life involves expressing reason well, but he claims that the fullest expression of human reason involves both knowing and loving God. It is not enough to contemplate God with our intellects, although that activity certainly requires reasoning. The fully rational person does not simply thirst for that kind of contact with God; she responds to it with love and joy. In this life, however, obstacles from the trivial to the serious constantly interfere both with our attaining true knowledge of God and with our responding appropriately to that knowledge. We get confused (and maybe even bored) reading Scripture, the phone rings while we are praying, and we are as likely to respond to a deepened knowledge of God and his plans for our lives with fear or resentment as with love. Although searching for happiness is our deepest life's goal, we cannot attain lasting, complete, and perfect human happiness until we have firsthand knowledge of God — that is, until the afterlife. Only then will all our desires be satisfied, all our questions answered. Only then can we rest content in union with our Creator.

Thus, Aquinas's reinterpretation of Aristotle's definition of happiness is grounded in a developed discussion of our capacities for knowing and loving. These abilities are not just what make human happiness possible in an abstract and detached sense; they are at the very heart of what makes a personal relationship with God possible, in the fullest sense of the word "personal."

What capacities need to be put into action in order for us to attain perfect happiness? In brief, the capacities of intellect and will; that is, our intellective and volitional capacities. To know and love God—or anything else, for that matter—we need to start with the capacity for knowledge and the capacity for desiring and enjoying the satisfaction of that desire. Our intellective and volitional capacities make up only one part of the total set of human capacities, however, and it is important to Aquinas's account that human beings do not merely have intellects and will. After all, human beings are by nature rational *animals,* and we possess a wide variety of capacities grounded in our physical nature. Indeed, many of those physical capacities are related in interesting and important ways to our intellective and volitional capacities. For that reason, the first goal of this chapter is to provide an overview of human capacities in general, in order to show how intellect and will fit into Aquinas's overall picture of human nature.

The second goal is to continue laying the groundwork for parts 2 and 3 of this book, where we discuss Aquinas's theories of human action and ethics. The capacities of intellect and will have a special role in human action and the flourishing moral life, as we will show by using the connection that Aquinas draws between being and goodness in order to illuminate how the flourishing human life involves actualizing distinctively human capacities. We are created in God's image, and we have certain capacities in common with God; most importantly, we resemble God by possessing intellect and will. Not surprisingly, then, Aquinas holds that—although our capacities for nutrition, sensation, and locomotion all play a part—intellect and will play the key role in attaining the flourishing human life. Because human beings are good (both metaphysically and morally) to the extent to which they actualize their natural potentialities, in developing these capacities we increase not only our knowledge of but also our likeness to the perfectly actual, perfectly good God.

ESSENCE AND CAPACITY

In *Summa theologiae* Ia.75–89, often referred to as the treatise on human nature, Aquinas follows up his discussion of the essential nature of the human being with a detailed discussion of human capacities. In fact, after spending only two questions addressing the rational soul's essence as the substantial form of the human body, he spends the next seven questions on the soul's capacities and the next six discussing in detail the operation of the most important of those capacities, the intellective capacity.

This attention to human capacities underscores Aquinas's belief that in order to understand fully what a thing is (its essence), we need to know what a thing *does*—or at least what it *could do*. Only God can know something's essence directly, or from the "inside out." Human beings can come to an understanding of something's essence only indirectly, or from the "outside in."[2] That is, we must begin with something's external features and work our way to an understanding of its true nature from an understanding of those features and their effects. So, for example, we see something small and metal and we hear it make a strange buzzing noise; we watch someone pick it up, flip it open, and talk into it, and we come to the conclusion from our observations that its nature—*what it is*—is a device for communication (in this case, a cell phone). We do not deduce its function from an inner understanding of its essence; rather, we arrive at an understanding of its essence from observing its function.

Importantly, for Aquinas, this general point about moving from observation of a thing's function to knowledge of a thing's essence applies to knowledge of our own nature as well. To understand the essence of human beings more fully, he claims that we need to examine what the "effects and proper attributes" of a human being are; that is exactly where a study of human capacities comes in. We will begin by addressing capacities in general and then examine the five main capacities Aquinas attributes to the rational soul—namely, vegetative, sensory, locomotive, appetitive (including the will), and intellective.

THE SOUL'S CAPACITIES IN GENERAL

The fact that human beings have a number of different capacities turns out to be an important feature of human nature. Human beings constitute the bridge between material and immaterial creatures, and so they possess both intellective and physical capacities.[3] We require a wide range of capacities in order to reach our ultimate end—happiness, or union with God. Although rocks and iguanas have their own special place in God's plan for the world, nonrational creatures cannot know God, and they cannot love God. Human beings are the only physical beings that can be happy. As we saw in chapter 2, however, human beings are the "slow students" of the intellective world; we need to do more work—gathering sense data, for example, and abstracting from it—than other intellective beings do in order to cognize. In the same way, human beings are "slow students" with respect to happiness; they need to actualize a number of capacities in order to reach union with God, whereas higher beings, such as angels, require only a few capacities, and the highest being, God, is pure actuality and does not need any capacities at all.

Imagine a knitting group whose goal is to make baby hats for preemies in the neighborhood hospital. The first night the group meets, it consists of several adults who already knit and one who doesn't know how to knit, along with a five-year-old child. The adults who already knit do not need to actualize any capacities at all in order to reach the goal of the knitting group; they participate in the goal of making baby hats as soon as the group meets. The other adult, however, has to actualize several capacities in order to participate in the group's goal: she has to learn how to hold the knitting needles, how to move the yarn in the right way with her hands, and so on. The five-year-old child would have to actualize even more capacities to reach the group's goal; for one thing, she still lacks the fine-motor skills sufficient for controlling the knitting needles.

God is like the knitters.[4] God doesn't need to actualize any capacities in order to reach the ultimate end: there is nothing that God lacks, and no sense in which God's happiness—his beatitude—is not already fully actual. Angels, on the other hand, are like the adult who does not yet know how to knit: they can attain perfect happiness, but they must actualize some capacities in order to reach that goal. They choose whether to actualize those capacities, and so although it is possible for them to reach perfect happiness if they use their intellective and volitional capacities properly, it is also possible for them to fail to do so, as evidenced by the fallen angels.

Human beings are like the five-year-old child. We need to develop and use a number of capacities in order to reach our ultimate goal. In fact, we need to use every power we have, since, as Aquinas puts it, "human beings are by nature at the outmost reaches among those to whom beatitude is given."[5] Only intellective beings can reach happiness. Human beings are the lowest intellective creatures, and so we are at the outer limits of those beings who can experience true happiness. Like the child who cannot yet knit on her own and who needs to develop a number of basic capacities before she is even in a position to begin learning, human beings cannot reach beatitude without actualizing a number of God-given capacities. We will also need God's assistance — God's grace — to actualize our capacities in the right ways. Even so, human beings are better off in this respect than rocks and iguanas, which cannot reach perfect happiness at all, in the same way that a goldfish could never learn to knit. No matter how many of its capacities it actualized, a goldfish simply lacks the sorts of capacities required for knitting; in the same way, no matter how many of its capacities it actualizes, an iguana can never reach beatitude. Human beings at least possess the requisite capacities to reach happiness; the pressing question for Aquinas is how we can do our part in actualizing those capacities that allow us to attain our ultimate goal.

What are capacities that allow us to reach happiness? Aquinas consistently refers to them as capacities of the *soul* and not as the capacities of the *human being*.[6] This might seem curious. After all, Aquinas takes pains to point out that human actions of all sorts — intellective and not — are properly attributed to the composite human being and not to the soul alone. Since our ability to perform actions stems from capacities for things such as locomotion, reason, and will, it seems as though Aquinas should also attribute these five capacities to the human being and not speak as though they belong exclusively to the rational soul.

Yet that is often how he talks, and there seem to be two main reasons for it. First, although the composite human being is what exercises various human capacities and what performs actions on the basis of those capacities, the human being has those capacities *in virtue of* her substantial form—the rational soul. That is, the body, taken either as a collection of bits of stuff or as a living organism, is what it is only in virtue of the soul that informs it. The rational soul is what accounts for all the things the body can do. Thus, it seems appropriate to talk about human capacities as capacities of the soul, even if the physical composite is what actualizes those capacities.

Second, the capacities that Aquinas is most concerned with, both philosophically and theologically—the ones that link us most closely with God—are, on his view, *nonphysical* capacities: namely, intellect and will.[7] Although our intellective and volitional capacities are what make us human, they are also what separate us most sharply from other physical creatures. One of the main reasons Aquinas believes human souls can survive death is that intellective activity can be carried out in separation from matter. In order for the soul to survive the death of the composite, the soul must have capacities that belong to it and not to the composite human being, properly speaking. Thus, there is a special sense in which it is appropriate to describe intellect and will as capacities *of the soul.* According to Aquinas, human souls possess intellective and volitional capacities even in separation from matter—when we are not, properly speaking, human beings—although capacities for such things as nutrition and sensation remain only in "root" form.[8]

Specific Capacities of the Rational Soul

To appreciate Aquinas's claims about how our intellective and volitional capacities play the primary role in our attaining a flourishing human life, we need to see how intellect and will fit into the broader scope of the soul's capacities taken as a whole. As we saw in chapter 1, Aquinas distinguishes between nutritive, sensory, and rational activities. Like Aristotle, he holds that to perform these three kinds of activities, we must—and do—possess five different sorts of capacities: nutritive, sensory, appetitive, locomotive, and intellective.

Human beings are able to grow, reproduce, digest, and be nourished by what they eat because they possess what Aquinas calls "nutritive" or "vegetative" capacities. Vegetative capacities are common to all living things. Every living thing possesses the ability to grow, not just in the random way an iceberg or a water stain grows but in a purposeful way directed toward the development of a mature, or "full-grown," member of a particular species. All living things also possess the capacity to reproduce, and they all possess the capacity for nutrition—the most basic requirement for continued life. In order to remain a living thing, a sunflower needs to be able to absorb nutrients and water from the soil, and a lion cub must have the capacity to digest the zebra thigh it has just eaten.

Unlike a sunflower, however, a lion cub can do more than simply grow, reproduce, and nourish itself; it can also see a zebra body, sniff it, and recognize it as food. The capacities that make such actions possible are generally characterized as "sensory" capacities: they are the abilities, common to all animals, that center around sense perception of the external world. Aquinas breaks these capacities into two categories: external and internal. Perception itself requires the five "external" sensory capacities—sight, hearing, smell, touch, and taste. Processing the information acquired by those external capacities requires "internal" sensory capacities—namely, common sense, imagination, the estimative (or, in the case of human beings, the cogitative) power, and memory.

The five faculties of external sense perception are well known to us, and we need not go into detail about their operation. According to Aquinas, the external sense capacities enable animals to acquire the sense data that grounds physical actions necessary for both their survival and their flourishing. So, for example, the lion cub feels pain when it gets too close to a brush fire; the cow sees luscious green grass a few feet away. In the special case of human beings, the information we receive from our senses forms the foundation not just for physical actions but also for cognition.[9]

The capacities of sense perception alone are not enough to explain animal activities, however; animals also require the ability to synthesize and react to their perceptions. Feeling the heat from a brush fire provides the lion cub with information it needs for its survival, but the cub must also process that information in certain ways before it can react appropriately. The cow must not only see the green grass but also recognize it as nourishment. This is where the internal senses come in. Aquinas identifies four distinct internal senses. These are capacities that are responsible for receiving, synthesizing, retaining, and/or preserving the sense data that we receive from our five external senses. The *common sense* receives and synthesizes sense data; it perceives the various sorts of sense data gathered from the five external senses, and thus allows us to combine the information received from different senses into one coherent picture. When we drink hot chocolate, the common sense is what allows us to process the brown color, the rich smell, the warmth, and the sweet taste not just as distinct sense data, but as different sensory perceptions of the same physical object. *Imagination,* on the other hand, stores the sensible forms gathered by our external senses. It allows us, for example, to picture the color of the irises in our backyard flowerbeds when we're in the library; it is also the capacity that allows us to combine different sense data into new arrangements we haven't personally experienced, so that we can picture what our gardens might look like with differently colored irises, or climbing roses.

The *estimative power*—or, in the case of human beings, the *cogitative power*—processes the sensible forms synthesized by common sense and stored in the imagination. The estimative power enables animals to move beyond merely experiencing sensible forms to recognizing how what they are currently perceiving might affect them.[10] It is what allows animals to "sense" danger, for instance. When a sheep perceives a wolf, Aquinas claims that the sheep perceives the relevant sense data as signifying something potentially dangerous. In the same way, the estimative power allows the cow to see green grass as potentially nourishing. Importantly, in human beings this capacity is called the cogitative power or *particular reason.* Because human beings are the only animals with rational powers, we are capable of more than simply apprehending intentions, such as the danger posed by a hungry wolf; we are also able to make comparisons between different intentions, such as weighing our chances of actively warding off a wolf-attack against our chances of escaping from it by running on foot. For human beings, particular reason plays an extremely important role in daily life. It is essentially the lowest-level rational power—it is the capacity that grounds deliberation about which breakfast cereal to eat, whether to drive or bike to work, and whether or not to ask someone out on a date. Finally, *sensory memory* preserves the intentions formed by the estimative or the cogitative power. Sensory memory allows us to put our current sense experiences in context; it explains why the dog runs toward the food dish at the sound of the can opener, and why the cat streaks out of the bathroom as soon as someone turns on the bathtub faucet.[11] In the case of human beings, sensory memory plays a role when we decide what to order at our favorite restaurant and when hearing a song on the radio makes us think of friends from high school. Together, our sensory capacities — both external and internal — provide us with information about the world around us and allow us to begin processing that information. Only then are we in a position to use our rational capacities to work toward a genuinely flourishing human life.

To actually perform actions, though, both human beings and animals require appetitive and locomotive capacities as well as sensory and vegetative powers. To see this, think again of the dog running toward the food dish at the sound of the can opener. Perceptive capacities alone are not enough to account for the dog's actions: running requires the ability to *move,* not just to perceive. Moreover, the dog would not move toward the food dish unless it were *motivated* to do so — and this motivation or desire is, in turn, distinct from hearing the can opener, remembering that this sound is associated with food, and moving toward the dish. In general, Aquinas believes that animals that can apprehend external objects also possess capacities to react to those objects, both internally, with desire, and externally, with movement toward or away from what it perceives. The locomotive capacity is simply this ability to move toward or away from the objects of perception. It allows the cow to stroll over to the green grass when it is hungry; it allows the sheep to run away from the wolf when it perceives danger. The locomotive power is what enables human beings physically to work toward their goals.

The appetitive capacity, on the other hand, is more complicated; in fact, Aquinas divides the appetitive capacity into two distinct categories. On the one hand, animals have a general desire for things that are pleasing to the senses and a general desire to avoid things that are displeasing or painful. Aquinas calls this the *concupiscible appetite;* it is what we are usually referring to when we talk about bodily appetites. The concupiscible appetite factors in our pleasurable anticipation of a warm bath, our desire for physical intimacy, and our disgust at the stench when we take out the garbage. On the other hand, animals do not always just move toward pleasure and away from pain; if our motivations were that simple, dogs would never leap into icy water to retrieve sticks, and there would be no professional athletes. For this reason, Aquinas believes that human beings and other animals also possess what he calls the *irascible appetite* — the capacity to resist the forces that interfere with our acquiring agreeable things or that bring us harm.[12] Colloquially speaking, the irascible appetite keeps us going when the going gets tough. It helps us attain the objects of pleasure we desire with the concupiscible appetite.

Suppose, for example, that David badly wants to climb Mt. Rainier. On the morning of the ascent, he wakes up in his tent eager to begin the hike. He bounds out of his sleeping bag full of desire to reach the summit and soak in the incredible view — his concupiscible appetite motivates him to get on the trail and start the trip. Hours later, though, he begins to get discouraged as he trudges up the umpteenth switchback. His feet are sore, he is sweating, and he is still a long way from the top. This is where the irascible appetite kicks in and keeps him slogging along the path instead of giving up; it keeps him climbing over the boulders in his way and slapping at biting flies that plague him. David wants the pleasure that will come from completing the hike, and the irascible appetite keeps him motivated in the face of adversity.

Obviously, there is an extremely close connection between the sensory capacities, appetite, and locomotion. We perceive something, we react to it with desire or revulsion, and we then move ourselves toward or away from it. In fact, all four sets of the capacities we have discussed so far — vegetative, sensory, appetitive, and locomotive — are closely linked in this way, and are all required for our survival. We all, for example, require nourishment for survival. If we cannot perceive our surroundings, however, we will have no way of identifying food in the first place. Simply perceiving something we can eat is not enough. We also have to desire it and to be able to move ourselves to it in order to eat the food, and we have to be able to digest the food once we have consumed it. Every animal requires the functioning of all its capacities for continued survival.

For our purposes, the importance of these basic capacities lies not in how they support animal life in general but in how they support human life in particular—and how they make possible not just human survival but human *flourishing*. For Aquinas, our flourishing involves actualizing all of our capacities to their fullest extent. More than anything else, though, it involves actualizing our rational capacities, since these capacities both distinguish us from other animals and link us with God. The natural question is how the lower-level capacities we have just discussed ground the operation of the rational capacities, which include intellect and will.

Intellect and Will

Aquinas is fond of hierarchies, as we have seen; the hierarchy he describes of the soul's capacities is particularly telling for his account of human nature and its ultimate end. In short, although the vegetative and sensory capacities play an important part in human life, the rational capacities rank higher; they are what distinguish human functioning from the functioning of other animals. Vegetative capacities are necessary for maintaining basic metabolic function and sustaining life. Sensory, locomotive, and appetitive capacities go beyond that in providing us with certain information, what Aquinas often calls "sensible forms"—the building blocks of human cognition. What makes human cognition and human flourishing possible, however, are the rational capacities, which have as their proper objects abstract concepts such as truth and justice.

According to Aquinas, there are two main reasons to consider the rational capacities superior to our other capacities. First, the rational capacities can "direct and command" the other capacities.[13] We hear what sounds like a friend calling to us in the distance, and we decide we should walk toward the noise to find out from whom it is coming. In this case, our rational capacities direct our locomotive capacities to move us closer to the noise so that our sensory capacities can gather more information. In the same way, Aquinas holds that even if someone is ravenously hungry, she will not begin rummaging around in the refrigerator unless her intellect judges that this is an appropriate activity. She will also not simply put the first thing she sees into her mouth; as human beings we think about what we want to eat, and we weigh the alternatives against each other. Moreover, this exercise of rational capacities over sensory powers does not involve only judgments of the intellect. Aquinas claims that we also have a rational *appetite* — the will — that can control our sensory appetite. Although the mere sight of juicy green grass is enough to motivate a hungry cow to begin eating, the mere sight of chocolate cheesecake does not automatically inspire a hungry human being to pick up a fork and dig into it. As Aquinas puts it: "A human being is not immediately moved by the irascible and the concupiscible appetite, but waits for the command of will, the higher appetite."[14] For a human being to eat the cheesecake, her intellect needs to judge that eating the cake is a good idea, and then her will needs to motivate her actually to eat it before she can actualize her capacity of locomotion in moving toward the cheesecake and devouring it, and her capacity of nutrition in digesting it.

Second, Aquinas considers the rational capacities superior to or "more perfect" than other human capacities because they are directed toward a higher or more perfect object — namely, being itself. This claim may sound a bit strange at first; we are used to thinking of capacities as abilities or powers *for* something, not as directed *at* something. We think of ourselves as having the capacity *for* sight, for example, more often than we think of our sight as a capacity directed *at* color. On Aquinas's framework, however, what a capacity is for immediately relates to what it is directed toward — that is, what its proper object is. Moreover, differences between the objects of capacities ground the distinctions between capacities.

Obviously, then, the vegetative, sensory, and rational capacities all have different proper objects. The vegetative capacities have as their proper object the body that exercises those capacities. As Aquinas puts it, vegetative capacities "[act] only on the body to which the soul is united."[15] That is, a sunflower's capacities for nutrition and growth are directed only toward sustaining that sunflower and not toward the ground in which it grows; in the same way, a skunk's capacities for nutrition and growth are directed only toward that skunk's body, not toward the neighboring squirrel. Another way to put this is to say that the powers of nutrition, growth, and even reproduction are "self-contained." They act on and are directed only toward the substance that possesses them.

In contrast, sensory capacities are directed toward anything that can be sensed—namely, physical objects in general. In this way, sensory capacities necessarily involve the relation of perceptive beings to other physical substances. Aquinas characterizes the difference between vegetative and sensory capacities by saying that the sensory capacities have "a more universal object." Rather than being concerned narrowly with only one body, as vegetative capacities are, sensory capacities are concerned broadly with *all* bodies.

Aquinas argues further that our rational capacities are directed even more generally; they are directed toward any and all existing things. Rather than concerning only physical objects, then, our rational capacities are "concerned with a still more universal object—namely, not only with sensible bodies, but universally with all being."[16] That is, our intellects are able to think about anything at all, from snowflakes to the nature of energy itself, and our wills are able to desire anything that exists, whether it is physical or not. We can, for example, both theorize about the nature of justice and deeply desire justice in our lives. To put the point in Aquinas's terms, the proper object of the rational capacities is *being itself*—certainly a "higher" object than just one individual substance, or even the entire class of physical substances. After all, God himself is pure being or pure actuality, on Aquinas's account. A capacity directed toward being itself is, most properly, directed toward God. Thus, our rational capacities are higher and more perfect than our other capacities because they are, ideally, directed toward the best possible object.

This point proves crucial to understanding the ultimate goal of human nature: human happiness. As we have seen, Aquinas claims that happiness consists in knowing and loving God, who is in his essence perfect, universal being. Our rational capacities (which, again, involve both our intellective and our volitional capacities) have as their proper object being itself—and so they are properly aimed at God. Directing our intellects and wills toward other things, such as memorizing the periodic table, is certainly *possible,* but our rational capacities will be completely and perfectly actualized only when they are directed at their proper object. It is certainly appropriate for us to use our intellective and volitional capacities to acquire a better understanding of Einstein's theory of relativity, but knowledge of that theory alone cannot perfectly actualize our rational capacities. Only knowledge of and love for God can do that, since only God is the first cause and final end of everything that exists.

This point also helps ground Aquinas's ethical theory, as we will see more fully in part 3 of this book. Since Aquinas equates being with goodness, he explains that we attain perfect human goodness only when we direct all of our capacities toward knowing and loving God. Everything we do is part of the moral life, whether it is praying, mowing the grass, or thinking about how best to care for our aging parents. When engaged in these activities, our capacities are put to proper use only if our desire in doing them — even in mowing the lawn — is grounded in a deeper desire to know and love God better.

Before we discuss the connection between human capacities and human goodness in detail, however, we need to say more about the nature of both the intellect and the will, and what it means to actualize those capacities fully. Intellect and will are both rational capacities; they both involve reason in some way or another. Intellect's connection to reason is obvious, since for us, intellection involves the activity of reasoning.[17] Roughly speaking, intellect is the capacity for cognition. More specifically, it is the capacity that allows us to comprehend the world around us — to recognize what is out there and to judge what might be worth pursuing. Our intellective powers enable us to recognize what courses of action are open to us and to make decisions about what we should do.

According to Aquinas, in fact, this is one of the central ways in which humans differ from all other animals. When a lion cub smells a dead zebra, for example, it instinctively scampers over to it; when it sees a crocodile at the waterhole, it instinctively runs away from it. It makes no judgments about the best course of action, and it does not (indeed, for Aquinas, cannot) consider the consequences of its action. Human beings, on the other hand, have the ability to make judgments about the best course of action; in addition, they have the ability to move from perception of material substances to the consideration of abstract concepts. So, for instance, if I see a dead zebra, I might initially be repulsed and want to run away from it. Upon consideration, however, I might decide it would be best to report the body to the park rangers before it attracts carrion birds. In this way, I am reasoning about what I think the best course of action is in this situation, not just reacting instinctively to the corpse. While waiting for the rangers to come, moreover, I could also begin to ponder the nature of death itself and think about what I want to accomplish before I die.

Aquinas believes that the proper object of the intellect is being itself, or true understanding of being. Intellects do not just allow human beings to respond to the external world in more complicated ways than nonrational animals can. Intellects allow human beings to reach beyond the physical world altogether. That is, the intellect is not meant just to decide which of two brands of cereal would be tastier for breakfast. Properly speaking, that is the work of the cogitative power, or of practical reason. The human intellect is meant to think about the nature of health itself and how it fits into the flourishing life, and then to use practical reason to deliberate about which choice of cereal would contribute more to that life.

In fact, the difference between contemplating the nature of health and deciding which cereal to eat for breakfast is dramatic enough that it leads Aquinas to distinguish between two different, corresponding aspects of the intellect: theoretical and practical.[18] Our theoretical or "speculative" reason, as Aquinas sometimes refers to it, is a capacity for recognizing and knowing the truth. It is at work when we evaluate the validity and soundness of an argument; it is at work when we contemplate the nature of God. Our practical reason, on the other hand, is our capacity for putting that knowledge into action — it is our capacity for determining how best to act on the basis of the truth we have comprehended. According to Aquinas, the proper object of practical reason is "the good directed to operation . . . under the aspect of truth."[19] Thus, our practical reason is at work when we try to determine whether we should specialize in pediatric medicine or go into occupational therapy, or when we try to figure out how best to comfort a friend who has just lost a parent. This distinction between reasoning about the truth versus reasoning about how to act on the basis of that truth helps us understand the difference we sometimes feel between, for example, the way the world *is* and the way the world *ought to be*.

This understanding of practical reason as directed toward the good "under the aspect of truth" also helps us see why Aquinas includes the will in the category of rational capacities. As we saw in chapter 1, Aquinas treats being as convertible with goodness; the fact that the proper object of the intellect is being thus entails that the intellect is also necessarily directed toward goodness. The contemplation of truth or goodness in and of itself, however, will not generate movement toward the good. Movement toward the good requires desire for the good — that is, it requires an appetite for the good. This appetite for what the intellect comprehends as good is the will, which Aquinas calls the *rational appetite*. Thus, our intellect involves the capacity to cognize being and to understand it as good; the will is the appetite specifically directed toward what the intellect presents to it under the description of "good."

In this way, the will straddles the divide between rational and appetitive capacities. It does not make judgments about the good; it merely follows reason's judgments about what is good, and it desires what is presented to it under that description. Yet Aquinas considers the will a *rational* appetite because it is our appetite for the good considered *as good*. Our sensory appetite desires things, such as cereal, simply because they look tasty or we are hungry. The will, however, desires the cereal *as a good* that contributes to a flourishing human life.

This difference can be made clear with a familiar example in which will and sensory appetite come into conflict. Suppose we have had two chocolate chip cookies, and we are already comfortably full. On the level of sense appetite, we want another one; it smells delicious, and we know it will taste good. On the level of the will, however, we do not want it; we are trying to stay fit, and we know — even before experiencing the sensation — that another cookie will leave us uncomfortably full. We exercise our will, then, in choosing not to eat another cookie; our rational appetite is directed toward what the intellect presents to it as good (namely, promoting our well-being) instead of what simply appeals to our senses.

Aquinas's explanation of the ways in which intellect and will interact is extremely complicated, especially when the concept of free choice enters the picture. In the second part of this book we discuss this interaction in detail, as well as how best to understand Aquinas's account of human actions. Here, however, what is important is the basic picture of how intellect and the will work together to produce human actions. In general, our intellect judges that a thing is good and presents it to our will, and our will then moves us toward that thing. Furthermore, the will must will some particular good or other, although it cannot make any judgments or deliberate about alternatives: that is the work of the intellect. The intellect performs its proper operation when it judges that something is good, and the will performs its proper operation when it desires that thing; both capacities need to be actualized for the whole human being to be actualized, or perfected. Moreover, we fully actualize those capacities only when we direct them toward perfect, complete truth and perfect, complete goodness—that is, only when we direct them toward God.

Being and Goodness Revisited

The pay-off of Aquinas's discussion of the soul's capacities (and in particular the discussion of intellect and will) is not just a deeper understanding of human nature, although that is certainly important. Rather, it is the insight into both how human beings *can* act and how they *should* act. An understanding of the soul's capacities allows us to see what is possible for human beings, how it could be made actual in human lives, and why that would be desirable for us—that is, why it would result in our flourishing. These topics lie at the heart of parts 2 and 3 of this book. In the remainder of this chapter, we set up that further discussion by returning to the connections Aquinas finds between potentiality, actuality, being, and goodness. We know that human beings are good to the extent to which they actualize their potentiality; more specifically, the best human beings are the ones who fully actualize all of their natural capacities. And, given our examination of human capacities, we are now in a position to see more clearly what that entails.

Again, according to Aquinas, "being and goodness are the same in reality; they differ only conceptually." Existence is a basic good. According to Aquinas, God's existence is completely actualized; God is, therefore, completely good. Furthermore, this God, who possesses absolute being and absolute goodness, causes everything else to come into being. Everything that exists owes its existence to God and is good insofar as it comes from God. Moreover, everything that exists was created for a particular purpose and with a particular nature, as a member of a particular species or natural kind. Things count as good, therefore, not merely by existing per se, but insofar as they live up to God's intent for them. Living things are good insofar as they exist fully as members of their natural kinds; they are good to the extent to which they exist *and fulfill their nature.*

Now, as we have already seen, something's nature (or essence) is closely related to its function—its characteristic activity. That is, what a thing *is* relates closely to what a thing *does.* A knife is, by nature, a cutting thing; its characteristic activity is thus cutting. A human being is, by nature, a rational animal; its characteristic activity is a life of activity expressing reason. In carrying out its function, a thing fulfills its nature. A thing's goodness, then, is intrinsically linked to how well that thing performs its function. To return to our earlier example, a knife that cuts a loaf of bread smoothly is good to the extent to which it exists and performs its function well. A blunt knife that crumbles a loaf of bread is good insofar as it exists, but it lacks goodness to the extent that it fails to fulfill its nature as a cutting thing. In the same way, a human being who reasons poorly about how to treat people and how to prioritize her life is good insofar as she exists, but she lacks goodness to the extent to which she is failing to perform her own characteristic activity successfully. A human being, however, who lives a life actively expressing reason *well* is good both insofar as she exists and to the extent that she performs her function well and fulfills God's intent for human nature.

In lumping moral agents together with bread knives, this general characterization of the relation between being and goodness might appear anemic in certain important respects. The ways in which human beings can count as bad human beings seem importantly dissimilar to the ways in which knives can count as bad knives. In particular, human beings, unlike knives, are capable of *moral* evil. A human being's conscious decision to torture a fellow human being seems bad or evil in a stronger way than a knife's crumbling a piece of bread does.

Aquinas holds, however, that the true explanation for moral evil should—and does—fit neatly into the general schema of being and goodness. Things lack goodness insofar as they fail to actualize the natural capacities that follow from their essences; moral evil results when human beings fail to actualize fully their capacities of intellect and will. To see this, it helps to return briefly to the four capacities that human beings share with other animals—the vegetative, sensory, sensory appetitive, and locomotive powers—and to look at the consequences of failing to actualize them well. We can fail to actualize our vegetative powers if we are unable to take in nutrition, grow, and reproduce successfully. For instance, David's esophagus could lack peristalsis, the muscular contraction that helps food move from the throat down to the stomach. In this case, David's vegetative capacity for nutrition is not fully actualized; he does not have a perfectly functioning esophagus, and to the extent that it does not contribute to his flourishing, Aquinas would say he has a bad esophagus. In the same way, David could be mostly deaf or blind. In either case, one of David's sensory capacities would fail to be actualized fully, and it would not be unusual to say that he has bad hearing or bad eyesight. Furthermore, defects in David's eyesight or hearing would impact his sensory appetitive capacities; his inability to see an oncoming car, for instance, would compromise his ability to actualize his desire to avoid danger. To give a less intuitive example, if David has an irrational fear of spiders, he might tend toward avoiding situations where he might encounter one, even if that means taking elaborate (and otherwise unnecessary) steps to avoid entering his basement. In this case, his irascible appetite is defective, since it fails in this respect to contribute to his flourishing and may, in fact, interfere with it. Finally, if David is hit by an oncoming car and becomes paralyzed, he would lose the ability to exercise his capacity for locomotion—something that would certainly have far-reaching consequences for the other aspects of his life.

In all these cases David fails fully to actualize certain human capacities, and in so doing, he falls short of fulfilling his nature as a human being. On Aquinas's schema, for these reasons, although David is still a human being, he does not count as a fully actualized, perfect member of the human species. Yet in all of these cases, the respects in which David fails to actualize his capacities seem out of his control, and so we are strongly inclined to say that David is not a *bad* human being simply because he cannot hear well, suffers from arachnophobia, or cannot walk on his own.

According to Aquinas, this simply shows that there are two ways in which we can fall short of human flourishing, one moral and one nonmoral. If David lacks locomotive powers he falls short of genuine human flourishing, but this defect does not make him *morally blameworthy* any more than a blunt knife's failing to cut well makes that knife morally blameworthy. If David fails to exercise his capacities for moral actions in the right way, on the other hand—if he ignores the stop sign in front of him and runs into another car, for instance—then he *is* blameworthy. Simply put, we need to actualize all of our capacities to reach our ultimate end, but the question of moral responsibility only enters the picture in the cases that involve actualizing the capacities we have control over, most particularly, intellect and will.

Intellect and will, as we saw, direct and command the other capacities; human beings generally can control how and even whether to actualize many of their capacities. We can, for instance, learn ballroom dancing, and we can choose not to reproduce; we can develop a keen appreciation for punk rock while avoiding country music altogether. A morally good human being, for Aquinas, is one who makes these decisions with the universal good for human life firmly in mind. Such a human being knowingly and willingly participates in actualizing her capacities in the best possible way; she consistently chooses the good. Moral failure results when we fall short of doing what we can to fulfill our nature. This kind of failure is quite different from not being able to hear or see. We have the capacity for both knowing and loving the good, and when we fail to actualize that capacity, we are actively—consciously—turning away from the good.

Thus, an individual human being is good in both the moral and the nonmoral sense to the extent to which she exists as a fully actualized rational animal. Ultimately, she is good insofar as she fulfills her potential for knowing and loving God. This activity involves all the human capacities, from vegetative on up—but it involves the intellective and volitional capacities most of all. In part 2, we will address how intellect and will work together to produce human actions, and how, in particular, Aquinas explains the existence of both moral goodness and sin. Only then will we be in a position to appreciate fully Aquinas's ethical account of the good life human beings are meant to live and how we can attain it.

Part Two
Human Actions

four

Actions and Ends

Given *Aquinas's account of human capacities, we are now in a* position to consider how he explains human action, which is foundational for his account of ethics. Aquinas explains such important moral notions as right and wrong, virtue and vice, in terms of the basic components of human action. Therefore, in order to understand his ethics, we need to understand what a human action is and what makes a particular action good or bad. This will allow us to see how Aquinas ties human actions to the development of virtuous and vicious character.

A grasp of the components of human action also helps us to see what differentiates our actions from the behavior of other animals. For example, we would hold our friend responsible for breaking a valuable antique vase, but we would not hold our dog responsible. We might be angry at the dog for knocking over the vase, but we would not think that the dog should replace the vase or exhibit the kind of remorse that we would expect of a human agent. There is something importantly different about the human case when it comes to praise and blame. Aquinas has a clear and concise explanation for what makes human action distinct.

Finally, we want to know *why* human beings do what they do. We want to know what motivates them to do what is right and equally what motivates them to do what is wrong, particularly when they are willing to grant that what they are doing is wrong. If we could understand what motivates violent events of the past and the rise of terrorism in our own time we might be better able to deal with them or even avert them in the future. Bad action is especially pertinent for this project because Aquinas is committed to the view that human beings are naturally oriented to their own good—and that their own good necessarily involves moral goodness. If Aquinas is to claim that all human actions are directed toward happiness, then he must explain why human beings perform bad actions that do not contribute to that good. Thus, he must explain how wrong action is in fact possible on his account.

To consider Aquinas's rationale for these claims and more, we begin by looking at Aquinas's general account of action, after a brief review of the basic capacities that enable human beings to act. Next, we will look at the end toward which human action is directed. Finally, we will examine what goes on when human beings act—the actual process that produces human action.

THE SOURCE OF HUMAN ACTION

What makes it possible for us to perform the actions we perform? On Aquinas's view, as discussed earlier, we need a body; we cannot do what we do without one. This is true even for what we might call internal actions, such as thinking about the weekend or yearning for the latest computer—that is, for actions that are not readily visible to an external observer. What directs the body's actions? As we have already seen, Aquinas's answer involves an appeal to powers or capacities that have their foundation in the human soul. The rational capacities of the human soul that primarily facilitate action are the intellect and the will. Working with the sensory capacities, the intellect—the cognitive capacity—has two main functions. It enables us to comprehend the world around ourselves in virtue of its speculative (or theoretical) capacity; this capacity allows us to recognize and understand the truth. The intellect also enables us to recognize possible objects of pursuit in virtue of its practical capacity; that is to say, it enables us to recognize what courses of action are open to us or what sorts of things we ought to pursue. This power of practical reasoning enables us to think about alternatives for action and make decisions about what to do; it allows us to know and recognize the good.

The will is what Aquinas calls a rational appetite — that is, an appetite that is capable of responding to a judgment from the intellect. Because it is an appetitive power, it inclines the human being toward particular objects of desire. In virtue of the will, we find ourselves attracted to various things out there in the world.

Human action is neither random nor arbitrary; it is purposive. According to Aquinas, it is always directed toward a particular goal or end; if it is not so directed, it does not count as a human action.[1] Instead, it is what Aquinas calls a mere "act of a human being," such as aimlessly scratching one's face or rubbing one's eye. "Acts of a human being" for him are brute responses to external stimuli. They do not involve the kind of thought and desire involved in human action, properly speaking, which is the result of what Aquinas calls a deliberate will.[2]

Aquinas implies two things by this locution, "deliberate will." First, he implies that when we perform a human action, we do something we intend to do; that is, our action is deliberate. Second, he implies that it results from the activity of the will. His description of a human action as the result of a deliberate will, however, seems to leave the intellect out altogether. What is the intellect's role in this process? For Aquinas, the intellect is found in the "deliberate" part; the intellect allows the agent to identify the various courses of action that are open to her and to consider the pros and cons of these alternatives. In considering them, the agent settles upon and inclines toward a particular course of action, which she ultimately performs. The action is deliberate — namely, something directly intended by the agent — insofar as the agent deliberates over various courses of action and settles upon one of them, the one she wants to do. The deliberation is made possible in virtue of having an intellect, while the desiring — the willing, the inclining — is made possible in virtue of having a will. Thus, action is the result of a deliberate will. We shall see that the process of executing an action is a bit more complex than this, but this description captures the basic idea.

Recall that for Aquinas, the will is not some neutral power that inclines willy-nilly toward everything out there in the world. Rather, the will is an appetite for the good.[3] This is not to say that the will cannot be directed toward something that is in fact bad. Aquinas is willing to grant that agents choose what is bad all the time. Instead, Aquinas's view means that whatever the agent chooses, she at least judges or perceives that there is something good about it. The cigarette smoker acknowledges that smoking is bad yet smokes anyway because of the pleasure she obtains from it. Furthermore, the will need not move toward something just because it is good. A thing's being good (or being perceived as such) is not a sufficient condition for the will to choose it; it is only a necessary condition. Thus, an individual might judge that the candy bar would taste good but still not eat it because she might also recognize that the candy bar is bad for her health; as a result, she does not choose to eat it. The reason she does not choose to eat it is that she values her health, in light of which she chooses to forego the candy bar. Thus, she pursues her health on the basis of her judgment of what is good.

Aquinas does not hold that the will pursues only things that are perfectly good. If it did, human beings would not do very much, since virtually all the things that we pursue lack goodness in some respect. The candy bar tastes good but is bad for one's health; health is a good, but it requires a great deal of effort to maintain it. Aquinas thinks that the things we desire in this life (as opposed to the next) always have some defect in them; none of them is perfectly good.[4] For Aquinas, it need only be the case that there is *something* good about a particular object for it to be a possible object of choice by the will—or at least, for the intellect to judge that there is something good about it.[5]

The will never wills only for the sake of willing; it always wills something—a particular goal or end, called its object. Thus, because human action has its source in the intellect and the will, all human action comes about for the sake of some end. It follows from Aquinas's view that human beings do not simply drift aimlessly about in life. All of us know people who always seem to be pursuing some goal and always seem to act with a specific purpose in mind. Nevertheless, we also know people who seem simply to drift from day to day without any purpose in mind. How is Aquinas going to explain these individuals?

Aquinas would argue that at the very least, the drifters drift because they regard drifting as a good. In their view, it is too much trouble to go off and do something—far better just to let life roll by. Most of us would reject such a life, but Aquinas need not criticize the drifter's life as far as his theory of action is concerned, for determining which kinds of life are worth pursuing is a task for ethics. All he needs to do is to account for the existence of such lives and such attitudes. It is of course a further question whether Aquinas's account is correct, but it does make sense on his account to argue that drifting just *is* the goal of the drifter, and that she sees a life of ease as a good.

THE ULTIMATE END OF ACTION

For Aquinas, not only is every action aimed at an end, which the agent regards as a good, but, in the final analysis, every action is aimed at an ultimate end, of which Aquinas argues there is only one.[6] This is a very strong claim. It has appeared implausible to many people, which is probably why Aquinas defends it at some length.[7] Here is his line of reasoning: The end is an object of desire, what one wants to accomplish. Above all else, human beings desire their own completeness. That is to say, human beings are created in such a way that they desire above all what fulfills their particular set of natural capacities. To fulfill these natural capacities is to achieve perfection, and to achieve perfection is to achieve that which one desires above all. Achieving perfection satisfies all of one's desires, which is what it means to be an ultimate end. For either a given object can satisfy our every desire or it cannot. If it cannot, then it cannot be the ultimate end because there would be something more we would need in order to be satisfied. On the other hand, if it does satisfy our every desire, then we have no need for anything further. We will have attained our ultimate end, and what we have attained will be the *only* thing that is the ultimate end.

The claim that everything we do is for the sake of some ultimate end seems problematic. If Leslie is relaxing in the local coffee shop, it is quite a stretch to say that she is doing so because she thinks it will somehow complete her as a person or increase her own perfection. Aquinas is well aware of the controversial nature of his views and in fact goes on to make even more controversial claims. He argues that not only is there one single ultimate end of all human action, but that the ultimate end is the same for all human beings. We need to look more closely at these claims to see whether Aquinas is able to defend them.[8]

Aquinas observes that whatever has a beginning is directed toward its completion and thus its perfection.[9] He thinks this is true both in nature and in human artifice: birds start out as babies and grow to maturity; the author begins writing a book intending to finish it; the builder builds a house and collects her money. Of course not everything makes it to completion: birds can die before they reach maturity; authors can give up; builders can go bankrupt. In these situations, the typical course of events has been interrupted before completion. This is also the case with our actions. What we want above all, Aquinas thinks, is the satisfaction of all of our desires. Once those desires are all satisfied, there is nothing left for us to want, and we will cease our searching and thus our doing. Thus, Aquinas thinks that either we choose directly what we at least perceive will satisfy completely all of our desires, or we choose what we at least perceive will help us attain the complete satisfaction of all of our desires. Aquinas thinks that these are the only two possible motivations for action; on his view, everything we do is for the sake of the ultimate end, either directly or indirectly.

Aquinas thinks that unless we had an ultimate end, we would never do anything.[10] The ultimate end functions as what he calls a "first mover" in a particular line of movers. Think of a freight train that consists of a locomotive and a long line of rail cars. The motion of the entire train depends upon the locomotive; unless it moves, none of the rail cars will move, and the entire train goes nowhere. Aquinas argues that the ultimate end operates in a similar manner. Unless there is a final goal, nothing would be desired, and no chain of action would result.[11] Aquinas, however, gives us no reason to think that an ultimate end functions like the locomotive in a freight train. He also gives us no reason to think that our actions can be motivated only by direct or indirect consideration of the ultimate end. His claims become more plausible if we consider what in fact Aquinas believes is the ultimate end of human life — happiness.

As we saw earlier, Aquinas believes that what we desire above all is the satisfaction of all of our desires, and what will satisfy all of our desires is happiness. Happiness is a notoriously difficult concept to articulate.[12] When we think about what it means to be happy, we often think about being content or tranquil or joyful; we focus on our emotional state. Aquinas would say that our emotional state might reflect our being happy, but that would be a side effect of happiness and not happiness itself. Alternatively, we might think of happiness as being a matter of getting what we want out of life, of having our desires satisfied. This is in fact closer to what Aquinas has in mind by happiness, but we must take care here. Aquinas is not advocating some simple-minded hedonism of instant gratification; not just any desires count. He also acknowledges that happiness means different things to different people and argues against various options: wealth, honors, fame, power, health, pleasure, or some good that pertains to the human soul.[13] Some of these things come close to capturing Aquinas's conception of happiness. He thinks, for example, that the soul plays an important role in the attainment of happiness, even if we cannot identify happiness solely with some state of the soul, such as temperance or another virtue.[14] The main problem with all of these possibilities is that they cannot fulfill human capacities adequately because they are not perfect goods, and so none of them constitutes happiness.

As we saw earlier, Aquinas thinks that genuine happiness involves our relationship with God.[15] We now know why. The desire for happiness is a desire for that which will satisfy us completely and fulfill all of our capacities — a good that is perfect in every respect.[16] Only God is perfectly good, and therefore only God has the wherewithal to make human beings happy.[17]

How does God make human beings happy? Aquinas's account is complex and seems to evolve as one proceeds from his theory of action to his ethical theory. As we have seen, Aquinas argues that happiness is knowing and loving God. When he is discussing the particularities of human action, however, he emphasizes the intellect's role over that of the will. He defines happiness as an intellectual vision of God, which he calls the beatific vision.[18] In fact, he argues that happiness cannot be primarily an act of the will, because an act of the will is not sufficient to guarantee that an end is actually attained. Aquinas gives an example of the greedy man who desires money. His mere desire is not enough to ensure that he will actually attain the money; he must engage in action in order to acquire it. Similarly, mere desire of the ultimate end is not sufficient to acquire it; something more needs to be done. It is through an act of the intellect (made possible by God) that the beatific vision, our final end, actually becomes present to us.[19]

Nevertheless, the will is necessary for attainment of the beatific vision, even if it is not primary. Human beings cannot arrive at this ultimate end unless they are properly ordered to it, and they cannot be properly ordered to it unless their wills are oriented in the right way—that is, unless they have upright wills. Thus, rectitude of the will is a necessary precondition for attaining the beatific vision, which is happiness.[20] Furthermore, Aquinas thinks that a certain joy or delight necessarily accompanies the vision of the divine, which human beings would not feel unless they had wills. The will enables us to have the attendant joy when we attain the ultimate end.[21] Hence, happiness consists in knowing and loving God, which comes about only when the intellect and the upright will are fully engaged.

Despite Aquinas's inclusion of the will, what we see here is an emphasis on the activities of the intellect over the will in the attainment of happiness. On the other hand, in his discussions of the virtuous life, Aquinas emphasizes the primacy of the will, which ultimately is directed toward God through charity—the virtue identified with love of God. Charity orients us toward our ultimate end, which is union with God. As we can see, Aquinas's discussion of the ethical life offers a more pronounced role for the will than is found in his discussion of action, the implications of which will become clear later. For now it is enough to note that both intellect and will, the capacities that distinguish human nature from that of other animals, play important roles in the attainment of happiness. Because the attainment of happiness requires the rational capacities of intellect and will, other animals cannot be happy. On Aquinas's account, knowing and loving God, the perfect good, completes and perfects our distinctly human capacities and as a result satisfies all human desire.[22]

Since God is a transcendent being that most human beings encounter only indirectly in this life, it is obvious that for Aquinas ultimate happiness is unattainable in this life.[23] Does that mean that we cannot be happy here? Aquinas thinks that we can approximate ultimate happiness in this life through contemplation—the human activity that most closely resembles what he thinks is going on in the beatific vision.[24] Contemplation involves the direct use of the intellect rather than the will, so it resembles happiness in that regard. In a life of contemplation, one engages in the deliberation of the eternal truth and the Supreme Good. On Aquinas's account, that just *is* God. As a result, whether one is conscious of it or not, when one considers eternal truth and the Supreme Good, one is directing one's attention to God. Thus, a life of contemplation bears a resemblance to ultimate happiness. Furthermore, many of the rejected candidates for happiness play a role in enabling one to engage in contemplation and thus enabling one to achieve this approximation of happiness.[25] One needs a certain amount of money, for example, to support a life of contemplation. Having one's health helps as well. And on Aquinas's view of cognition, prior acts of sensory apprehension are a necessary condition for engaging the intellect, at least in this life.[26] For example, our understanding of the structure of the DNA molecule is rooted in empirical observation. So, while happiness does not consist in wealth, health, or sensory apprehension, these have a connection to whatever happiness we can approximate in this life, insofar as they bring about the conditions under which contemplation is possible and can flourish.[27]

Finally, Aquinas argues that human beings are not able to acquire genuine happiness solely through their own powers, although they are able to attain its approximation through their own efforts, and their good acts help them to merit genuine happiness as a reward.[28] Since happiness is the vision of something infinitely beyond us, its attainment exceeds our natural powers.[29] Thus, in the final analysis, our acquisition of happiness relies upon God's power—in particular, God's grace.[30] In part 3 of this book we will look more closely at the role that grace plays in Aquinas's ethical theory.

What we have seen so far is that for Aquinas, all human beings have an ultimate end, and they do what they do for the sake of that end. He does not think that we always have to be conscious of choosing what we think will help us achieve our ultimate end.[31] Aquinas uses the analogy of a journey. One can walk from Jerusalem to Jericho without always being conscious that one is doing so; yet if asked, the traveler will surely reply that her destination is Jericho. It is similarly the case with the ultimate end. If we ask Leslie why she is hanging out in the coffee shop, initially she will say that she wanted a cup of coffee. If we ask her why she wanted a cup of coffee, she will say that coffee tastes good to her, or it wakes her up in the morning, or she finds it a satisfying drink. We could persist in our questions, and eventually Aquinas thinks that Leslie will describe how coffee fits into her vision of a satisfying life. In other words, eventually she will answer, "Because it makes me happy." If we persist in our annoying questions and ask her why she wants to be happy, she will be puzzled. There is nothing further she wants, and so there is no further answer she can think to give. The question simply makes no sense. The reason it makes no sense is that she has no further ends, nothing more she wishes to achieve than happiness. Aquinas would say that this demonstrates that there is an ultimate end for human beings and that ultimate end is happiness, which for Aquinas is the vision of the divine essence, a vision that involves the intellect and will.

Next, we consider Aquinas's account of the process of action, which also involves the activities of intellect and will. This, in turn, will help us better understand the elements of Aquinas's ethical views. For example, Aquinas defines virtue and vice as habits that move us to act well, in the case of virtue, or badly, in the case of vice.[32] Habits themselves arise from repetitions of actions. Thus, there are fundamental connections between the process of action and the elements of Aquinas's ethics. So we need to look more closely at the process by which an action comes about, on Aquinas's view.[33]

THE PROCESS OF ACTION: INTELLECT AND WILL

One must keep in mind that although Aquinas frames his discussion of the events that constitute an action in terms of the intellect and will, he recognizes that it is the human being who acts.[34] Human beings are able to act because they possess the capacities of intellect and will. Also, although these events are presented sequentially, an event that occurs earlier on the list is not necessarily *temporally* prior to one listed later, although certain events will be *logically* prior to others. For example, one cannot make a choice unless one has at least one possibility in mind from which to choose. However, Aquinas need not be committed to the view that one has to deliberate over what to do before one is able to choose at some later time — although, of course, with any given action, it may turn out that that is what transpired. The point is that this sequence of events often comes about very quickly in reality, and some events may be simultaneous in time even though we can recognize a logical priority of some events over others.

In the sequence of events that terminate in a particular action, first the will intends a particular end.[35] Suppose it is Friday night, and Leslie is trying to decide what she should do. She could finish up her philosophy paper, or she could simply relax since it has been a tough week. Since the will is not an apprehensive power, it depends upon the intellect to apprehend or identify ends that it, the will, could intend. Thus, the will's intention of any given end presupposes an act of the intellect.[36] Unless Leslie, in virtue of her intellect, recognizes that there are any number of things she could do on a Friday night, she would never have a particular goal or end in mind for Friday night. Suppose Leslie decides to relax. Once the end, relaxation, has been identified, the intellect engages in its activity of deliberation to identify the means by which the end can be attained; that is, Leslie has to think about what sorts of things she could do in order to achieve her goal of relaxation.[37]

Aquinas places two conditions upon deliberation. First, he maintains that deliberation takes place only when there is more than one way to achieve the end, or when there is some question of how to achieve the end, since if there is an established way to accomplish a given end, which the agent understands, then there is no deliberation over the means required to achieve the end. Aquinas argues that the scribe does not think about how to form each letter when he is copying the manuscript.[38] There is an established method for writing the letters, which the scribe has internalized, and so it is not necessary for him to think about what he should do in carrying out his duties. On the other hand, if there are several ways of accomplishing a given end, or if the agent is unsure of how she ought to go about achieving her goals, then she needs to think about what options are open to her and what she ought to do. In Leslie's case, there are lots of things she could do to achieve her end of relaxation: she could go to the movies; she could invite friends over and have an impromptu party; she could stay home and watch television; she could read a book; she could play board games with her roommate. So she deliberates over how she could achieve her end by identifying a number of alternatives that could serve as the means for achieving that end.

Aquinas's second important condition for deliberation is that there is no deliberation over ends, only over the means for achieving these ends.[39] This is bound to appear implausible. Surely there are plenty of ends over which we deliberate: we think about what we want to do on a Friday night, about where we want to live, about what career we want to pursue. All of these are ends about which we think and about which we sometimes think long and hard. Aquinas acknowledges this fact, but he thinks that we deliberate over these ends not insofar as they are ends, but insofar as they are means for some further end, and especially as they relate to the ultimate end—that is, to happiness, about which Aquinas thinks there is no deliberation.[40] On Aquinas's view, since all human beings desire their own happiness, happiness, the ultimate end, is simply a given. Thus, every other end is not solely an end but also a means to this further (ultimate) end, and the reason we deliberate over them is that they are means to the ultimate end. On Aquinas's view, Leslie deliberates over what to do on a Friday night because she is thinking about what will make her happy. Relaxation may be an end, but she adopts this (intermediate) end as a means to the ultimate end.

Leslie's end is relaxation, and she has identified a number of ways to achieve that end, considering the pros and cons of each of them. The next step in the process is what Aquinas calls consent. Consent terminates deliberation. As long as there is uncertainty over what alternatives are acceptable, or doubt about what to do, deliberation continues. Consent is the final decision about what to do.[41] Calling consent a decision suggests that it is a function of the intellect, but Aquinas characterizes consent as an activity of the will, albeit one that is responsive to prior activity of the intellect.[42] The intellect judges that one or more potential courses of action are suitable. Insofar as they are suitable, the will inclines toward them. It does not incline toward anything the intellect judges to be unfit for action, since such alternatives are not perceived as good, and the will is an inclination for the good. This inclination of the will toward the suitable alternatives is called consent.

In the example under consideration, suppose that Leslie judges that going to the movies and playing board games with her roommate are suitable courses of action. The party is too much work; she is rather tired from the week. There is nothing worth watching on television. Reading a book is attractive, but she would prefer to spend some time with her roommate, whom she has not seen all week, and the roommate likes both movies and board games. So her intellect has narrowed things down to two possibilities for Friday night. Both are good; both are things Leslie would enjoy doing. At this point, Leslie has finished her evaluation of the various alternatives for Friday night and has settled upon these two in virtue of her intellect. In virtue of the will, she feels an attraction to either of these possibilities. She has consented to each.

The pattern that Aquinas has presented so far is the following: first, there is an apprehension of an end, followed by a desire for the end; next comes deliberation over the means for achieving the end—what Aquinas calls "the things that are for the sake of the end"—followed by a desire for the means.[43] Each of these steps consists of a paired set of activities, one from the intellect and one from the will. Thus, what we have seen so far is that the intellect and the will work together in producing an action.

In deliberation, the intellect may come up with several possible ways to achieve the end, or perhaps only one way. If there are several that are acceptable, the will consents to each one. If there is only one live possibility, the will consents to it, and in doing so, essentially achieves the next step, which is choice.[44] In other words, when deliberation uncovers only one suitable alternative for accomplishing the end, consent collapses into choice. If Leslie consents to both the movie and the board game, then she feels an inclination toward each of these possibilities. Now suppose she looks at the movie selections and determines that none of the movies currently playing in town look very interesting. She could of course go to the video store and rent a movie, but that is too much trouble. So she decides that there is really only one alternative that is plausible, and that is playing the board games. In this case, given the disadvantages of the other alternative, she no longer regards it as attractive; that is, she no longer consents to it. At this stage, she has made her choice.

Although it seems a simple matter to us in virtue of its familiarity, choice is a very complex notion for Aquinas. He holds that choice is an act of the will that presupposes an act of the intellect, which orders the act of the will.[45] What this means is that the will is not able to choose something that has not been presented to it by the intellect. In other words, we cannot choose something of which we are not aware. If the only alternatives

Leslie has considered for Friday night are going to the movies and playing board games, she cannot choose to go to a party, since it never occurred to her that she could do so. Since the intellect is that power by which we come to recognize potential courses of action, the will, in making a choice, depends upon the activities of the intellect in order to have alternatives for choosing. In Aquinas's words, appetite (i.e., inclination or desire) follows cognition.[46]

Aquinas's claim that the will depends upon the intellect has both a stronger and a weaker interpretation. When he says that the intellect orders the act of the will, he might mean that the intellect comes up with one or more alternatives for action and the will chooses among those alternatives; that would be a weak interpretation of the claim. However, Aquinas might mean something stronger; he might mean that the very alternative that is chosen by the will is determined by the intellect. His characterization of choice implies that he holds this stronger interpretation.

Aquinas characterizes choice as materially an act of the will but formally an act of the intellect.[47] What he means by this is that while the will does the actual choosing—the "material" act—the intellect forms or structures the content of the choice—the "formal" act. Thus, he implies that it is the intellect that determines which alternative for action is actually chosen. In fact, he holds that the process of choosing *requires* that the will desire the alternative that the intellect has determined is to be preferred.[48]

Aquinas's characterization of choice does not mean that the will has no role to play in bringing about a choice. On the contrary, unless the will engages in its activity, there will be no choice. Unless the will inclines the agent toward the alternative that the intellect presents to be chosen, the agent fails to choose. Thus, the fact that a choice comes into being at all depends directly upon the inclination of the will. In this sense, then, choice is materially an act of the will. Nevertheless, the intellect determines which particular thing is chosen, thus configuring the nature of the choice. Just as on the Aristotelian model of form and matter, the form configures the matter, making it into a thing of a particular sort, so too, in specifying *what* the will chooses, the intellect makes the choice a choice of a particular sort. One chooses to eat ice cream rather than choosing to walk past the sweet shop.

Returning to our example, Leslie has figured out that her only "live" option, so to speak, is playing board games with her roommate, and she does so in virtue of her intellect. At this point, however, she has not actually chosen to play board games. She has not suggested it to her roommate; she has not asked her which game she wants to play; she has not actually gotten the game out yet. It is still just a judgment she has made on the basis of her deliberation. Something more needs to take place, namely, an act of the will. Leslie must be moved, in virtue of her will, to choose the board game option. In Aquinas's terms, Leslie's intellect presents the board game option to her will, which then moves her toward that option. The choice is set up by the intellect's process of deliberation, but that an actual choice is made is due to the motion of the will.

Choice directly initiates the process of executing the action, which involves two aspects: command and use. After the will makes the choice directed by the intellect, the intellect commands that the will activate the appropriate powers and limbs of the body to execute the action.[49] The will activates the appropriate powers and limbs through an activity that Aquinas calls "use."[50] In an act of use, the stimulation of the appropriate parts of the body by the will brings it about that the actual visible action takes place.[51]

In terms of the rational capacities involved, we can analyze Leslie's choice to play board games this way: Leslie's intellect commands her will to activate those parts of the body that need to be activated in order to fulfill the choice. In other words, once she chooses to play board games, she asks her roommate if she wants to play, they decide what game or games to play, they get the games out, and they play them. Aquinas thinks that the will's moving the appropriate limbs of the body in response to the direction of the intellect produces Leslie's externally observable action (or in this case, a sequence of her actions).

Thus, the pivotal part of the whole process for Aquinas is choice. Choice determines the action that will take place and initiates the final cascade of events that culminate in the performance of the action. It is, as Alan Donagan puts it in the title of his 1987 book of essays, the "essential element in human action."[52]

Once we perform a particular action and achieve a particular end, we enjoy and delight in our achievement. We experience enjoyment in virtue of the will,[53] although Aquinas argues that only the ultimate end brings about perfect enjoyment, for until we have achieved the ultimate end and all of our desires are satisfied, we remain restless. Even though the achievement of intermediate ends does not satisfy us fully, still, we get a certain pleasure from these ends, for they themselves carry with them a particular, albeit imperfect, form of delight.[54] Leslie could not play board games forever; she would get bored after a while. For a Friday night's entertainment, however, board games can bring her some enjoyment. Aquinas is also willing to grant that we can receive a particular pleasure from the anticipation of our achievements, even before we accomplish them, although once again, he argues that this is an imperfect form of enjoyment.[55] Anticipating a vacation trip, say, to New Zealand can bring a certain amount of enjoyment to an agent even before she steps on the plane; the mere idea of it can bring a smile to her face.

To sum up, Aquinas gives us this picture of an individual action: a human agent intends an end in virtue of the will, an end that has been identified previously by the intellect. If necessary, the will moves the intellect to deliberate over various means of achieving that end. The intellect identifies appropriate means and other matters pertinent to the end, and the will consents to these means. The intellect judges which alternative for action is to be performed and presents this alternative to the will, which chooses the alternative in question. Intellect commands the will to execute the alternative by acting upon the appropriate parts of the body. The latter actually produce the action that is visible to an external audience, but the limbs of the body would be unable to complete the action without the carefully coordinated and orchestrated activities of the intellect and the will. Finally, in virtue of the action (or sequence of actions), the human agent experiences a state of enjoyment and delight in the achievement of the end, once again in virtue of the will.[56] Thus, human action, although ultimately a function of the body, is made possible by the integrated activities of the intellect and will.

This all sounds very complex; we are often unaware of doing all of this when we act. Keep in mind that Aquinas does not take himself to be giving a strictly empirical account of what transpires in every case of action. For example, we may not make a conscious and explicit act of deliberation in a particular situation. We might simply recognize what needs to be done and do it.[57] Aquinas would grant the point. He would argue, though, that if we were asked why we did what we did, we could give reasons for our action, and that fact demonstrates that there is at least some (very quick, unself-conscious) activity of the intellect going on. Similar points can be made for other steps along the way.

The picture we have been considering makes it clear that action comes about in virtue of close interaction between intellect and will. Aquinas argues that the activities of intellect and will are ordered toward one another.[58] That is to say, they are directed toward the same sort of thing, and something of the other power is found in each of their own domains. As we have seen, Aquinas argues that there is something of the intellect in the will's activity of choosing—namely, a prior judgment of what to do.[59] There is something of the will in the intellect's activity of deliberation insofar as the intellect deliberates over how to accomplish what the agent *wishes* to do, and wishing is a function of an appetitive power.[60] Furthermore, in carrying out their specific roles, intellect and will act upon each other and in that sense share each other's activities. The will inclines toward a particular object because the intellect presents this object to the will, and the will moves the intellect to its activities of deliberation. Thus, there are very tight connections between intellect and will as they work together to bring about a given action.

THE PROCESS OF ACTION: PASSION

Although Aquinas argues that human action comes about primarily in virtue of the interaction between intellect and will, he is well aware that another important influence motivates our actions—the passions. As we shall see, passions have an important effect upon intellect and will and, therefore, upon action. Their influence affects the moral appraisal of action, which we will consider in the next chapter. Furthermore, insofar as there are virtues and vices that affect the passions, passions will also be important in our discussion of Aquinas's ethics in part 3.

The term "passion" implies something that is passive, something that happens to a thing rather than something a thing does. It suggests a reaction rather than an action that one has initiated. This idea is reflected in Aquinas's account of the passions. The passions arise as a result of changes in the body in response to an external stimulus.[61] Because they can move us, Aquinas locates them in an appetitive power, and because they have to do with the body, he locates them in the sensory appetite.[62]

We saw in the earlier chapters that the sensory appetite has to do with pleasures and pain, and that Aquinas divides the sensory appetite into two parts: the concupiscible power and the irascible power. Each part has its own passions; what distinguishes them is their relationship to the pleasurable good.

The passions found in the concupiscible part are love, desire, joy, hatred, aversion, and sadness.[63] Aquinas argues that the concupiscible power moves the agent toward what is pleasant and away from what is painful. It has to do with the pleasurable good in and of itself—that is, the pleasurable good without qualification. One loves, desires, and finds joy in the good insofar as it is good, and one hates, avoids, and is made sad by evil insofar as it is evil.[64]

The irascible power moves the agent toward a good that is difficult or arduous to achieve. It also has to do with the pleasurable good, but only in a particular respect—that is, insofar as it is difficult to obtain.[65] It helps us to keep on going in the face of the arduous situation that tempts us to give up. Thus, we have hope that we can accomplish a particular good despite the obstacles in our path, and we dare to pursue it. Or we despair that we can bring about a particular good because of the obstacles in our way. We dread a looming evil because to overcome it will be arduous or even impossible, and we fear that there is no way around it. We become angry in the face of an offending evil and are moved to oppose it.[66]

The effects of our passions on our actions can be good or bad depending upon their relationship with the intellect. Aquinas follows Aristotle in holding that passions are responsive to the intellect; insofar as they do not oppose what the intellect has judged as good, they add to the perfection of human nature and increase the goodness of our actions.[67] In other words, when the passions stay in line with the judgments of (right) intellect, human beings are functioning as God intended. Suppose that Nick has the good goal of maintaining a good relationship with his friend and recognizes that his hot temper is interfering with that goal. If his passions are orderly, then although he might feel some regret at restraining his anger and frustration when he would prefer to vent it at his friend's expense, by and large, he manages to hold his tongue and refrain from blowing off steam over small irritations, and feels satisfied with having achieved a more constructive friendship as a result. His passions are in line with what his intellect tells him is the right thing to do, and so they add to the goodness of his actions.

When the passions are unruly and oppose the good identified by the intellect, human beings act in opposition to the intentions of God. If Nick's passions are disorderly, then he struggles to restrain his anger and may in fact even give in and blow up at his friend on the slightest provocation. His passions incline him in opposition to his good judgment and make it harder for him to do the right thing.

The passions can also make a particular alternative look good that ordinarily would not look good.[68] This too can operate in a positive or negative way. Suppose that ordinarily Sue would never consider buying a brand new BMW. Now suppose she gets a promotion at work, which stimulates a desire for a status car and makes it appear to be a good thing. Or, to consider a different case, most drivers would never dream of ramming another vehicle on the road or shooting at the vehicle with a gun, but under the influence of anger at being cut off by an inconsiderate driver, those options might all of a sudden appear attractive. On the other hand, consider an individual who is usually timid about caves, or perhaps is claustrophobic. Ordinarily she would not want to enter a cave. If her child is lost in the cave, however, all of a sudden she finds the courage to enter the cave and rescue her child.

Besides enhancing formerly distasteful options, the passions can also distract us from considering particular ideas and options that we could and should be considering.[69] For example, Kim could be so overcome with excitement that she forgets to check the bungee cord to make sure it is fastened securely as she jumps off the bridge. Or Tom could become so paralyzed with grief and sorrow at his wife's death that he fails to notice that his children need to be fed dinner. It is apparent from these examples that passions have their effect upon our deliberation and judgments about what to do.

Passions can also augment our rational abilities. For example, Aquinas argues that we gain feelings of pleasure from engaging our intellectual capacities. The pleasure we feel can spur us on to greater intellectual achievement.[70] The timid parent who rescues her lost child is stimulated by the passion of daring to face the potential danger of the cave.[71] It enhances her judgment that entering the cave is the right thing to do. It helps her intellect and will to overcome her usual fears.

Because passions are motions that happen to us, as opposed to motions that we bring about, in a certain sense we have no control over them. A pit bull lunges out at him as Mark walks past its yard; he can't help but feel fear. Sue receives a promotion at work; she naturally feels joy. In and of themselves, passions are neither good nor bad; they are simply feelings that arise in us in response to various situations we face in our daily lives. They are morally neutral. However, Aquinas thinks that although the brute occurrence of passions is not something we can control, what we do in light of the passions we feel is within our control, as long as we are functioning normally.[72] Thus, acting on passion is something for which, ordinarily, we are held accountable; we can be praised or blamed for the resulting action. If Sue rushes out and buys a brand new BMW in light of her promotion at work, she may be judged to have acted rashly if her corresponding raise in pay is not sufficient to cover the payments on the car, or if she has other bills toward which the increase in pay should be directed. She did not have to buy the new car, even though her sudden rush of joy at the unexpected promotion led her to think that buying it was a good thing to do. Because she is a human being who possesses the capacity to think and act on the basis of her deliberations, she could have stopped herself and thought about whether it was in fact a good idea, given her circumstances.

Thus, Aquinas argues that although the passions can and do affect our actions, primarily by affecting our deliberative process and ability to make judgments, still, if an agent possesses a functioning intellect and will, those passions cannot determine the resulting actions.[73] As long as our intellects and wills are functioning properly, it is within our power to stop and think about what action is appropriate. Even if we go on to act on the basis of the passion, we do so having acquiesced to the passion. If the acquiescence is in accordance with one's (correct) judgment of the good, then the resulting action is praiseworthy. If it is in opposition to one's good judgment, then the resulting action is blameworthy. Aquinas does not think that, ordinarily, human beings are simply overwhelmed by their passions. He acknowledges that passion can arise very suddenly and make it very difficult to step away from the passion's influence. He also acknowledges that mental illness may interfere with the intellect's ability to control the passions, and hence affect culpability.[74] Nevertheless, as long as we have the ability to reflect on what we are tempted to do, we are able (at least in principle) to resist the influence of the passion. Even though the action has been influenced by the passion, its influence is always mediated by the intellect and will.[75]

Now that we have considered Aquinas's basic account of action in general, we are in a position to understand his account of the moral appraisal of actions. Although moral appraisal is generally taken to be a part of ethics proper, Aquinas considers it within the context of his theory of action insofar as discrete actions lay a foundation for the broader topics of ethics. Because individual actions lead to the formation of habits, they contribute to the development of our characters, given that Aquinas defines the virtues and vices, which make up our character, as good and bad habits. Therefore, we need to see which actions are good and which are not, and what makes good actions good and bad actions bad, in order to understand the development of these habits.

five

The Moral Appraisal of Actions

In this chapter we begin by examining Aquinas's account of good and bad action in general and then consider some specific types of bad action, the so-called sins of ignorance, passion, and willful wrongdoing. His account of the performance of good and bad actions underlies his account of habits, which we consider in the next chapter, and which in turn is necessary for understanding how the virtues and vices operate in Aquinas's ethics.

GOOD AND BAD ACTIONS IN GENERAL

Especially interesting about Aquinas's view of action is his claim that every particular human action is either good or bad. This is bound to strike us as startling. There are many actions that we consider to be morally neutral or morally indifferent. How could Aquinas think that all actions are either good or bad? What about picking up a pencil or raking leaves out of the yard?

Aquinas would agree that actions can be neutral as long as we are referring to a kind of action rather than a specific instance of action. He classifies actions into three kinds or species — good, bad, and neutral — on the basis of the principles of human acts.[1] As we saw earlier, Aquinas argues that the principles of human acts are the will and the intellect.[2]

Since the will moves us to act in virtue of being presented with an object by the intellect, the fundamental principle of our action is the intellect or reason. Reason, however, is ambiguous between two different (although related) interpretations. Reason might mean merely our cognitive power, by which we come to comprehend the world or figure out what we ought to do. Or, reason might mean what is rational for us to do. The principle of human acts has to do with both notions of reason. The intellect's presenting the will with a course of action to choose brings about an action (assuming no impediments such as sudden paralysis, for example). This is the first notion of reason, reason in the sense that the cognitive power sets up the conditions by which an action takes place.

The sorting of action into the species of good, bad, or morally indifferent ultimately rests upon the second sense of reason — that is, whether or not a particular type of action in and of itself is rational. What is rational for us to do is a function of what promotes or contributes to the ultimate end for human beings.[3] That is to say, what is rational for us to do is to pursue those courses of action that develop our capacities and promote flourishing. Actions will be classified into good, bad, or indifferent to the extent that they contribute to the ultimate end of flourishing. Listening to the woes of a sorrowful friend promotes flourishing insofar as it comforts the friend, about whom one cares; it is a good action. Murder is a bad action insofar as it cuts off the victim's flourishing and contributes nothing to the flourishing of the one who kills. Picking up a pencil off the floor in and of itself neither contributes to flourishing nor detracts from it; it is a neutral action.[4]

On the other hand, one might argue that obtaining the pencil helps one take an exam, which helps one achieve one's educational goals, which contributes to the development of human capacities, and hence, to human flourishing. So maybe picking up a pencil is not so neutral after all. Aquinas would agree. Remember that actions classified as neutral are so by their very nature. With a neutral action, nothing about the action itself contributes to achievement of the ultimate end. Rather, the use that one makes of the pencil determines whether the pencil is part of a flourishing life. If Leslie uses the pencil to help achieve her educational goals, picking up the pencil is a good thing. If she uses it to stab her roommate, then picking up the pencil is not a good thing, unless of course her roommate is a homicidal maniac and Leslie is trying to defend herself, and even then Aquinas has some qualifications and reservations.[5] In other words, evaluation of action depends upon more than the kind of action that is chosen.[6] On Aquinas's view, evaluation of the action also depends upon the end for which the action is performed and the circumstances under which the action is performed. Thus, moral appraisal of action depends upon a trio of factors for Aquinas: species, end, and circumstances.

This means that although an action can be indifferent with respect to its species, once that action is performed, it is no longer possible for it to be so. It will always be either morally good or morally wrong.[7] This is because actions are always performed under a particular set of circumstances and for a particular end. In neither of these cases can there be neutral actions. The circumstances are always either appropriate or inappropriate for the performance of any particular action, and the end is always either good or bad. Since both the circumstances and the end affect the goodness or badness of a particular action (as we will see below), even actions that are of a neutral kind or species will, in the final analysis, be either good or bad. Thus, an agent can be blameworthy for raking her neighbor's leaves if her reason for doing so is the bad end of clearing the way for her partners in crime to make a smooth getaway after burglarizing the house. An individual can be praised for taking a walk if his goal is to improve his health. On the other hand, if he takes the walk during a blizzard, then even this good end might not be enough to render his action good. Although there are circumstances in which it is appropriate to take a walk during a blizzard—for example, to get help for someone who might otherwise die—in most situations, it will be more appropriate to postpone the walk, even if one intends by the walk to achieve a good end.

Aquinas argues that an action that is bad according to its species is bad, period, and in this case, one need not consider at all the end or the circumstances. For Aquinas, the end never justifies the means. One is not allowed to adopt an immoral action even to accomplish what would otherwise be a perfectly good end. Extortion is not justified even if the money extorted goes to charity. Also, there are no circumstances under which performing a bad kind of action is morally permissible, and so, in the case of an action that is bad in species, we need look no further.[8] We need to consider circumstances and end only for actions that are neutral or good in kind.

In order for an action to be considered good, it must be performed under the appropriate circumstances.[9] An action that falls into the species of good (or neutral) actions and yet is performed under the wrong sort of circumstances is in fact a bad action. Ordinarily we think that helping someone with her homework is a good thing to do, but if the tornado sirens are sounding and the sky outside is darkening with clouds swirling, it is surely the right thing under those circumstances to forget about the homework and head down to the basement to safety. Insisting on helping with the homework would not be the virtuous thing to do even though helping with homework falls into the species of good actions.

Aquinas also argues that the end makes a difference to the moral appraisal of a particular action.[10] Performing a good or neutral type of action cannot justify a bad end. To use Aquinas's own example, one's action of giving to charity is bad if one does it for the sake of vanity. Therefore, in order for an action to be morally good, it must not only be a good (or indifferent) type of action, but it must be appropriate for the circumstances, and it must be performed for the sake of a good end. A deficiency in any one of these conditions renders the action morally wrong.

What we have seen, then, is that there are three conditions that must be fulfilled in order for an action to have moral goodness; the action must be of a good or neutral type, it must aim at a good end, and it must be performed under appropriate circumstances. The failure to fulfill even one of these conditions renders the particular action morally problematic.[11]

There is one other important consideration for moral appraisal, and that has to do with the consequences of an action. Aquinas does not believe that the consequences of an action determine whether the action is right or wrong, but he does think that under certain circumstances, consequences add something to the moral appraisal of an action. This is determined first by whether or not the agent recognized what was likely to happen, and second, if he did not recognize what was likely to happen, whether he *could* have recognized what was likely to happen.[12] If the agent recognizes that the action is likely to have bad consequences and performs it anyway, the action is worse than it would have otherwise been. If the agent recognizes that the action he is about to perform is likely to have good consequences, his recognition is to his credit and increases the goodness of the action.[13]

If an agent did not foresee the consequences of her action, then the case is more complicated and depends upon whether or not the agent *could* have foreseen the consequences. Aquinas argues that if the consequences of a particular action are such that under usual conditions, they are built into the nature of that action and as a result generally come about whenever an action of that type is performed, then the agent could have foreseen the consequences and could have been in a position to recognize what is likely to happen. In that case, what actually happens does contribute to the goodness or the badness of the action. If Nick fails to consider what is likely to happen if he runs the red light, the fact that he did not consider the consequences does not lessen the wrongness of his action, because he certainly could have and should have considered the consequences. If he runs the red light at a busy intersection, and there is a car in the intersection, which is likely to be the case, he will hit the car, and he will be culpable for hitting the car.

If the consequences of a particular action are such that they would occur only under atypical conditions and only in rare instances, then the fact that such consequences do in fact come about does not add to the goodness or badness of the action, since the agent was not in a position to apprehend what was going to happen as a result of performing that action. For example, suppose that Leslie goes to the local mall with the intention of shooting the first person she sees.[14] Ordinarily her action would result in at least injuring and quite possibly killing that individual. She could reasonably be expected to foresee these consequences. Suppose it turns out that the person she shoots was actually a terrorist who intended to blow up the mall and in fact would have done so had she not shot him. It turns out that her action has some very good consequences,[15] but on Aquinas's view, she did not do the right thing because she could not have foreseen that her action would have those consequences. Preventing terrorist attacks is not what usually results from a random shooting and is not an essential part of the act of shooting someone. The actual consequences of her action are not what would have followed in the usual case, so her action is not a good act.

On the other hand, suppose that, unbeknownst to Nick, terrorists wired his car during the night in such a way that the next morning, when he turns on the ignition, the engine initiates a chain reaction that results in an explosion of dynamite that destroys his neighbors' house and kills them in the process—all of this without damaging his car or maiming him. The terrorists are very skilled; they hid the wires so well that Nick would not have noticed them even if he had inspected his car prior to starting the motor (although he had no prior reason to inspect his car). Surely, in this case, Nick is not blameworthy in starting his car even though the result was that his neighbors' house was destroyed and the neighbors killed; he had no reason to think that merely starting his car would initiate such a horrific chain of events. Turning the ignition key does not ordinarily set off a bomb, and Nick had received no warnings that terrorists were going to use him in this way. Therefore, the consequences in this case were not of the sort that he could have reasonably foreseen; they are not essential to that type of action. Thus they do not turn what is ordinarily a permissible action into a blameworthy one.[16]

Leslie cannot be praised for killing the terrorist and Nick cannot be blamed for killing the neighbors and destroying their house, because in neither case could it have been predicted that those actions would have had the consequences they did have. Thus, the consequences make no difference to the moral appraisal of the actions. On Aquinas's view, consequences can have an effect upon the morality of a given action, but by themselves they do not determine the morality of an action. This accounts for our basic intuition that sometimes consequences do matter in our moral judgments, but other times they do not. Consequences can make things better or worse and are among the things we need to consider when trying to decide what to do, but according to Aquinas, what ultimately determines the goodness and badness of an action is the extent to which reason properly orders the action to the ultimate end. It is irrational to perform an action that ordinarily has bad consequences in the sense that such an action ordinarily does not contribute to a flourishing life. Nevertheless, consequences are not the fundamental thing that determines the morality of the action. If they were, then we would end up with a number of counterintuitive cases, such as the ones described above, where a bad action would count as morally good (the mall case) and a permissible action would count as morally bad (the car case). Aquinas is able to acknowledge the fact that consequences matter but is also able to explain exactly why the mall case counts as a bad action and the car case is not blameworthy.[17]

A Closer Look at Bad Actions

Now that we have considered the goodness and badness of action in general, we need to examine Aquinas's account of particular kinds of bad actions, namely, what Aquinas calls sins of passion, ignorance, and deliberate wrongdoing. His account of these sins follows directly from his moral psychology, and it gives us a nonarbitrary way to think about the sources of bad action. Besides helping us to understand the motivations of the agents, it shows us all of the different ways in which rational activity—the defining activity of human nature—can go wrong and interfere with our flourishing. First we will consider Aquinas's general framework for what he calls sins, and then we will look at each type of sin individually.

Aquinas differentiates between sins and vices, calling vices a type of disposition or inclination toward what is not suitable for a human being to do, and calling sins "disordered acts."[18] Insofar as a vice is a disposition, it is a habit, namely, that which disposes us to act either well or badly.[19] Habits that dispose us to good acts are virtues. If Leslie has the virtue of prudence, then she is in the habit of making the right decisions about what to do.[20] Habits that dispose or incline us to act badly are vices. If Leslie has the vice of boastfulness, she is inclined to speak more highly of herself than she is entitled to do.[21] If she actually engages in a boastful act, then she commits the sin of boasting. While vice is a disposition that inclines us toward bad actions, the bad actions themselves, once they have been committed, are sins. Although the having of a vice makes it more likely that we will commit bad actions, nevertheless, having a vice is not yet to sin. The reciprocal case is true as well; one could sin without having a disposition to do so—that is, without having a corresponding vice.[22]

Vices will be considered in more detail in part 3, as belonging to Aquinas's account of ethics. At this point we want to examine individual kinds of sin rather than dispositions to sin, because insofar as sins are a type of action, Aquinas classifies them as part of his theory of action. To commit a sin or a disordered act is for Aquinas to perform an action contrary to right reason—that is, contrary to what will contribute to the achievement of the ultimate end.[23] Such an action is, of course, bad. However, on Aquinas's account, humans are always directed toward what is good, so there is a puzzle here—namely, how are we able to will what is bad, especially when we recognize such an action as the wrong thing to do and yet do it anyway? Aquinas argues that the one who commits a sin does not really want to stray from what she knows is right. Instead, she neglects what she knows is right in order to pursue some lesser good that she desires—for example, some kind of indulgence or pleasure that conflicts with her duty.[24] That she also acts against right reason—namely, what her rational power tells her is right (or would tell her is right, should she pay attention to it)—is beyond her immediate intention. Her will remains oriented toward the good even as she pursues what is objectively bad.

Aquinas's classification of sins follows directly from his theory of action. Insofar as there are three sources of human action, there are three types of sin: sins of the intellect; sins of passion; and sins of the will, which Aquinas calls "deliberate wrongdoing." As we saw above, human action results from the interaction between intellect and will and is often influenced by the passions of the sensory appetite. Aquinas argues that sin results from a breakdown or a defect in any of these three powers.[25] We will examine how this comes about in each case.

First, however, we need to address a worry. If sin results from a defect in a particular power, then why think that human beings can be held responsible for their sins? After all, if Nick has a defect in his leg, then he cannot be blamed for failing to walk up the stairs. If someone has a developmental deficiency, allowances are made for that individual, and she is not blamed for her deficiency. Why should it be any different for sin?

As we shall see in more detail in the discussion below, Aquinas agrees with this basic intuition. The reason that we do not blame people for physical or mental defects is that the defects are beyond the control of the individuals who suffer from them. Aquinas argues that the defect in this case is a "nonculpable defect."[26] For example, Aquinas argues that an individual's intellect can be impaired by disease to the extent that the intellect is no longer able to control the passions, and in that case the agent is not blamed for acting inappropriately. Nevertheless, Aquinas argues that there are many cases where we are responsible for the defect in question, and hence, we are culpable for the bad action that results from that defect.

Although we will concentrate on the internal defects that give rise to sin, Aquinas identifies two other factors external to the soul that can influence our actions negatively: the devil and other human beings.[27] These give rise to sin insofar as they can affect the internal powers in virtue of which we perform actions. Nonetheless, neither of them is necessary nor sufficient. They have their effects either by stimulating the sensory appetite to pursue some pleasure or by persuading the intellect to abandon right reason, thus moving the will to choose a sin. However, since a properly functioning intellect is not moved necessarily either directly or indirectly through the influence of the sensory appetite, neither the devil nor another human being is able to force one to sin. Thus, temptations from these external sources are not sufficient for sin, and of course they are not necessary either, since one can move oneself to sin independently of these influences.

Since external influences have an effect on sin only as they affect the internal principles of human action, we need to consider next the ways in which there can be defects in these internal principles. In other words, we need to consider, in turn, the sins that arise from the intellect, the sensory appetite, and the will.

SINS OF IGNORANCE

A sin of ignorance results from a defect in the intellect, given that ignorance involves a lack of knowledge about something. One might wonder why anyone should be culpable for a failure to know, since it is impossible for mere humans to know everything. An individual might simply be moving along, just living her life, and not even realize that she lacks knowledge about some sort of thing. Why, in fact, would she even realize it? She does not know it. Why then should she be blamed for this lack of knowledge?

Ignorance is a complex notion. We will talk more about voluntariness later, but Aquinas argues that one cannot choose something about which one is ignorant, and so there is a sense in which ignorance makes an action involuntary. If an agent does not realize that there was a stop sign at the intersection, then no matter what else is true of her, she could not have chosen at that moment to stop for the sign. She did not know that she should stop, and she could not have chosen something of which she was not aware — so her action is involuntary. How can she be blameworthy for something she could not have avoided?

Aquinas responds that some actions from ignorance are blameworthy and some are not. If one is blameworthy for acting out of ignorance, the ignorance itself is voluntary, and so the subsequent action is voluntary.[28] There are two ways in which ignorance itself is voluntary. First, an agent might will to be ignorant in order to have an excuse for not doing the right thing. We could call this kind of ignorance "willful ignorance." Suppose that Nick walks into the kitchen and sees a plate of brownies on the counter. He could go find his mother to ask her what the brownies are for and whether he may eat them, but he might tell himself that he is not going to bother doing so; he is just going to help himself. Later, when his mother asks in dismay what happened to the brownies, Nick can say that he did not know that they were for the PTA meeting. Alternatively, he could walk into the kitchen, spy the brownies, and just start eating them. In this case, it never occurs to him that he should ask whether the brownies are being saved for a particular purpose. We could call this kind of ignorance "negligent ignorance."

In both cases, Nick lacks knowledge of his mother's intentions for the brownies. In both cases, Aquinas would say that Nick could have and that Nick should have acquired the knowledge that the brownies were intended for a purpose that did not include his pleasure. So, although there is a sense in which his action is involuntary because he lacked knowledge, the ignorance itself is voluntary insofar as the knowledge was accessible to him, had he made the effort that he should have made in order to obtain it. Therefore, Nick's action is blameworthy.

Of the two kinds of ignorance, negligent ignorance and willful ignorance, Aquinas thinks that the latter is a worse sin than the former.[29] Negligent ignorance, of course, does not excuse us if we neglect what we could have and should have pursued. If a driver fails to stop at a stop sign, she cannot get out of a ticket by claiming ignorance of the traffic laws. But if we will not to know something so that we have an excuse for doing something that turns out to be wrong, then there is a sense in which we orient our wills directly toward sinning. We intend a sin—ignorance—in order to try to get away with another sin. If we are merely negligent, our wills are not directed toward those sins. We remain guilty of them insofar as we did not have to be ignorant and therefore did not have to engage in wrongdoing. However, there is something worse about directly intending a sin than failing to avoid a sin, at least in Aquinas's eyes.

On Aquinas's account, not all actions involving ignorance are sins. A lack of knowledge is sinful only if it involves knowledge that one ought to know and is able to know before acting. The knowledge that we ought to acquire includes moral knowledge, the articles of faith, and whatever knowledge one needs to fulfill the duties of one's station in life.[30] An agent can be held accountable if she performs an action out of a lack of knowledge in any of these areas.

Aquinas's position raises a question in the other direction. If one can be held responsible for one's lack of knowledge on moral matters, matters of faith, and civic, familial, and job-related duties, why not think that ignorance is always culpable? It is surely the case that an agent ought to make sure she has sufficient knowledge before she acts. If she fails to gain that knowledge, then is it not a case of either negligence on her part or willful ignorance? In other words, why should we think that there are cases of nonculpable ignorance? Remember that two conditions must be fulfilled for an action to count as a sin of ignorance. It is not sufficient that the missing knowledge be knowledge the agent ought to have known; it also must be the case that the agent was able to acquire that knowledge. Suppose that you stop at a stop sign and look carefully in all directions before you move out into the intersection. As far as you can tell, the coast is clear, and it is safe for you to proceed, but just as you do, a child on a bicycle darts out into the intersection. You hit the child. You certainly would have avoided the accident had you been able, but the fact is that you were unable to do so through no fault of your own. You were ignorant of the fact that the child was coming, and your ignorance is nonculpable because you followed the correct procedures for appraising the traffic conditions at the intersection. Aquinas would argue that you cannot be blamed for your ignorance in this case.

So far we have seen two conditions for a sin of ignorance: the ignorance has to involve knowledge that the agent could have and should have acquired. There is a third condition. In a genuine sin of ignorance, the agent's lack of knowledge *causes* the particular action the agent performs. Had the agent possessed the knowledge in question, she would have performed an action different from the one she did perform. Recall the case of Nick and the brownies. Suppose that Nick would not have eaten the brownies had he known that they were being saved for a special purpose — if, for example, his mother had left a note next to them stating that they were for the PTA meeting. Because she did not write such a note, the missing knowledge has an effect upon what action is performed; therefore the lack of knowledge causes (at least in part) Nick's action of eating the brownies. If the information in the note would not have made a difference to what Nick ultimately does, then Aquinas thinks that the ignorance does not cause the action; it merely accompanies the action. If Nick would have eaten the brownies whether or not there was a note, Nick's sin would not be that of ignorance but of some other type.[31]

Thus, there are three conditions for a sin of ignorance: a lack of knowledge that the agent could have obtained, should have obtained, and that would have made a difference in what she would have done. If the agent could not have obtained the missing knowledge or the missing knowledge was such that the agent was not obligated to obtain it in the first place, then the resulting action is not a sin to begin with. If the final condition is not met, then there is a sin, but the sin is not one of ignorance; rather it is of another type.

Aquinas considers a further case. Sometimes the agent's knowledge is partial and incomplete, and so the ignorance involved is not total ignorance.[32] Aquinas argues that if the possession of whatever knowledge the agent does have should be enough to prevent the action from being performed, then the fact that he does not possess total knowledge of the situation does not excuse his action. Consider the case of Oedipus,[33] who knows that the obnoxious stranger ordering him off the road is a man and that murder is wrong, but who does not know that this man is his father. Presumably, the knowledge that this man is his father would prevent the murder. Thus, the lack of knowledge makes a difference to what Oedipus chooses to do. However, he remains guilty of murder because the knowledge he does have should prevent him from killing the man who turns out to be his father. His ignorance does not excuse him.

SINS OF PASSION

Sins whose origin is primarily the sensory appetite are sins of the passions.[34] The sensory appetite, the source of the passions, is able to influence and interfere with the operations of the intellect and will, which are the immediate causes of human action. Since the will's activity is mediated by the intellect's activity, ultimately the passions affect the will insofar as they impede the operations of the intellect by interfering with the intellect's consideration of what it actually knows.[35] As we saw in the last chapter, first, the passions can distract the agent so that it never occurs to her to think about her situation and consider what might be right or wrong to do. Consider an agent who seeks pleasure by engaging in gossip without stopping to think about how he might damage someone's good name. Second, the passions can make an alternative look good to an agent that ordinarily would not look good to her.[36] Road rage is a classic example of this case. Even individuals who are ordinarily mild-mannered sometimes judge that cutting off another driver is a good thing to do when the other driver has done so to them. Such a judgment arises in the light of the passion of anger.

Since the passions occur naturally in a human being, the mere having or feeling of a passion is not a sin. Even acting on a particular passion is not necessarily a sin; whether actions performed out of passion are sinful depends upon the extent to which the intellect is functioning as it should.[37] If the agent retains her capacity to reason even in the face of a strong passion, she is (at least in principle) able to step back and consider what she really ought to do—that is, whether the direction in which the passion is inclining her represents what is in fact in her interest to do.[38] The capacity to think through reasons for acting one way rather than another enables an agent to resist the pull of passion. As long as she retains this cognitive ability, she is guilty of sin if she gives in to a passion and does the wrong thing. Aquinas thinks that in cases where the agent is distracted by the passion or the passion makes something appear good that ordinarily would not look good, the average agent with a functioning intellect is able to resist the pull of the passion. Therefore, actions performed on the basis of the passions' influence are ordinarily culpable. The driver who judges that cutting off another driver is a good has the capacity to rethink that judgment, calming herself down by bringing to mind all of the reasons why it is not good to act on such an impulse. Thus, she is culpable if she subsequently cuts off the other driver.

Aquinas's discussion here raises an important concern, and that is why sins of the passions are not reducible to sins of the intellect, since acting or not acting on passion ultimately depends upon what the intellect does or fails to do. The easy answer is that Aquinas defines sins of the intellect in terms of ignorance; given that there is no ignorance in a sin of passion, it does not fall into the category of sins of the intellect. This is not a very satisfying answer, however, for two reasons. First, perhaps Aquinas should have broadened his notion of sins of the intellect to include cases where the intellect originates the sin insofar as it judges that a particular action is to be done despite having the knowledge that that particular action is morally impermissible. Second, cases of distraction by passion might look like cases of ignorance insofar as the agent is not actually considering alternatives she ought to be considering.

The latter case is easy to dismiss. Although the agent does not actually consider the alternatives she ought to consider, she still has the knowledge she needs to be able to consider them. The knowledge is dispositional rather than occurrent. In other words, she possesses the requisite knowledge; it is simply not currently present to her mind, in the same way in which a parent knows the date of his child's birth even though it is likely that he is not now thinking of it. Since the agent has the requisite knowledge but simply fails to bring it to mind, it is not really a case of ignorance.

Even if one broadens the concept of a sin of the intellect to include cases of the first sort, ultimately, sins of passion are not reducible to those of the intellect because there is something present in the sin of passion that is importantly absent in a sin of the intellect—namely, the passion. While it is true that a sin of passion does not qualify as a *sin* without the operation of intellect, that is because (as we shall see in the next chapter), nothing counts as a sin unless it is voluntary, and Aquinas defines voluntariness in terms of the intellect. What differentiate kinds of sins on Aquinas's account are their origins. A sin of the passions originates in the passions. A sin of the intellect originates in the intellect.

SINS OF THE WILL

The third category of sin has to do with a defect in the will—what Aquinas calls sins *ex certa malitia*. Although *malitia* resembles our word for "malice," the English word has connotations that are not present in the Latin term. *Malitia* literally means "badness," which has broader and more neutral implications than malice, but "badness" is an awkward term in English. To avoid these complications, these sins will be referred to as sins done from deliberate wrongdoing.

There is of course a sense in which all human actions are deliberate on Aquinas's account, insofar as we intend a particular end whenever we act; in this sense, *all* sins are cases of deliberate wrongdoing. Aquinas has a technical meaning in mind, however; sins from deliberate wrongdoing are sins whose source or origin is the will. Although all other sins eventually involve an act of the will insofar as they are actions at all (and the will is necessary for an action to take place), sins of ignorance originate in the intellect while sins of passions originate in the sensory appetite. Sins from deliberate wrongdoing have their source directly in the will.

These sins arise when there is disorder in the will—that is, when the will loves a lesser good at the expense of a greater good and chooses to suffer the loss of the greater good in order not to be deprived of the lesser good.[39] For example, an agent who buys a bottle of wine instead of food for his malnourished child pursues a lesser good (the pleasure of the wine) over a greater good (satisfying his obligation to care for his child). Aquinas argues that the pursuit of a lesser good at the expense of a greater good is a bad thing without qualification—that is, a bad thing simply speaking. And so he adds that an agent pursuing the lesser good at the expense of a greater good does so on purpose, as if he chooses evil knowingly.

How can an agent pursue evil knowingly? Does this not contradict Aquinas's claim that the will always chooses what is at least perceived to be good? Aquinas acknowledges the worry and goes on to argue that the agent chooses evil not for the sake of that evil, but rather for the sake of obtaining a lesser good, which he does not wish to relinquish even though it means the surrender of a greater good. There is still some good that the agent pursues; the agent does not choose something wholly evil. He chooses something evil insofar as forsaking a greater good for the sake of a lesser good is itself an evil, but not for the sake of evil itself.[40]

Many philosophers have found this view unconvincing. Some point to Satan's famous dictum "Evil be thou my good" in Milton's epic poem, *Paradise Lost,* as a paradigm declaration from one who pursues evil for its own sake.[41] They argue that in pursuing evil as if it were a good, Satan pursues evil for its own sake, for Satan also says that "all good to me is lost." Aquinas would be unconvinced; he would argue that what Satan's characterization expresses is in fact his motivation to pursue evil precisely because he regards evil as a good. In saying that "all good to me is lost," Satan acknowledges that in sinning, he loses all objective goods; what is left to him is in fact what is bad. But he loses what is *in fact* good precisely by his own choice to pursue something else he *judges* to be a good (at least good in a certain respect—the pursuit of power, for example, or the opportunity to be like God, subject to no other will),[42] and which he prefers to the objective good.

In responding to the objection that the agent appears to pursue evil for its own sake, Aquinas uses the example of an individual who pursues a certain kind of pleasure even though he knows that doing so is an offense against God.[43] In this case, the agent prefers to offend God rather than to be deprived of this particular pleasure and so pursues something evil. Given that this case involves the pursuit of pleasure, why is this a sin from deliberate wrongdoing and not a sin of passion?

Aquinas argues that two major differences separate sins done from deliberate wrongdoing from sins of passions. First, passions often arise rather suddenly, distracting the agent away from the good ends toward which he is ordinarily disposed. The student who ordinarily would sit down and focus on her studies is distracted by the sudden idea that lying on the beach would be extremely pleasant right now, and before she realizes it, she has spent half an hour thinking about a trip to Florida.[44] In a sin from deliberate wrongdoing there is no such distraction. The agent is well aware of what she should be doing and chooses not to do it; she makes her choice clear-eyed, so to speak. For example, the office manager knows she ought to be writing up a report but instead chooses to chat with her friend on the phone for half an hour. She recognizes what she owes to her employer but deliberately pursues her own interests.[45]

Second, agents who sin on the basis of their passions on the whole are oriented toward correct ends. When they sin, they choose alternatives they would not have chosen had it not been for the passion,[46] and when the passion subsides they regret their sinful choices and go back to their good ends. This is not so with agents who sin from deliberate wrongdoing; they choose as they do because they are badly disposed toward their ends. In other words, there is a problem with their basic orientation; they view what is objectively bad as something good and therefore suitable to choose.[47]

This last point helps Aquinas to explain how sins from deliberate wrongdoing are possible, given his view that something's being good is a necessary condition for an agent's choosing it, but it raises another question: how is it that an agent distorts her orientation toward the good in such a way that she sees what is bad as something good? That is to say, how does an agent come to be the sort of agent who prefers what she knows to be bad? She is willing to grant that lesser goods should not be preferred to greater goods, yet she prefers the lesser good. How can this be? We will consider this question in more detail in the next chapter, but part of the answer has to do with habit formation: the agent develops a *habit* of regarding such ends as good. This answer raises a question pertinent to the discussion here about the relationship between the intellect and the will. The agent *regards* the disordered end as good. The act of regarding implies an activity of the intellect. This raises the concern that sins from deliberate wrongdoing originate in the intellect, not in the will, and therefore could be reducible to sins of the intellect. There is a sense in which this is correct. The origin of the disordered preference lies in the intellect's presenting disordered alternatives to the will again and again until the disordered preference is inculcated within the will; over time, the will acquires a misshapen or disordered preference. So, yes, the disordered preference has its origin in the intellect. The question then is what is distinctive about sins from deliberate wrongdoing.

While a preference may arise out of a mistaken judgment of the intellect, it is still a disordered *preference,* and once the disordered preference is present in the will, *it* is what shapes subsequent choices. What distinguishes sins done from deliberate wrongdoing from sins that result from disorder in the intellect is the very presence of this preference, which is not found in a sin of the intellect. Since the will is an appetitive power, preferences—including disordered ones—fall under its domain. In a sin from deliberate wrongdoing, the intellect is functioning normally; it still determines the content of the choice, but now it does so in light of the agent's disordered preference. Thus the alternative chosen, which is a disordered choice, is ultimately a function of the will's disordered character.

Furthermore, Aquinas could argue that once one has the habit of disordered preferences, those preferences structure the content of what the intellect submits to the will for the choice. If the will did not have disordered preferences, the intellect would not even present a lesser good to be chosen over a greater good. This explanation, while in keeping with Aquinas's account of deliberate wrongdoing, raises another problem; it gives the will more autonomy than his account of action allows.

Aquinas can resolve this objection in the following way: the increased autonomy in the will is only apparent, because the will remains dependent upon the intellect for the content of its choice. It is true that one's skewed preferences have an influence upon one's deliberative process; one has become the kind of person who habitually prefers a lesser good or goods to greater ones and so has developed a certain kind of character. Nevertheless, the will would not have made such choices in the past unless the intellect had presented them to the will as good choices. Why the intellect would do such a thing is of course a further question and one that will not be answered here.[48] For now we want simply to say that on Aquinas's account, the intellect and the will function in this way, a way that preserves the priority of intellect over will. Thus, even though disordered preferences move the agent's deliberation in certain ways, the origin of those preferences lies ultimately with the intellect. Nevertheless, the origin of the sin itself is found in the will, since the will is the source of preferences.

To summarize, then: the intellect contributes to the will's habit of choosing disordered ends by presenting such ends as good. Once the will has the habit of inclining toward such ends, the will moves the intellect to present objects in accordance with its inclinations or preferences. This preserves the consistency of Aquinas's account of action, since the will is willing in accordance with a judgment of intellect. It also maintains his distinctions between sins of deliberate wrongdoing and sins of intellect insofar as the disordered preference is present in the former and not in the latter.

This explains those cases where the agent has a habit of choosing the lesser good, but Aquinas thinks that human beings do not have to acquire a habit in order to commit sins from deliberate wrongdoing. How do we distinguish cases of deliberate wrongdoing where there is no bad habit from sins of the intellect? Cases of this sort come about because of the removal of some previously present impediment to the bad choice.[49] For example, consider the individual who avoids looting only because he is afraid of getting caught. He has a desire for obtaining goods without paying for them, but he judges that avoiding the police is a better good. Then along comes a hurricane, and all of a sudden, in the chaos that results, it seems highly unlikely that he will get caught, and he goes on a spree of stealing jewelry and designer clothing from the abandoned stores. The fear of punishment that previously served as an impediment is no longer operative, and so the agent commits acts he knows full well are wrong.

Thus, Aquinas identifies two mechanisms by which sins from deliberate wrongdoing can come about. One is the result of a disordered preference produced by the formation of a bad habit, and the other is the result of removing a prior impediment. The question remains as to how an agent becomes the sort of person who comes to have such disordered preferences, a process that will be considered in the next chapter.

We have looked at the mechanics of Aquinas's account of wrongdoing and now understand how he structures the various types of wrongdoing that result from disorder in the basic principles of human action. What we need to consider next are the very important refinements that Aquinas makes to his basic account. First is the notion of habits, which, as we have seen from our discussion of deliberate wrongdoing, plays an important role in explaining the motivation for this type of sin. We will also need an understanding of habit for the discussion of virtue and vice.

The second important refinement is Aquinas's account of the freedom of human action. As we shall see, habits have important implications for human freedom, and freedom is an important precondition for ethical judgments. Ordinarily we do not hold people responsible for their bad actions or praise them for their good actions if we think that they did not commit them freely. For example, suppose that a former soldier from the Cold War is brainwashed by an evil agent to shoot a presidential candidate when he sees a certain playing card.[50] If he does in fact succeed in the assassination, we would not hold him responsible for the action because it was not his own choice to kill the candidate. He could not have chosen *not* to kill him. Similarly, we would not praise people for their good actions if we thought that they were simply robots doing what they were programmed to do. Given the importance of such judgments, we need an explanation of what makes such judgments possible.[51] In other words, we need to look at Aquinas's account of how human beings are able to act freely.

six

Habits and Freedom

Habit Formation

Up until now we have been considering discrete, individual actions. A further concept that follows from Aquinas's account of particular actions is that individual, discrete acts performed repetitively enable us to develop what he calls habits. The habit is a key concept in Aquinas's ethics, since virtues and vices are habits. Thus, they are important for our character and (as we have seen) play a significant role in Aquinas's explanation of sins that originate in the will. Aquinas has a rather complex and very broad notion of habit. He defines a habit as a disposition or inclination that moves one to act either well or badly with respect to a particular operation or end in accordance with one's nature.[1] He also describes habits as the perfection or completion of a power.[2] Habits come in different types; Aquinas describes things as diverse as beauty, health, wisdom, virtue, and vice as habits. Habits perform different functions for human beings. For example, without habits, our abilities or powers to engage in certain activities would not be very efficient or even possible. Habits perfect our powers of acting so that we are able to perform many of our ordinary day-to-day activities. Furthermore, particular kinds of habits (virtues and vices) play important roles in our pursuit of the ultimate end and for moral appraisal.

Habits are necessary for beings who possess (at least some) powers not determined toward one particular way of acting. Aquinas argues that in powers or entities determined to one particular act, there is no need of habits, and therefore such powers or entities develop no habits.[3] Thus, for Aquinas, stones have no habits. The human nutritive system is determined to specific activities and so has no need of habits. For example, Nick eats a banana and the components of the digestive system begin to operate, breaking down the banana into nutrients the body can use. Each part of the digestive system is automatically activated and carries out a specific task on its own, so the system has no need of habits and is not able to develop them.

On the other hand, human beings have a number of powers and capacities that are not predetermined to particular acts, so not only do they develop characteristic ways of acting, but they *must* do so.[4] Without habits, they would not be moved to act in particular ways, ways that are conducive to human function and ultimately human flourishing. For example, habits are found in the sensory powers insofar as the sensory powers respond to the dictates of the intellect.[5] Thus, our eyes can be moved by the intellect (and will) to focus on a particular part of the landscape — say, the highway ahead of us so that we can anticipate a slowdown in the traffic. Without habits such as temperance in the sensory appetite, the human agent would struggle to act in accordance with what her intellect tells her is the right thing to do. Habits are also found in the intellect as well as in the will,[6] due to the unspecified nature of their activities. Thus, there are certain habits of the speculative intellect — our coming to recognize particular analytic truths such as the law of non-contradiction, for example — that make thought possible. Prudence is a habit of the practical intellect that enables us to judge rightly about what to do. Justice is a habit of the will that inclines us to give to others what is due to them.[7] The possession of these and other habits enables the agent to perform these actions easily and efficiently.[8]

We are not born knowing how to do (at least most of) these things; instead, we have a natural capacity to learn how. And we acquire the habit of doing them by actually doing them over and over until it becomes, as it were, second nature to us.[9] Aquinas argues that in most cases, it takes more than one act to develop a habit, because, in general, the power in which a particular habit resides is incapable of developing in virtue of performing that activity only once. For example, a court reporter has the habit of hitting certain keys in order to produce individual words. That pattern must be learned and practiced over and over again until the court reporter becomes proficient in the requisite manner.

Most of the examples we have considered so far have to do with ordinary activities in ordinary life, but habits have an essential connection with the moral realm for Aquinas, insofar as he defines them in terms of enabling us or disposing us to act well or badly in accordance with our nature.[10] When we possess a habit that inclines us to perform what is appropriate for our nature (i.e., what is rational for a human being to do, what is in accordance with reason in Aquinas's terms), we are well disposed, and we have a virtue. When our habits incline us to indulge in what is not appropriate for our nature, we are badly disposed and possess vices. Good habits—the virtues—are those habits that dispose us and move us to act in ways that are conducive to our flourishing. That is to say, they move us to act in accordance with reason. Habits that move us to act against what is in our long-term best interests—namely, what fulfills our human nature—are bad habits or vices.[11] Thus, habits can be either good or bad and subject to moral appraisal.

Aquinas also thinks that God is capable of infusing habits into human beings.[12] Some of these infused habits are required in order to orient us toward our ultimate end of union with God, an end we could not achieve without them. Grace falls under this category. Since the ultimate end, union with God, is beyond our natural capacities, we human beings are not able to achieve this ultimate end on our own and so depend upon God to give us what we need—namely, his grace.[13]

On Aquinas's view, God can infuse other habits, such as knowledge of Scripture and the ability to speak in different languages. He has in mind here the passage from the Christian scriptures where the apostles were given the ability to speak to the crowd, to each in his own language (Acts 2:4–6). Although it might appear that God has bypassed altogether the usual route by which one acquires this habit, still, Aquinas argues that in infusing a habit, God builds upon previously existing habits—for example, the already developed capacity to speak a language.[14] Nevertheless, if a non-Greek-speaking person were to be granted the habit of understanding Greek by divine infusion, it is true that he would not have gone through the process of learning that particular language.

Given the nature of habits and the fact that they are acquired through repetitive actions, it is obvious that habits can become stronger and stronger.[15] Aquinas also argues that at least some habits can diminish in strength or become corrupted or destroyed altogether. This is important because virtues and vices are habits; if habits could not be weakened or lost, those with vicious habits could not reform, and those with virtuous habits could not fall into vice. Nevertheless, Aquinas does think that certain habits of thought—or intellectual habits—are not able to be destroyed.[16] Aquinas has in mind certain self-evident principles, such as the law of non-contradiction or the innate human tendency toward the good. As long as one retains one's ability to think, one will agree that the proposition that it is both raining and not raining at the same place at this very moment cannot be true. Such a proposition violates the law of non-contradiction. As for the innate tendency toward the good, Aquinas argues that as long as an agent retains her ability to think, she will never pursue what she has judged to have no redeeming qualities whatsoever. Some habits of thought, on the other hand, can be destroyed. Human beings can fall prey to fallacious reasoning so that what they previously thought to be correct no longer seems correct to them. If an individual becomes sloppy in her thinking so that she no longer thinks things through carefully, she will lose her previously cultivated valid patterns of reasoning.[17]

Habits that govern one's passions can be lost as well. Aquinas ties the loss of these habits ultimately to problems in the intellect.[18] The loss of one's appetitive habits—those that regulate the passions—comes about when the judgments of the intellect have been misdirected due to ignorance, or when the passions interfere with the operations of the intellect, or when the intellect presents the will with bad choices. For example, Aquinas argues that meekness or gentleness moderates the effects of anger.[19] This habit can be lost over time if the intellect and the will do not restrain excessive anger. The same mechanisms can merely diminish the strength of the habit, or habits can be lost or weakened by a failure to use them.[20]

In summary, habits make human life possible. They also form the basis of our characters insofar as we develop good or bad habits—that is, virtues or vices. Although our characters are fixed to the extent that our good or bad habits are firmly entrenched, they are not so firmly entrenched that we become unable to lose them or unable to act out of character. This is important because it explains some of the puzzles we saw in our discussion of sins from deliberate wrongdoing.

In our discussion of such sins, we noted that at least some agents guilty of this kind of sin have distorted their characters in such a way that they prefer the lesser good to the greater good; they pursue what is in fact bad as if it were in fact good. An important question is how agents become individuals who prefer the lesser good to the greater good. How do they develop these kinds of disordered preferences? Aquinas does not answer this question directly, but we can see how he might reply. Suppose that Nick is tempted to steal a candy bar without paying for it. The first time he does it, he might feel guilty. After all, it is stealing, and Nick has been taught that stealing is wrong. Nevertheless, Nick might think to himself, *it's only a puny candy bar,* and candy bars taste good, and maybe one of his friends is daring him to do it, a friend he wants to impress. So he does it, and he gets away with it. Then, the next time he goes to the store, he thinks about it again. He remembers how he got a little thrill from shoplifting before, and he wants to see if he can get away with it again. Pretty soon, Nick develops a habit of shoplifting. After a while, he no longer feels so bad about it; it is a thrill, and he gets the candy without having to give up anything for it. He has become the sort of person who at some level recognizes that shoplifting is wrong, but whose behavior is no longer guided by that recognition. His habit moves him to pursue something bad—the lesser good of a thrill, impressing his friends, getting for free something that tastes good—at the expense of the greater good. He habitually commits sins from deliberate wrongdoing.

As we saw earlier, Aquinas agrees that if the disorder involved in a sin of any kind arises from factors beyond the agent's control, we cannot blame the agent for the subsequent action. But how can we know that the disorder involved is in fact within the agent's control? We can raise an analogous claim about good actions. Insofar as good actions result from the inner workings (intellect and will) of the human agent, why should we think that such actions are any more praiseworthy than, say, the digestion of food, which also results from the inner workings of the human agent? We do not praise human beings for being good digesters of food because the digestive system is by and large beyond our control. Of course, we have some control over the process insofar as we can choose what foods to eat and thereby avoid foods that we are allergic to or that upset our system, but we can be praised or blamed for these choices precisely because we have control over them.

Thus, ascriptions of praise and blame depend largely upon whether we control the actions being considered—that is, whether we perform those actions voluntarily or freely. Aquinas agrees with this common intuition,[21] but it is not obvious from anything he has said so far that human beings are able to act freely. Thus, we must consider Aquinas's account of human freedom.

FREEDOM OF ACTION

On Aquinas's view, only rational beings act freely. Nonrational animals are capable of some flexibility of action, but they are not capable of choosing in the same way in which human beings (and other rational beings, such as angels and God) are capable. What makes the difference here is the possession of rational capacities—that is, intellect and will. Aquinas argues that what is most characteristic of those actions that are distinctively human is that they are voluntary and hence free, because the will is what Aquinas calls "a rational appetite"—that is, an appetite that is responsive to reasons for acting in one way rather than another.[22] Aquinas presents three specific conditions for voluntariness.

Since all action is for the sake of an end, Aquinas sets up the conditions for voluntariness in terms of the agent's apprehension and understanding of the end. The three conditions are: (1) an apprehension or perception of an end; (2) an understanding of the concept of an end—that is, what it means for something to be an end; and (3) an understanding of the relationships among ends and between a given means and a given end.[23]

On Aquinas's account, those things that lack the ability to perceive the world around them, such as stones, still move toward an end but of course have no awareness of doing so. Aquinas thinks that built into the nature of the stone is a natural end, that of "seeking" the lowest place. Aquinas did not know about gravity. For him, stones naturally roll down hills, thus fulfilling their natural ends but without any perception or understanding of doing so. If the conditions are suitable, they roll down the hill; if the conditions are not suitable, they stay put. The conditions that determine their activities are external to the stones and beyond any "influence" they can bring to bear upon the situation. Thus, the "actions" of stones are not voluntary insofar as stones fail to satisfy the first condition.[24]

Other types of beings — other animals as well as humans — are able to apprehend things in the world that can serve as ends for their actions. The sheep is able to perceive the lovely green grass and to graze upon it as a result. The abilities for apprehension and subsequent motion are internal to the sheep (in virtue of its soul). Aquinas argues that the sheep thus has a kind of control and flexibility of action that is lacking in the case of the stone. It moves itself in response to the environment; it does not depend upon the external conditions to determine its movements fully. And it does this in virtue of being able to apprehend things in the world that are possible ends for it. Thus, the sheep satisfies the first condition.

Nevertheless, apprehension of an end is not the only condition for an action performed freely, for all animals satisfy this condition; yet Aquinas thinks that there are important differences between the actions of non-rational animals and humans. He distinguishes between what he calls perfect cognition, which only human beings have, and imperfect cognition, which other animals have.[25] Beings with perfect cognition not only perceive ends but also satisfy the second and third conditions. That is to say, they understand *both* what it means for something to be an end (condition 2) and the relationships among things that are for the sake of an end (condition 3). Condition 3 includes the ability to identify one or more means for achieving various ends as well as an understanding of how ends relate to one another and how they fit into a plan for one's life.[26]

Only rational beings are capable of such activity, and so only rational beings have perfect cognition.

Because nonrational animals have only imperfect cognition, they are capable only of imperfect voluntariness. The sheep is able to apprehend grass, the consumption of which constitutes something good for the sheep. The sheep is unable to understand what it means for something to be an end or a good for it and is not going to think about whether it is in fact good for it here and now to graze on the grass. If the sheep is hungry, it will nibble. If the sheep is not hungry, it will not nibble. So the sheep's action of chomping on the grass is not perfectly voluntary, since the sheep lacks perfect cognition. Nevertheless, the sheep is able to move itself in response to its perceptions of the grass, and so Aquinas thinks there is something voluntary about its actions. The sheep has a certain flexibility in its movements because it is able to perceive the world around it and move accordingly, unlike the stone, which just sits there until an external force (such as an earthquake or an eight-year-old boy) operates upon it, setting it into motion. In contrast, human beings need not eat even when they are hungry because they can recognize that there might be good reasons not to eat at that particular time. There might be other goals to attain—for example, having blood drawn for a fasting glucose level. Human beings need not act on their basic physiological appetites, for they can choose to satisfy them or not. In virtue of their greater capacity to reason things out, they have perfect voluntariness.

Aquinas specifies the conditions for voluntariness in terms of cognitive activities—that is, in terms of activities of the intellect. We satisfy the conditions for voluntariness in virtue of our ability to comprehend the world and in virtue of our possessing the concepts that enable us to judge what to do. As we saw above, however, Aquinas defines voluntariness in terms of the will. Where is the will in this explanation of voluntariness? It seems to have been left out.

The explanation for voluntary action lies in the will insofar as the will is a rational appetite—that is, an appetite that is responsive to reasons.[27] That action comes about at all is due to the will, but the will is unable to move the agent unless the intellect first identifies alternatives for action and reasons for choosing a particular alternative over its competitors. The will has a role in the voluntariness of action insofar as the will has a role in bringing about an action; nevertheless, it is the intellect that enables human beings to satisfy the actual conditions for voluntariness.

Thus, Aquinas's discussion of the voluntary implies that the intellect has the greater role in enabling human beings to act freely. This is not surprising, given the account of action, and especially of choice, that we described in chapter 4. Aquinas maintains that the will is free, but he has a rather surprising explanation of what freedom in the will amounts to and how it comes about. On Aquinas's account, the intellect is the primary source of human freedom, and the will performs its functions freely only to the extent that the intellect is free in performing its functions. That is to say, freedom in the will is dependent upon freedom in the intellect.[28]

Aquinas sets up this claim first by noting that action follows the activity of the appetite (i.e., the will), which in turn follows the activity of the intellect.[29] Because of these tight relationships, it follows, according to Aquinas, that if the intellect is not in our power, neither is the will, nor is the action that results from the will's activities. In this case, we would not act freely; our actions would be determined. But Aquinas holds that the intellect is in our power because we are capable of reflecting upon our cognitive activities.[30] That is to say, at the end of the deliberative process by which we have identified a particular alternative for action, we are capable of stepping back and reflecting upon whether we have done a good job making the decision we have just made or whether there are other things we ought to consider. We might not engage in this process of reflection, but Aquinas argues that it is always open to us to do so— even under the influence of passion. Even in the event that an agent becomes enraged, Aquinas would argue that she retains the ability (in virtue of her intellect) to calm herself and reconsider the action she is tempted to take in light of her anger. Our ability to do so enables us to have control over our deliberations, and hence our subsequent choices and actions. As a result of having this ability, Aquinas claims that "the entire root of freedom is established in reason."[31]

Aquinas says that freedom is in the will insofar as the will is a *subject* of freedom. What it means for the will to be a subject of freedom is that freedom is found or located there. Nevertheless, the will is not free on its own accord, for Aquinas argues that the will is not the *cause* of its freedom; rather, the *intellect* is the cause of freedom.[32] Thus, the will is free, but only insofar as the intellect is free.

The texts we have just examined support the view that the intellect is the primary bearer and source of freedom. Nevertheless, other texts in Aquinas's canon suggest that the will is the primary source of freedom. Aquinas argues that freedom of action has to do with the will's activity of choosing and that the will is able to move the intellect. He also distinguishes between what he calls the exercise and the specification of the will's act. These claims imply that the will is autonomous with respect to the intellect. We will now examine them to see if Aquinas's account is in fact consistent.

As we saw above, Aquinas associates acting freely with the human ability to judge. Sometimes, however, he connects judging freely with the act of choosing.[33] Though he gives no reason for this leap from judgment to choice, it is clear from his account of action that a judgment of what to do terminates in a choice.[34] What is puzzling and in need of explanation is his claim that human freedom is located in the will's capacity to choose.[35] This claim implies that freedom is a function of the will, not the intellect, which appears to contradict the account of freedom we examined above.

Aquinas defends his claim that freedom is a function of choice by observing that we act freely because we are able to accept one thing while declining another, which is the central idea of the ability to choose. That is to say, in an act of choice, the agent pursues a particular alternative and rejects the others, independently of constraint. The fact that we are not constrained in our choices accounts for our *freedom* of action, since if we had chosen a different alternative, we would have performed a different action. Recall that for Aquinas, choice involves both the intellect and the will. Choice involves deliberation and judgment on the part of the intellect; it also requires an act of the will insofar as the will accepts and inclines toward what has been judged suitable by the intellect.[36] Aquinas states that insofar as we choose what we choose for the sake of a given end, choice is the object of the will, which, as we saw in our discussion of action, has to do with ends and means to the end.[37] Ultimately, then, a freely performed action is due to the will, for without an inclination of the will, there would be no action. This claim, however, is compatible with the idea that freedom in the will depends upon freedom in the intellect, for what the will chooses is directly dependent upon what the intellect presents to the will as its object of choice. Had the intellect presented a different alternative, the will would have chosen differently, which is to say that the will's choice is not constrained; but this means that the will's choice is not constrained because of activity in the intellect, not in the will itself. Thus, freedom in the will is tied to the intellect's freedom to consider various courses of action.

Another part of Aquinas's theory implies a more autonomous role for the will. He argues that the will and the intellect are able to act upon each other; the intellect is able to move the will, and the will is able to move the intellect. The will moves the intellect with efficient causation, while the intellect moves the will with final causation.[38] The intellect moves the will with final causation insofar as it presents the will with an object to be willed. The will moves the intellect efficiently insofar as it is able to move the intellect to perform its characteristic operations of cognition and deliberation. The distinction is important because efficient causation is sometimes considered to be a stronger form of causation than final causation, insofar as the will moves the intellect *directly* toward a particular activity—deliberation, for example—while the intellect moves the will *indirectly*—presenting it with an object toward which the will then moves itself. This implies that the will has some "wiggle-room," so to speak. The fact that the intellect is not acting on the will directly implies that the will is able to move toward the object or not, whereas the will's acting directly on the intellect implies that the intellect moves in response to the action of the will, just as a billiard bill moves across the pool table when it is hit by the cue ball. To act with efficient causation implies that the movement of the thing being moved is in the hands of the mover, not the thing being moved. If the mover acts with sufficient force, the thing being moved moves. This makes it appear as if there is no "wiggle-room" for the intellect in the face of the will's moving it. Thus, Aquinas's discussion of the manner in which the intellect and will act on each other implies that the will has more autonomy and the intellect less.

That Aquinas accepts these implications is suggested by his distinction between the exercise of the will and the specification of the act of will. The exercise of a capacity has to do with whether that capacity acts or refrains from acting, whereas the specification of the capacity's act has to do with the content of the act. For example, the exercise of the will has to do with whether one wills or not. The specification of the act of will has to do with what is willed, for example, whether one wills to eat ice cream or to take out the garbage or to study philosophy. Aquinas argues that with respect to its exercise, the will is never necessitated. That is to say, one is able either to will or to refrain from willing. With respect to the specification of the act of will, the will is necessitated in only one instance, and that is if it is presented with a perfectly good object by the intellect.[39] Since nothing we encounter here on earth is perfectly good (although we might mistakenly judge something to be perfectly good), nothing here on earth necessitates what we will.[40] This discussion implies that the will has a certain autonomy with respect to its own activities, which contradicts Aquinas's claim that the will wills what the intellect presents to the will as a good to be chosen.

In order to resolve this apparent contradiction, we need to look more closely at Aquinas's discussion. The reason the will need not will any particular object, Aquinas argues, is that the intellect is capable of perceiving the defects of any particular object.[41] The intellect carries the will to a particular object on the basis of its judgments of what is good to will and what is not good to will. The will's flexibility in choosing any particular object over a different object is tied to the intellect's ability to conceive objects from different points of view.[42] Thus, the intellect's abilities make possible the will's freedom to choose. This does not imply that the will is able to act independently of the intellect's considered judgment, for the will rejects an imperfect good not on its own initiative but rather on the basis of the judgment of intellect that doing so is good.

The claims that we have just considered have to do with the specification of an act of will. What about the exercise of the will? Aquinas argues that will is never necessitated with respect to its exercise because it is always in the agent's power not to think of any particular object and hence in his power not to will any particular object.[43] Once again, Aquinas ties the agent's ability to act freely not to any autonomous power the will possesses but rather to the intellect's capacities and activities. Freedom in the will is tied to and made possible by freedom in the intellect.

On the other hand, recall that, according to Aquinas, the will is able to move the intellect, which implies that the will moves the intellect not to consider a particular object and hence enables itself not to will it. This position also implies that the will moves the intellect to focus on the bad aspects of a particular course of action, thus enabling the will not to choose that action. For example, suppose you are reading a magazine and come across an advertisement for an overseas relief agency that features a picture of a starving child. You know at some level that if you read the advertisement, you will feel guilty and end up mailing the organization the money you were planning to spend on something else.[44] So you quickly turn the page and go on to read the next article. Aquinas would explain this scenario by arguing that your will moved your intellect not to read the advertisement but rather to turn the page. Thus, while the will has no direct autonomy over its activities, perhaps it is indirectly autonomous; that is, the will does not directly contradict a judgment of intellect concerning what to do, but rather it moves the intellect to give it a different directive upon which it—namely, the will—acts. There is still a judgment of intellect informing the will and specifying the contents of the will's activities, but the will determines which judgment specifies its activity by directing the intellect's activity.

Aquinas does hold that the will can act in this manner with respect to the intellect, but we need to be careful not to read more into this position than is there. On Aquinas's account, the will is not a cognitive power and therefore depends upon the intellect for its object. What this means is that if the will moves the intellect to consider an alternative for action in a particular light, then there is a prior judgment upon which the will is acting, namely, that doing so is a good. Although every act of will requires a prior act of intellect, not every act of intellect requires a prior act of the will.[45] Even though it might appear that the will is able to act independently in virtue of directing the intellect's acts, its directing the intellect's acts remains tied to and dependent on a prior judgment of the intellect. In the magazine example we just considered, your will moves you to turn the page because your intellect has judged that turning the page is good. In this way then, Aquinas maintains the priority of the intellect over the will with respect to acting freely.

What we have seen is that some texts suggest that Aquinas holds that human beings act freely primarily in virtue of the intellect, while other texts seem to support the position that human beings act freely primarily in virtue of the will. Nevertheless, as we have also seen, it is possible to interpret the texts that seem to favor the will in a manner that renders them compatible with those that assert a stronger role for the intellect. Furthermore, it is not clear that the reverse is the case — that is to say, it is not clear that one could interpret those texts that suggest that it is the intellect that enables human beings to act freely in such a way that they are compatible with an interpretation that the will is the primary bearer of freedom. Thus, it seems reasonable to conclude that Aquinas holds that human beings act freely in virtue of their intellectual capacities.

AQUINAS IN THE CURRENT DEBATE

The medieval debate over freedom is couched in very different terms from the debate currently waged in philosophy. Medieval thinkers took it for granted that human beings act freely, and they took their task to be (at least in part) explaining which human capacities enable this to be so. The debate largely focused on whether human beings act freely in virtue of the will or the intellect. The fact that philosophers currently debate over the question of free *will* seems to indicate that, over time, the position that human beings act freely in virtue of their wills eventually won out, a conclusion supported by an examination of history.[46] Thus, Aquinas's position that intellective capacities enable human beings to act freely is an historical anomaly. The current debate centers on a different question: whether or not free will is compatible with causal determinism — that is, the view that every event is determined or caused by certain events (or chains of events) that precede it plus the laws of nature.

Those who argue that free will is compatible with determinism are known as "compatibilists," while those who argue that it is not are known as "incompatibilists." Incompatibilism comes in two varieties: determinists, who argue that human beings have no freedom of action, all of their actions being determined by antecedent causes beyond human control;

and libertarians, who argue that human beings do act freely, at least on some occasions. Thus, the libertarians agree with the compatibilists that free action is possible but deny that free action is compatible with determinism. Libertarians agree with determinists that free action is not compatible with determinism but do not accept the view that there is no free action (thus accepting the position that *complete* causal determinism is false).

Although some historians of medieval philosophy would argue that to insert Aquinas into the current debate would be anachronistic, since his concerns were not our own, the fear of anachronism does not stop philosophers from doing so. The question, then, is this: What reasons are there for thinking that Aquinas is a compatibilist, and what reasons are there for thinking that he is a libertarian?[47] That he is not a determinist is something that everyone can agree on, since he obviously argues that human beings act freely (at least on some occasions).[48]

THE ROAD AHEAD

We have seen that human flourishing requires the actualization of human capacities, and especially the actualization of the intellect and will. Aquinas's theory of action shows us what it means to actualize those capacities insofar as individual discrete actions produced by the inter-action of intellect and will are aimed at the achievement of the ultimate end, which is union with God. Of course, not all action contributes to the flourishing of human lives; we saw in particular the stringent conditions an action must satisfy in order for it to be evaluated as a good action — that is, an action oriented correctly toward the ultimate end. We also saw the ways in which human capacities can go wrong, resulting in particular kinds of sin or wrongdoing. Finally, we looked at habits, which are produced by the repetition of discrete actions of the same type, and which are important for understanding Aquinas's account of virtues (the good habits) and vices (the bad habits). We also considered Aquinas's account of freedom, since for Aquinas (and for many others as well), morality and moral appraisal are meaningless if human beings do not perform their actions freely.

Nevertheless, the elements that give Aquinas's ethics its distinctive character also threaten elements of his theory of action. In part 3 of this book, we shall see that Aquinas's ethics focuses on the notions of virtue/vice, law, and grace. Each of these notions raises questions about the origins and freedom of our actions, that is, questions about whether our actions are in fact truly our own. For example, virtues and vices move us to act in certain ways. Can they become so strong that we cannot act against them? Aquinas also thinks that God can infuse habits into us; in particular, God gives us grace, as well as infused forms of the virtues. Grace and infused virtues move us to act in particular ways; do they determine our actions? If we act from something such as grace or infused virtue that has its source external to us, do the subsequent actions count as our own? And finally, as we shall see, Aquinas characterizes the natural law in terms of natural human inclinations. If we act on the basis of inclination, do our actions deserve moral praise?[49] After all, nonrational animals act on the basis of natural inclination, and Aquinas does not think that they are subject to praise or blame.

Thus, Aquinas's ethics will generate a number of interesting questions for his theory of action. Part of what we will see in the next chapters is how he is able to answer these questions. We will also finally come to see exactly how his accounts of human nature and of action form the foundation for his account of ethics and how, with all of these diverse elements assembled together, we arrive at a single coherent, comprehensive, and useful moral theory.

Part Three
Human Flourishing

seven

The Virtues

W*e have set out in this book to integrate Aquinas's metaphysics of* human nature, his action theory, and his ethics. His metaphysics of persons tells us what sort of beings we are; his action theory tells us what beings of this sort are able to do; and his ethics tells us how human beings can live a good, flourishing life. At one level, we have seen that Aquinas's story about these three areas can be told in the language of Aristotelian philosophy: We are rational animals, composed of form and matter; our nature includes a set of potentialities and capacities, most notably intellect and appetite, which fit us for action. When we fully develop those natural capacities, we reach actualization or perfection as flourishing members of the species. As our study of Aquinas's metaphysics and action theory has already made clear, however, there is more to the story than that. In this third part of the book, our study of Aquinas's ethics will put us in a position to see how his theological commitments transform and transcend his Aristotelian views of a flourishing human life, even as they incorporate and build on them.

Aquinas's ethics is framed by his discussion of human nature and human action, since the goal of the ethical life — human flourishing — consists in knowing and loving God. These activities express the perfection of intellect and will, and thereby also the perfection of our rational nature.[1] After laying out his view of human nature and describing the rational capacities of intellect and will, then, Aquinas goes "behind the scenes" to examine three specific influences on the intellect and will: virtue, law, and grace. All three guide and shape our actions in ways that enable us to realize our ultimate end. Aquinas calls virtue an interior source of influence because virtues perfect the sources of human agency, intellect and will.[2] He counts law and grace as exterior influences because God, an agent distinct from the human intellect and will, is their source.[3] As we will see, things soon become more complicated. For now, we simply note that all three are treated in the ethics because they each involve human participation or action in some way; that is, they are still *human* ways of achieving our end because they involve, at some level, the contributions of intellect and will.[4]

Understanding Aquinas's ethics well requires that we pay attention to the overall structure and context of his discussion. A cursory glance at Aquinas's ethics reveals a lengthy and detailed discussion of the virtues—first in general, and then in particular.[5] The *Summa theologiae* includes forty questions on virtue and vice in general and one hundred seventy questions on individual virtues and vices, compared to only nineteen on law and six on grace.[6] Lengthy discussion (or an increased number of objections and replies in a given question) often indicates an area of controversy; at other times it indicates importance, or an area in which Aquinas's synthesis of traditions calls for extra explanation. When we notice that the vast majority of his ethical instruction on human flourishing is devoted to virtues and virtuous living, and that in the *secunda secundae* (the second half of part II of the *Summa theologiae,* or *ST* IIaIIae) Aquinas organizes discussions of law and gifts of the Holy Spirit under the superstructure of the three theological virtues and the four cardinal virtues, we may wonder why the three principles of human action in the *prima secundae* (the first half of Part II, or *ST* IaIIae)—virtue, law, and grace—are apparently so unevenly distributed in the discussions in *ST* IIaIIae.

This extensive attention to the virtues may puzzle readers of Aquinas's ethics for other reasons. Many scholars and textbooks frame Aquinas as a natural law theorist, and their accounts of his ethics say little or nothing about the virtues. Given the text before us, however, the sheer amount of energy Aquinas spends on virtue begs for an explanation: how do virtue and law fit together in his ethics?[7] Moreover, given the theological commitments operating in Aquinas's ethical work, how can

we explain the paucity of attention he gives to the more obviously theological concepts of law and grace, while the virtues—a Greek philosophical inheritance—are discussed in great detail? In response to these questions, we will argue that for Aquinas, virtue is deeply integrated with law
and grace, to the point of being inseparable from them. Moreover, his
account of the virtues is deeply transformed by his theological commitments, both structurally and in substance.

Our task in part 3 will thus be to explain how the integration of virtue, law, and grace is the key distinctive feature of Aquinas's ethics—
one that requires attention to his theological commitments for its full appreciation. This integrative reading will also highlight the ways in which
Aquinas's ethics incorporates his theory of human nature and his analysis of human action. This chapter will explain the role of the virtues in
perfecting our rational nature and its capacities for action. It will show
how Aquinas's account of the virtues is thoroughly informed by his theological commitments, in his account of the foundational role of the theological virtues and also in his treatment of *moral* virtues infused by grace.
Chapter 8 will explain how Aquinas's treatments of law and grace are essential for understanding the role and operation of the virtues. Finally,
chapter 9 will study a specific vice and a specific virtue to show how the
central role Aquinas gives in his ethics to the virtue of charity—which
fulfills the law and comes only by grace—transforms Aquinas's account
of particular virtues and vices and thereby shapes the character of the
moral life in a fundamental way.

What Is a Virtue?

The transforming influence of Aquinas's theological commitments
is most evident in his treatment of the various types of virtues, and his introduction of the infused virtues makes clear the necessary integration of
virtue with grace. Before we discuss the different kinds of virtues, however, we need to consider further what a virtue is.

Not surprisingly, Aquinas's definition of virtue highlights the connections we are trying to make in this book. He calls virtue both "the
perfection of a capacity" and "a habit ordered to action."[8] His account of

virtue starts from a capacity, or potentiality, of human nature and traces it through two stages of its actualization—first, as the natural capacity is perfected by virtue, and second, as this perfected capacity issues in virtuous action.[9] This picture reflects both Augustine's definition of virtue as "a good quality of the soul by which we act rightly" and Aristotle's definition of virtue as a habit that "makes its possessors good and their work to be done well."[10] It also sets the virtues in a pivotal role in the teleological, or actualization-directed, picture of human flourishing.

Virtues are the sorts of habits that both perfect human nature and in so doing also properly order their actions to their ultimate end. For example, a person with the virtue of prudence[11] is both a *practically wise person,* the sort of person we can count on to make good judgment calls, and someone who regularly *judges well,* dispensing insightful advice and making good decisions about how to achieve the human good concretely here and now. Her natural capacity—the practical intellect—is perfected, and this shows in the way its characteristic action—making wise judgments about what should be done—is also good. This is just what it means to have a virtue—to have a habit that makes the person and her actions good.

A capacity's perfection is measured and confirmed by its action or operation, the outward sign of its inner direction or aim. Virtues that perfect our capacities, while good, will not by themselves enable us to attain the full human good; they also need to be expressed in action through the operation of intellect and will. To put it simply, the point of having a habit is to use it, since human flourishing consists in rational activity and the attainment of happiness requires excellence embodied in action. Virtues rightly "aim" our capacities toward the end, and thus enable us to "hit the target" in action. Describing what virtues are and what they are for requires a grasp of Aquinas's teleological theory of human nature and its capacities, as well as his action theory. Thus his ethics depends on his metaphysical and action-theoretical views, treated earlier in this book.

Aquinas's capacity-based analysis of the virtues helps us understand why we act the way we do and how to figure out what goes wrong when our actions misfire. In other words, he analyzes capacities and action for the sake of practical application and living well, not just for the philosophical pleasure of multiplying distinctions. His approach helps us to think of ourselves and our moral character as being an interlocking system of smaller systems. An overall malfunction is hard to fix unless we know how the systems impact each other, what the function of each system is, and what the right result was supposed to be. Aquinas's ethics, including most particularly his analysis of the virtues, is supposed to work like a comprehensive owner's manual for the moral "system" that is you.

All human capacities, when properly functioning, work together in harmony to produce a life of total human fulfillment. The role of the virtues in this process is to perfect and direct our rational capacities, the internal sources of human action, so that the action that flows from them realizes our ultimate end, actualizing our nature as human beings and yielding a flourishing life.[12] To put it technically, Aquinas explains the function of virtue in terms of rightly ordering our rational capacities toward their proper "objects." The objects of the capacities are the ends, or goods, toward which the capacities and their actions are ordered. Rightly directed capacities yield rightly ordered acts—that is, acts that appropriately achieve good ends and that together constitute the human good.

The capacities relevant to ethics are those that are responsible for properly human action. In his discussion of human nature, Aquinas has already declared himself to be most concerned with "the intellectual and appetitive powers, in which the virtues are found."[13] These capacities include not only those that are themselves rational—the intellect and will, or rational appetite—but also those that are rational by participation—the sensory appetites.[14]

As we discussed in chapter 1, Aquinas distinguishes each capacity by a difference in its object—the good toward which it tends. Every capacity involves an internal inclination toward something,[15] and that something—that object—defines the capacity. For example, the intellect is the capacity by which we are able to know the truth—through activities from insight to judgment to complicated reasoning. Built into this capacity is a natural tendency to seek truth as the knowable good that perfects it. The appetites, on the other hand, have as their natural object the good as lovable or desirable. The object of the rational appetite or will is the good presented to it by reason—goods that are conceivable (universal and spiritual) and not merely perceivable (particular and material). The object of the sensitive appetite is the perceivable good—what is available to us through our senses.[16]

Aquinas thinks that all objects, all goods, and with them, all capacities designed to achieve them, are hierarchically ordered. Reason's job is to discern this order and direct us to acts that respect it. Divine goods are ranked highest, then human goods, including (in descending order) spiritual goods, bodily goods, and external goods. When integrating human action into a unified life ordered to a single ultimate end—namely, God, who is the Good itself—one must preserve the proper ranking. External goods should be sought and used according to what is good for our bodies and physical well-being; our ability to seek and attain bodily goods should be directed by our spiritual good (the well-being of our intellect and will); and spiritual goods are to be sought always for God's sake. For example, sometimes our love for God will require fasting for a time; other times, it will require feasting. But in either case, our eating is to be directed not merely to our physical good but also to the spiritual goods of communion with God and others. Sometimes sacrificing lower goods is necessary, as when we endure physical hardship or inconvenience to help a friend in need, or when we compromise our loyalty to our country or our friendships if those allegiances demand that we dishonor God.[17] Aquinas also addresses the proper order of love for God, others, self, and body in the treatise on charity.[18]

The virtues, following the capacities they perfect, are also defined in terms of their objects.[19] Perfecting and directing our capacities toward their proper goods, they enable those capacities to attain those goods in a properly ordered way. Consider the case of a college student who frequently gives in to the temptation to overspend at the movie concession stand and as a result cannot pay her rent on time, creating friction in her relationship with her roommates. In the proper ordering, the virtue of temperance (controlling one's appetite for sensible things) would serve justice (one's ability to give to others what is due), which would ultimately contribute to charity (one's relationships of love with others and God).[20] Individual, sensible goods are supposed to serve common goods and goods of the soul, while goods within human relationships must be ordered to our ultimate end. Having the requisite virtues is the same as having one's capacities rightly directed and disposed toward the goods that enable us to flourish as human beings.[21]

It is essential in Aquinas's ethics to understand that not only is the pursuit of a good (or apparently good) object behind every movement in the universe,[22] but also that for the rational creature in particular, one's loves must respect the proper *ordering* of goods if human fulfillment is to be attained. Ordering our love is an ethical task, however, not just a natural given.[23] Our inclinations, unlike those of most animals, do not guide action like instincts; many of our inclinations can and need to be taught to listen to reason and obey it, as a child is subject to the direction of a parent. (This is why Aquinas says the inclinations of the sensory appetite are part of our rational nature "by participation"—because they can follow reason's judgments about the good, even if they cannot recognize or desire higher-order goods themselves.) In addition to their untutored state, however, our inclinations are also corrupted and misdirected by sin.[24] Thus, we need the virtues to direct our capacities toward goods appropriate to our whole person, the goods that we ought to desire in order to fulfill our nature. As Aquinas puts it, "in us, love is ordered through virtue."[25] Because human beings are rational animals, Aquinas calls the standard by which virtuous action is ordered and measured "the order of reason"—that is, reason directing us rightly to the good that befits the perfection of rational nature.[26] The whole point of developing the virtues is to perfect one's capacities so that one becomes the sort of person who, at every level—from passion to will to intellect—consistently aims at and achieves the human good, the good of reason, in her action.[27] For all of us, this moral formation requires lifelong effort.

Because Aquinas thinks that we cannot desire evil as evil, but can only desire it under some good description, one of the chief hallmarks of sin on his account is the tendency to seek goods in violation of the order of reason. Recall the example of the student who impairs her relationship with her roommates in order to satisfy her desire for popcorn, candy, and soda. These sensory desires override her judgment about what is most important and her will to give others their due. The order of goods under the influence of sin opposes the order of reason.[28] The proper order is for the higher capacities—the rational capacities that mark us as human beings—to direct the lower capacities to serve them and their inclinations.[29] What we cannot see, when we are misdirected intellectually and appetitively by sin, is that only in serving the higher capacities can the whole person—*including* her lower capacities—be fulfilled and perfected.[30]

Thus, it is not the aim of the moral life to rid us of the desires of the sensitive appetite, as if they were the source of evil. Rather, goods are to be desired and sought in a rightly ordered way, so that all our capacities might be fulfilled and perfected in a way that harmonizes with all the others. While Aquinas recognizes that bodily impulses and appetites, among other influences (including defective operation in the intellect and will), can be an occasion of sin, he is always concerned to respect our whole nature, and his ethics integrates the passions accordingly, rather than recommending that we eradicate them altogether. In fact, if what reason commands is not only done willingly but done wholeheartedly and with passion—that is, with the collaboration of the sensory appetite—Aquinas thinks this contributes to the moral perfection of the act,[31] just as it is better to give to the poor with compassion and a generous heart than out of a sense of burdensome obligation. If the student in our example is virtuous, she will take more pleasure in a good relationship with her roommates than she would in acquiring another transitory pleasure for herself. Likewise, a meal shared with them is morally better if it brings her sensory and social pleasure. Our moral formation must therefore apply to our intellect, will, *and* sensory appetite if we are to achieve perfection and full integrity as human beings.[32] Aquinas accordingly assigns virtues to the sensory appetites—those emotions and inclinations that are dependent on the body and its dispositions, but can listen to reason—as well as the properly rational capacities of intellect and will.

In fact, virtues of the sensory appetite play an important role in moral formation, since disciplining and directing certain passions is essential for good human action.[33] For example, it is difficult to understand the different ways that acts of aggression and endurance can exemplify the virtue of courage for Aquinas unless one refers to his descriptions of fear, hope, sorrow, and anger.[34] A courageous person must maintain hope, resist fear, use anger, and overcome sorrow in the face of threats to his bodily well-being; thus, he may have to restrain some passions to act virtuously, while cultivating and encouraging other passions to enhance the moral perfection of the same act. Similarly, an agent will experience disruption in the work of the virtue of prudence if her appetites are disordered by lust or covetousness—for she will not be able to see clearly what is to be done if her overriding desire is to satisfy herself with pleasures or possessions.[35] Moreover, Aquinas claims that the fullest form of prudence is achieved only when one's will is shaped by love for God.[36] His ethics, therefore, is intent on harmonizing all human powers through virtuous formation. Virtue is meant to perfect all aspects of our character, all the way down.

KINDS OF VIRTUES

Intellectual Virtues. Aquinas has defined virtues as dispositions of rational capacities that direct them to their proper goods. When distinguishing between kinds of virtues, then, Aquinas appeals to the different capacities that are perfected—the "subjects" of virtues. As we have seen, these capacities and the different virtues which perfect them are further defined according to their "objects" or the goods that are their respective ends.[37] For example, our intellectual capacities are aimed at truth as their object—either the truth about reality or the truth about what action is called for in a given situation. Intellectual virtues perfect the work of the intellectual capacities and help them achieve truth. In the case of speculative reason, the virtues of wisdom, reasoning, and insight enable it to achieve a true and full grasp of the way things are. In the case of practical reason, the virtue of practical wisdom, or prudence, perfects the work of practical reason, enabling it to make good judgments about what we should do and to command the will accordingly. We will concentrate our attention here on the virtues of the practical intellect, not the speculative intellect, because of their direct application to ethical action.[38]

Moral Virtues. Aquinas counts prudence an intellectual virtue because it, like the other intellectual virtues, is located in the intellectual powers on account of its object, truth. Because of its ability to command the will concerning the means to the good,[39] however, Aquinas follows Aristotle in treating it in close conjunction with the moral virtues. Why? The moral virtues are so called because they all are located in or involve the appetites — and our moral character concerns the good, which is the object of appetite. That is to say, as an intellectual virtue, prudence is aimed at the truth, but as a director of the appetite and its movements, prudence is aimed at the truth about the good that is to be done, and *that* good is the object of the moral virtues.[40]

The moral virtues thus perfect the appetites, whose object is the good as loved or desired, rather than the intellect, whose object is truth as known. Aquinas recognizes an extensive range of moral virtues, many of which are familiar to us, such as generosity, honesty, gratitude, and chastity. He follows Aristotle's pattern of organizing the virtues and vices, by assigning a vice of excess and a vice of deficiency to each virtue.[41] For example, generosity (liberality) is opposed to the vice of prodigality on the one hand, with its excessive spending, and the vice of covetousness on the other, with its deficient spending. The prodigal undervalues money, and the covetous person overvalues it. Generosity is defined as the mean between these two extremes, since the generous person rightly values money — neither too little nor too much — and thus can both use it wisely and give it away freely when and where she ought.

The Four Cardinal Virtues. Prudence and the three main moral virtues — justice, courage, and temperance — comprise the cardinal virtues.[42] All other moral virtues are organized in relationship to them in Aquinas's ethics.[43] Aquinas's list of four follows a tradition that runs from Plato through Augustine and Gregory the Great.[44] The term "cardinal virtues" comes from the Latin word *cardo,* which means "hinge"; these four virtues are taken to be those on which the moral life hinges or depends. As the representative moral virtues, prudence, justice, courage, and temperance cover the full range of human rational capacities — from intellect to rational appetite to sensory appetite, with the latter dividing into the irascible and concupiscible powers.[45] Prudence, also known as practical wisdom, is the main virtue of the practical intellect, as we already noted. The virtue of justice perfects the rational appetite or will, conforming it to reason's judgment about the good and implementing its commands in action. In the sensory appetite, the virtue of courage rightly orders our reactions to bodily pain and difficulty so they do not deter us from worthwhile goods, while the virtue of temperance directs our desires for bodily pleasures so that all these movements of the appetite support, rather than detract from, our pursuit of what reason has judged is good.

The cardinal virtues work together to achieve the human good. Aquinas calls prudence and justice "executive virtues": prudence expresses right reason by directing us rightly to our end, and justice itself realizes the good of reason, in the sense of making it real in action. The type of goods to which prudence and justice direct us are rational goods—goods it takes a rational nature to be able to recognize and desire.[46]

Courage and temperance, as perfections of the irascible and concupiscible powers, are "enabling" or protecting virtues, virtues that keep temptations and obstacles at bay so that the realization of the human good proceeds unhindered. Given their location in the sensory appetite, they have particular bodily goods and evils as their immediate object.

Structure of the Human Soul	Capacity and Its VIRTUE	Object
Essentially Rational Part	Practical Reason PRUDENCE	truth about the good to be done (e.g., good judgments about action)
Rational-by-Participation	Rational appetite (will) JUSTICE	goods apprehensible by reason (e.g., friendship, obligations, common goods)
	Sensory appetite	goods perceivable by sense (material objects)
	Irascible power COURAGE	sensible goods blocked by difficulty (e.g., goods we need to work hard for or face evils in order to attain)
	Concupiscible power TEMPERANCE	sensible goods, taken simply (e.g., physical pleasures)

Nevertheless, their function is to pursue those objects in a way that fits the larger program of human fulfillment.[47] That is why they must be directed by prudence, which has the good of the human person *as a rational being* in view.[48]

Take, for example, the action of participating in a blood drive at the local blood bank. Prudence directs us to this action because it judges it a good way to contribute to the human community and its well-being, a community of which we ourselves are a part, and to contribute a resource we may need ourselves someday. Using reason to weigh various goods and order them rightly actualizes one's rational nature. The intellect perfected by prudence then commands the will, which—as a rational appetite—is able to desire the good of the human community and appreciate the long-term value of our contributions to it. The will in turn mobilizes us to execute this action. Courage keeps fear of pain in the irascible appetite from interfering with our willingness to get pricked and curbs impatience at the inconvenience of waiting, and temperance restrains our concupiscible desire to make an impulsive stop for a cappuccino and pastry on the way, with the result that we miss our appointment.

The work of prudence illustrates Aquinas's view of how practical ends can be "nested" and goods properly ordered—that is, the way different goods and projects can be pursued for the sake of further goods and larger projects, with the highest aim being the fulfillment of the whole person over a whole human life. Although prudence enables one to make a judgment about a single action, this action is determined to be an acceptable means to some further end, which is then ordered to another end (at least implicitly), and so on up to the ultimate end. Judgments of prudence about what is to be done here and now, therefore, are always (at least implicitly) made in the light of the ordering of goods that will make for a whole flourishing human life. Aquinas repeatedly quotes Aristotle to make the point: "prudence is ordered 'to living well as a whole.'"[49] This broad conception of the human good functions as the basis of all particular moral reasoning. Good deliberation is always measured against a background conception of the whole human good and our ultimate end. Having the right ultimate end is thus essential to the proper operation of prudence, in all particular cases and with respect to all particular ends. Moroever, prudence's direction in light of that ultimate end is essential to the proper operation of all the other moral virtues. We will see later how charity's orientation of the will toward the ultimate end links it with prudence and makes it, too, indispensable for the proper operation of all other virtues.

The Three Theological Virtues. Aquinas distinguishes the four cardinal virtues from another important set, the three theological virtues: faith, hope, and charity.[50] These seven virtues together form the backbone of Aquinas's account of how we achieve our ultimate end, and they likewise form the structural principle of Aquinas's treatment of each of the moral virtues in detail, a treatment that comprises nearly all of *ST* IIaIIae. Instead of organizing his ethics around, say, the Ten Commandments, or even the heuristic device of the seven capital vices — a popular motif among pastors and scholars in his own day — Aquinas keeps its attention on striving for excellence, on living a flourishing human life, as exemplified by faith, hope, charity, prudence, justice, courage, and temperance.

What makes the theological virtues theological, since all virtues can be ordered to the good — that is, union with God? Since the theological virtues also perfect the intellect and will, they are distinguished from the moral virtues on the basis of their object, as well as their divine source.[51] Aquinas explains that the three theological virtues have God as their direct object rather than their indirect object.[52] For example, the immediate object of prudence is whatever is the right thing to do here and now according to right reason that best achieves the human good — that is, reason rightly ordering human nature to God as its end. Prudence concerns the means to our ultimate end, rather than intending union with God directly. Similarly, courage helps us stand firm against bodily evils so that we can hold fast to the good, but the bodily evils it withstands are its immediate concern. By contrast, faith, hope, and love all intend union with God, in some mode or other, as their immediate object.[53] Faith unites the intellect with God, while hope and love unite the will with God. Because the end to which they direct us is a supernatural one, for the operation of these virtues, divine reason must supplement the ability of human reason to direct our action.[54]

Faith, hope, and especially love are also distinguished by their role in the moral life. The three theological virtues function as the roots of *all* other virtues, shaping the deepest orientation of our person and informing every other inclination and movement relevant to moral action. They operate as first principles: like natural inclinations, they are fundamental sources of motivation.[55] Given to us directly by God—in Aquinas's terms, "infused" by the grace of the Holy Spirit—the theological virtues expand our natural capacities and inclinations and direct us to a supernatural end, an end *above* our nature, which we could not apprehend or achieve with our own natural power.[56] Theological virtues therefore have a supernatural source corresponding to their supernatural end—God.[57] Human flourishing is still the goal, but flourishing now includes not only this life and its relationships with other human beings, but also a life beyond this and a life lived even now in relationship with God.[58]

The theological virtues do not therefore replace the cardinal virtues; they give them a new range of operation. As we will see in a moment, this means that the cardinal virtues will have both an imperfect form—the form Aristotle discussed—and also a perfect form. In their perfect form, they are manifestations of charity, as Augustine conceived them.[59] The cardinal virtues serve as instruments and implementers of the theological virtues in the matter of concrete acts, but these acts are now done with the *ultimate* end in view. Without the theological virtues, the cardinal virtues operate simply in view of the end as human reason can perceive it. While the virtue of faith reveals our perfect, supernatural end, Aquinas assigns charity the premier role in directing the cardinal virtues to that end: "Charity, because it orders human beings to their ultimate end, is the principle of all the good works that can be ordered to the ultimate end. For that reason, all the moral virtues must be infused together with charity, since it is through them that they accomplish each different kind of good work.[60]

Charity orients everything we do toward the goal of knowing and loving God. Practical wisdom is still required to determine whether love is best expressed by spending time with one's children this afternoon or writing another chapter of a book, and love can be expressed both by cooking a magnificent feast for one's neighbors and friends and by devoting oneself to a lengthy fast. In these examples, prudence and temperance, respectively, function as channels of love, each choosing its particular expressions and regulating its mode of expression in concrete actions of different sorts.[61] As the example of fasting implies, what counts as a temperate act may look very different in the context of our ultimate end.[62]

Ultimately, the function of the theological virtues is to make us "partakers [*consortes*] in the divine nature," a phrase Aquinas uses to describe our union with God.[63] These virtues have as their purpose to make us perfect by making us more and more like God. This is why Aquinas uses the Aristotelian notion of friendship to describe charity—the bond between persons is based on similarity of nature and a shared goodness of character.[64] Thus Aquinas says that "the theological virtues . . . should properly be called not human virtues, but superhuman or divine virtues," since human rational nature has them only by participation in the divine nature and by them human beings are able to reach a happiness beyond nature "only through divine power."[65] In what sense these virtues and the acts that come from them are still our own we will consider later. Attention to the divine source of the theological virtues, however, alerts us to another important distinction in Aquinas's ethics—that of acquired and infused virtue.

Acquired and Infused Moral Virtues.   This distinction—along with the role of charity as the principle and end of all other virtuous action— is the key place where we see how Aquinas's theological commitments saturate the rest of his moral theory. Rather than leaving the influence of grace neatly relegated to the theological virtues, Aquinas argues that all the cardinal virtues—indeed, the whole range of moral virtues—have an infused form. We acquire some virtues by practicing their characteristic acts, a process which Aquinas, following Aristotle, calls habituation. Hence their name, "acquired virtues." Moral virtues like truthfulness can thus be inculcated by the usual means: consistently telling the truth, imitating truthful role models, and reinforcing truth-telling by praise, especially when it is difficult.[66] Infused virtues, in contrast, are created in the soul by the direct action of God: "Virtue which orders human beings to the good as measured by the Divine Law, and not by human reason, cannot be caused by human acts, the principle of which is reason, but is produced in us *by divine operation alone.*"[67] Hence Aquinas adopts

Augustine's definition of virtue to describe infused virtues as something "'which God works in us without us.'"[68] But the paradigm has shifted away from the Aristotelian model here: Aquinas says that the acquired virtues count as virtues only in a qualified sense, and the infused virtues are "perfect" in that they "order human beings well to their ultimate end without qualification," while other virtues direct us toward good in a more restricted sense.[69]

While it is true that God causes infused virtue in us "without any action of ours," Aquinas also adds that God does not do so "without our consent."[70] Once God gives us a virtue, furthermore, it is up to us to act on it, and acting according to an infused virtue in turn strengthens the habit.[71] God is the direct cause of the virtue itself, therefore, but human beings in turn must use these virtues to direct their own acts. Moreover, they are free *not* to act according to the infused virtues, for moral habits still require the will for their exercise, and the will remains free to act or not to act. In fact, as Aquinas will note in the treatise on charity, they are free to act against virtue as well.

As an analogy, imagine a singularly ungainly and uncoordinated person being miraculously given the ability to win an Olympic gold medal. Even with this gift, our new "athlete" would not necessarily be able to compete and win the gold instantaneously. He would still need physical training, good coaching, and a venue for competition. Nevertheless, the actual gold medal-winning performance will properly belong not to the miraculous giver, nor to the coach, but to the performer. Infused virtue is something like the miraculously-given athletic talent, and the actual gold medal performance is like our ultimate end. Even enabled by divine grace, Aquinas will argue, the activity will be our own.

Even though he thinks acquired and infused forms of courage, for example, are distinct species of virtue and can have correspondingly different acts,[72] Aquinas typically draws little attention to the differences between the acquired and infused forms when discussing a particular virtue. He also does not usually employ the terms "acquired" or "infused" to mark major distinctions between the two, which can lead to confusion about which type he is referring to in a given text (or whether his comments include both). This absence of distinction can make the transition from Aristotle's ethics to his own Christian perspective on ethics appear more seamless than it is. For example, his treatise on courage discusses fear and daring and basically follows Aristotle's *Nicomachean Ethics,* naming death in battle as the principal act of courage.[73] But a small comment about battle as including "single combat" opens the door for an abrupt paradigm shift—from facing death in battle, on the Greek conception of acquired courage, to Christian martyrdom, an act of infused courage. Infused courage, however, not to mention the opportunity for Christian martyrdom, only comes to us by grace. Aquinas continues discussing the component virtues of courage and the opposing vices as if he had never made a distinction between acquired and infused forms, but then mentions in passing that patience and perseverance (parts of courage) have *only* an infused form.[74] Thus much of the work of distinguishing the two types of courage is left an exercise for his reader.

Perhaps the best explanation for this ambiguity is the fact that Aquinas, writing for a Christian audience,[75] was primarily concerned with the infused forms of the virtues, so he sprinkles them through the text without further explanation.[76] After all, his ethics, though replete with philosophical elements, is located within the discipline of theology. Moreover, Aquinas's ethics has the practical objective of helping others attain the end of human flourishing in its fullest sense. The inclusion of virtues that come only by God's power and gift would be of primary ethical significance for him, since all human beings have God as their ultimate end. Under the rubric of discussing the four cardinal virtues, then, he includes—without further comment— discussions of obedience, humility, religion, piety, and the like —virtues most at home in the theological framework that he and his audience would have shared.[77]

Unlike the moral and cardinal virtues, the theological virtues have *only* an infused form. Faith, hope, and charity are received as a gift from the Holy Spirit. Because these three theological virtues function as the principles of the moral virtues, all other virtues and virtuous actions may be done for the sake of love of God. Like the theological virtues, the infused moral virtues are marked not only by their divine source but also by their orientation to our ultimate end. Thus, when Aquinas describes an act of infused courage, he quotes Augustine with approval: "Courage

is 'love bearing all things readily for the sake of that which is loved'"—
where the loved one is God, who is loved above all.[78] Despite Aquinas's
appropriation of Aristotelian passions in his moral theory, then, the passions of fear and daring are reshaped by love and raised to a level that
Aristotle could not have anticipated, by their direction to God as the
greatest good.[79] Calling the virtue of charity "the root and mother" or
"commander" of all other infused moral virtues, Aquinas gives charity
the premier role in this ordering.

Insofar as charity orders the infused virtues, both theological and
moral, to God as their last end, Aquinas designates them "true and perfect" virtues in the strictest sense.[80] Perfect virtues dispose our acts to God
as our final end and most fully actualize our nature by uniting us with
God. Acquired virtues are still worth having because they enable human
life to be better than it would be without them—even though they are
not fully perfecting of our nature, nor do they enable us to reach our ultimate end.[81]

The two types of virtue can work together, however. For example,
a person well-trained in facing difficulty for the sake of another's good
may find acting courageously after receiving the virtue of infused courage much easier than someone who has spent most of his life indulging in
comfortable cowardice. Similarly, someone who has persevered for many
years pursuing a scientific research project in the face of her colleagues'
skepticism may also find it easier to hold to her religious faith against the
pressures of scorn or even persecution, compared to someone who is ac-
customed to working with the support and affirmation of others.[82] Because the infused virtues are received as a gift from God, along with other
gifts of the Holy Spirit, rather than being gradually cultivated by practice
over time, like the acquired virtues, their presence is not usually accompanied by passions which have been gradually retrained through habituation.[83] Aquinas says that an infused virtue enables one to act well despite the influence of lingering disordered passions.[84] He acknowledges
that this initially gives acts of infused virtue the "feel" of acts that are self-
controlled but do not include pleasure in the good, which is the traditional
hallmark of virtue. As we act on the infused virtues time and time again
after their reception by grace, however, the passions eventually undergo

the same transformation that they do with the acquired virtues. This is another way in which grace leaves room for human agency—we need to act on infused virtues to train our appetites to accord with them and so to make these divinely bestowed dispositions become "second nature" to us.[85]

A Closer Look at the Theological Virtues

We have said that Aquinas distinguishes between the virtues on the basis of their objects and the moral capacities—or subjects—that they perfect. Since all three theological virtues have God as their object, and two of the three have the will as their subject, Aquinas needs to do extra work distinguishing their mode of operation.

Given Aquinas's theory of action, the virtues of the intellect always come first in order of acquisition, for the intellect must apprehend an object before the will can incline toward it as good. Thus, among the theological virtues he treats faith before hope and charity.[86] Faith is a virtue of the speculative intellect; like wisdom (*sapientia,* not *prudentia*), its object is the ultimate source of truth—in Aquinas's words, God as "first truth."[87] Because we cannot see this truth fully, the will must aid the intellect in holding fast to it with a certainty based not on what is seen but on the trustworthiness of the giver of truth.[88] Therefore, the "living faith [*fides formata*]" of a human believer, because it requires the engagement of the will, must also be informed by charity.[89]

In the treatise on happiness (*ST* IaIIae.1–5), Aquinas describes the beatific vision of the speculative intellect—the comprehensive vision that perfects and succeeds faith's imperfect grasp—as the essence of happiness.[90] As in his treatment of the virtue of faith, his emphasis here on happiness as the vision of the intellect is balanced later in his ethics, in *ST* IIaIIae, by the foundational role of charity, or the virtue of love found in the will—a point easily missed by those who read only *ST* IaIIae to learn his ethical views.[91] Complete happiness, or union with God, engages *both* intellect and will, and the activities of each mutually perfect each other. The union with God, as the fullest perfection of human nature, cannot, for Aquinas, be a purely intellectual exercise. So while his account of happiness in the ethical part of *ST* begins with something very much like Aristotelian contemplation, it is neither complete nor fully accurate without the account of our union with God that also includes the friendship of charity.[92] Happiness is a beatific, transforming gaze of love, not merely a clear-sighted contemplation of truth—reflecting Aquinas's conviction that the truth known by this gaze is knowledge of a person, another rational being who is capable of love, rather than knowledge of a set of facts or propositions.[93] As he puts it elsewhere, "vision is a cause of love."[94] Just as prudence and the moral virtues mutually depend on each other, so also charity is the necessary complement to both the virtue of faith and the beatific vision that perfects faith.[95]

Faith therefore perfects the intellect,[96] whose object is the highest truth, in concert with the affirmation of the will. Hope and charity, by contrast, both perfect the rational appetite or will, whose object is the good. When Aquinas is discussing love, he distinguishes between delight, which is love's present possession of the good it loves, and desire, which is love's yearning for a loved good that is not yet or not yet fully possessed. Because in this life our attainment of the highest good, God, is both already partially and not yet fully realized, Aquinas thinks that we need two distinct theological virtues to perfect the will.

God is present in us already, through the infusion of charity. The vision of God that completes faith and our perfect union with God in charity, however, is also not yet fully realized, leaving room for hope. Aquinas defines hope as regarding a future good, one that is possible to attain in some respect.[97] Furthermore, charity is related to God as our end, while hope regards God as the one without whom we cannot achieve that end.

Attainment of a desired end is possible for us in two ways: by our own power or by the help of another. Hope seeks to attain our ultimate fulfillment not on our own but with God's help. Aquinas describes the object of hope in terms of "divine assistance."[98] Because God is united to us in the "friendship of charity," however, Aquinas can explain how the attainment of an end is possible *for us,* even if it is achieved through God's grace, by invoking Aristotle's notion of friendship: the friend is "another self," and "what we can do with the help of our friends, we can in a sense do by ourselves."[99] While for Aristotle, human beings need others—such as legislators, parents, educators, and friends—to attain happiness, for Aquinas, human beings also need the help of a divine legislator, parent, educator, and friend to achieve their ultimate end. The virtue of hope stresses human dependence on God; we must accept divine agency in order to actualize our own.

Aquinas's treatment of hope highlights human dependence on God for divine assistance. His characterization of charity, in contrast, focuses on the relationship of love between human beings and God. He also describes the friendship of charity as uniting us with God and as the "spiritual life whereby God dwells in us," since love effects union and mutual indwelling between those who love each other.[100] The love that is charity unites us with God by making us like-natured friends of God, in communion with him. Here is Aquinas's fullest definition of charity:

> Charity is the friendship of human beings for God, founded on the fellowship [*communicationem*] of everlasting happiness. Now this fellowship is not according to natural goods but gratuitous gifts, for, as Romans 6:23 says, "the grace of God is everlasting life"; thus charity itself surpasses our natural faculties. . . . Charity therefore cannot be in us either through our natural or our acquired powers, but by the infusion of the Holy Spirit, Who is the love of the Father and the Son. Our participation in the Spirit is created charity.[101]

Human nature is transformed by its participation in the divine nature through charity, and human capacities are enhanced by grace. Given that Aquinas's account of human flourishing is based on his account of human nature and its capacities for action, we should expect, therefore, to see the impact of this transformation in every element of his moral theory, and to find charity at the heart of change.

We can understand better now why Aquinas makes charity the principle of all the other virtues and the source of their unity. With the virtue of charity, he argues, one receives all the infused moral virtues as well.[102] Aristotle held a similar thesis about the unity of the virtues, except that the moral virtues were connected through the virtue of prudence, the *sine qua non* for them all. Aristotle, however, was concerned with human flourishing in this life and the virtuous activity required for that end. Aquinas has eternal life in view in his account of virtue, and his ultimate end includes not only Aristotelian contemplation but also a loving union with a personal God. Thus, while he accepts Aristotle's thesis of the unity of the virtues through prudence, he adds rootedness in charity as an additional and necessary unifying principle. Every virtuous act has charity as its underlying source and seeks to attain a more perfect union with God as its end. As we will see further in chapter 9, this has the effect of shaping the very substance of the other virtues and the species of their acts.[103]

The other infused virtues depend on charity, then, but the opposite is also true: it would frustrate the purpose of charity, which is to direct action toward our ultimate end, if charity were infused without the necessary instruments—the infused moral virtues—to carry out its purpose.[104] As we saw earlier, love needs to be concretely expressed *through* temperance and prudence and the other infused moral virtues. Since love is the root of all the other movements of the appetite, it only makes sense that charity would inform the whole network of human virtue and action.[105]

We noted earlier that the seven virtues—the three theological virtues and the four cardinal virtues—form the backbone of Aquinas's account of all the other virtues. Charity appears after the other two theological virtues because in the logical order of infusion it is the last: faith, as an intellectual act, must precede the movement of the will, in keeping with the general principles of Aquinas's action theory.[106] Charity appears *before* the cardinal virtues, however, because just as it orders and informs the other two theological virtues, it also directs the moral or cardinal virtues to the ultimate end of human nature.[107] Thus, we find charity, with prudence immediately following, at the center and apex of the section in the *Summa* on the seven main virtues. With charity as the root, mother, and commander of the virtues, each virtue's character and operation now does its work shaped by supernatural love for God.

In the treatise on charity we also find links between virtue, law, and grace. For example, Aquinas holds that the gift of wisdom—which perfects moral judgment—is infused together with charity.[108] As a gift of the Holy Spirit, this type of wisdom is a work of grace.[109] While the virtue of charity perfects the appetite, wisdom perfects the intellect by enabling it to judge rightly in light of the Eternal Law, which orders all things to God as their end.[110] What the study of charity and infused moral virtue in this chapter has shown, and what chapter 8 will consider with respect to law, is the way that Aquinas's account of the perfection of intellect and will through virtue and law is suffused by grace. His picture of human flourishing and the role of virtue in achieving that end are shaped through and through by his theological commitments.

eight

Law and Grace

In *chapter 7 we examined the virtues in Aquinas's ethics and* argued that the theological virtue of charity is central in his account of the virtues. Virtues, or good habits, are the "interior" directors and perfecters of human action. In the present chapter we introduce Aquinas's account of the "exterior" principles of human action, sources external to us that perfect our nature and direct us to our ultimate end. In treating the exterior principles of law and grace, our emphasis will be on how Aquinas integrates these with the virtues and how, again, his theological commitments inform this move.

LAW

Aquinas's discussion of law begins with God, who orders the universe and all its motion back to himself as its ultimate end and good.[1] Wisdom (in all its forms) and goodness, the perfections of the intellect and will, respectively, involve right order.[2] The duty of the wise person is to understand the order of reality, and moral perfection requires living in accordance with that order. The fundamental function of a lawmaker is to order things toward the good, and God's providential ordering of the universe, a rule marked by wisdom and goodness, explicitly frames Aquinas's discussion of the law.[3] Human beings, as creatures who have "power" [*potestam*] over their own actions, reflect in their intellects and wills their participation in God's rule.[4] By participation, Aquinas means both the way our natural inclinations reflect God's law and the way we can actively share in God's activity of governing ourselves and other created things.

Law in general names the ordering of action to the common good. Lawgiving requires reason, since it involves ordering and commanding the things under the lawgiver's care to the proper end of the whole — whether that whole is the universe, a human community, or even an individual, who is the common subject of various capacities.[5] Law therefore presupposes a person in charge of the common good; it presupposes that there is a community or whole made of parts that has a good and that is capable of being ordered; and it presupposes that those subject to it can take orders, since — to count as law — those orders must be "promulgated" or made known.[6] Under this general description we can see how Aquinas's view of law is modeled on God's nature and action: God, a person capable of both directing and commanding others by virtue of his rationality, is in charge of the world that he created and orders all things to himself as their end and the perfect good.[7] Law is also closely identified in Aquinas's ethics with divine agency, since by means of law, God is the extrinsic principle of human action.[8]

Aquinas treats four main kinds of law: eternal law, natural law, divine law, and human law.[9] He further divides the divine law into the Old and New Law, with the New Law providing a fitting segue to the discussion of grace. Despite these distinctions, the different types of law overlap substantially in content. Aquinas begins his discussion of the types of law with the eternal law as *the* archetypal law from which all other laws derive their status as law.

Eternal law is another name for God's providential direction — his master planning — of the universe as a whole. God's rule of law is evident in the workings of the natural world as well as in human inclination and history; it guides and orders everything to its proper *telos*.[10] All other kinds of law, in order to count as law, must reflect and accord with the eternal law.[11]

Natural law, the second type, names the extent to which human nature, especially the human intellect, participates in God's law and imitates

God's lawgiving.[12] Directing our own actions according to an end and a good that we grasp as such is a law-like ability. Our nature, with its internal principles, capacities, and *telos,* is designed to conform to eternal law, as are all other natures; however, we uniquely imitate God in our ability to apprehend a common good and direct ourselves and others to it. Law's work of directing and commanding not only locates it within the scope of the work of the intellect, as Aquinas already noted when discussing the will's act of "command," but also connects it closely with the work of prudence.[13]

Calling our participation in eternal law "natural law" stresses both that we have this ability by our nature, as rational beings, and that all law must befit nature—the nature of all reality and God's design for it.[14] Law is not a purely spontaneous or creative activity for us; in our lawmaking, we can only apprehend and work from the structures God has set in place already. The ability of rational creatures to direct their own actions in light of certain given natural principles is what Aquinas means to pinpoint in his discussion of the natural law. When our legislation breaks from the nature of things, including our own nature, it is invalidated, since law is legitimate only when it is consonant with eternal law.

Aquinas thinks that we have certain principles embedded in our nature that express our various natural inclinations to the good; this is why they count as precepts of the *natural* law. He also says they are "naturally known" by us, because they are, as it were, written on our nature. We find his famous list of principles in *Summa theologiae* IaIIae.94.2. These natural law precepts express our directedness to the human good (the good of reason) at several levels, including our natural inclinations, for example, to preserve ourselves, reproduce, enjoy companionship with others, and seek truth. Notice that Aquinas's list maintains a concern for our whole nature as rational animals.

It may be helpful to think of the principles of the natural law as something like "the laws of human nature"—analogous to the laws of nature in science, or what Alvin Plantinga calls "a design plan."[15] This means that we often act according to natural law without ever having gained explicit knowledge of it, just as we operate a vehicle without knowing the principles of physics according to which the engine was designed. The first and most fundamental principle of the natural law is,

"Good is to be done and pursued and evil is to be avoided."[16] Thus Aquinas thinks that all human action aims at some good, at least implicitly; it is part of human nature to aim at something under the notion "this is good for me." We may not be able to articulate any of the precepts of the natural law in so many words; however, the fact that this assumption is essential in order to make sense of any human action as such tells us that we have hit upon a fundamental law of human nature.[17]

When human beings are functioning as they were designed and their natures are aimed at flourishing, these fundamental laws of human nature simply describe their actions, according to Aquinas. However, given the fall into sin, our natures have become disabled and disordered, so that our "natural" inclination is no longer a reliable guide to the laws that rightly order human nature. Further, Aquinas gives examples of occasions when our grasp of the natural law is marred, blurred, and even sometimes entirely obscured, due to the double defects of sin and error.[18] The difficulty we have in discerning what is part of our design plan and what constitutes a defect in it is illustrated, for example, in recent debates on the bounds of "natural" human sexual behavior. Hence, in our current state, the natural law is no longer merely descriptive; it is also normative.[19]

Aquinas is perfectly candid about the limitations of human knowledge and experience when it comes to discerning the specific ways we are designed to be and to act at anything more than a very basic level. We know we are supposed to pursue the good, and our desires are "hardwired" that way.[20] To the extent that we understand our own nature, the natural law is (and certainly was, before our fall into sin) sufficiently promulgated. To the extent that our nature is both limited and disordered by sin, Aquinas thinks that the natural law will need to be augmented by divine law, a point we will consider below.

"Human law," the sort of positive law that political leaders make and judges uphold, specifies how the principles of natural law best apply in a given community at a given time. For example, *that* certain crimes be punished and restitution be made for them—namely, that justice be done—is part of the natural law, but *how* they are punished and *what* restitution is required is largely a matter to be determined by particular peoples in particular historical situations.[21] For example, some moralists argue that today's penitentiaries are sufficiently secure to justify giving up the death penalty for those who commit murder, whereas in the past, execution may have been a necessary measure to safeguard the community against such criminals. While these matters may sometimes prove difficult to decide, Aquinas is clear that when humanly-made laws depart from the natural law, they forfeit any genuine moral authority.

Laws are framed to cover what should be done in general, even though at times and in some cases the law will fail due to the contingency of human affairs.[22] Moreover, what the good is for these sorts of cases, for this group of people, or for this time and place is not always clear.[23] Aquinas argues that because of the overwhelming number of contingent and particular factors to consider in individual actions and the limited time in which to make decisions, our judgments and practical decisions will inevitably be marked by uncertainty and error.[24] One can appeal to the spirit of the law when a particular formulation does not adequately cover a given case, but discerning this and deciding what to do in exceptional cases requires virtues such as prudence and equity in order to be done well.[25]

The ultimate aim and effect of law, as a dictate of reason, is to make people virtuous, although its ability to do so is limited.[26] Law, through the threat of punishment, can give people a reason to do good acts, or at the very least restrain them from acting badly.[27] The hope, however, is that the law will function, at least at a basic level, as a source of habituation.[28] In the best cases, our acts will no longer be done merely *according* to virtue, as the law commands, but instead will be done *as* the virtuous person would do them — that is, from an interior love of the good which no longer needs external coercion.

Aquinas is forthright about the inadequacy of human reason to discern the human good and the laws consonant with it. He offers the following as one of the reasons we need divine revelation in addition to the natural law:

> On account of the uncertainty of human judgment, especially in contingent and particular matters, different people form different judgments regarding human acts; which result in different and contrary laws. Therefore, so that human beings may know without any doubt what they ought to do and what they ought to avoid, it was necessary

for them to be directed to their own acts by a God-given law, for it is undisputed that such a law cannot err.[29]

Even without the effects of sin, moreover, he thinks that the "light of grace" must be added to the "light of nature," just as our intellectual grasp of God in this life needs to be enhanced now by the light of faith and perfected later in the beatific vision.[30] As infused virtue is added to acquired virtue, similarly, divine law is added to the natural law.

"Divine law," the final type of law, is thus the portion of the eternal law that God explicitly reveals, primarily in Scripture. In theological terms, the divine law is to special revelation what natural law is to general revelation, but we must keep in mind how much the divine and natural laws overlap in content. Aquinas thinks, for example, that much of what God revealed in the Ten Commandments is a reiteration of what we in principle could have known through natural law, were we not corrupted and blinded by sin.[31] The Ten Commandments imply general claims about conduct that go beyond their explicit commands or prohibitions. For example, Aquinas holds that rightly ordered sexual desire in all of its forms is the good at stake in the commandment against adultery, and maintains that the commandment explicitly mentions only adultery because many of us are too morally corrupt to recognize the other forms of disorder that the commandment, in its intention, prohibits.[32] Thus, we need to listen to the morally wise to figure out the rest, but adultery should strike most people as morally wrong despite the distorting effects of sin.[33]

The main negative purpose of the divine law is therefore to correct for defects and imperfections in human perception and understanding of the natural law, but its positive purpose and end is to direct human beings to an end above their natural capacities. In Aquinas's words, the end of the divine law is nothing less than charity: "the intention of the divine law is, principally, to establish human beings in friendship with God."[34] For this reason it is called the "law of love."[35] Again, law points to virtue and is completed by charity: "the end of the commandments is love (1 Timothy 1:5)."[36]

The divine law is divided into the Old Law and the New Law, corresponding, roughly, to what God revealed to Israel in the Old Testament and what God revealed to the Church through Jesus Christ.[37] The moral precepts of the Old Law are still obligatory, but they are no longer written merely on tablets of stone and enforced by temporal punishments. Rather, these precepts form part of the New Law "of liberty."[38] Our obedience is motivated not by an external lawgiver and the coercive threat of punishment, Aquinas says, but by the Holy Spirit within, who prompts in us a desire to comply with all that love requires. The New Law is written on the heart of a person by the Holy Spirit and obeyed out of love and devotion to God, rather than out of fear of punishment.[39] Aquinas's description of the New Law therefore not only interweaves divine and human agency but explicitly links law and grace: "Since then the grace of the Holy Spirit is like an interior habit infused [*infusus*] in us inclining us to act rightly, it makes us do freely those things that are becoming to us by grace, . . . and freely fulfill those precepts and prohibitions, insofar as we do so by the interior instigation of grace."[40]

As Aquinas's reference to an "interior habit" indicates, this new type of law provides a further link to virtue as well. Take, for example, the distinction Aquinas makes between servile fear and filial fear—both of which can be gifts of the Holy Spirit that accompany the theological virtue of hope.[41] The distinction directly applies to our motivation for obedience to different forms of law. In the Old Law, servile fear—that is, fear of temporal punishment—motivated adherence. By contrast, in the New Law, the greatest fear of followers of the law of love, animated from within by the Holy Spirit, is that by their disobedience of the law they will be separated from a God whom they love. Their "filial fear" (from the Latin *filius,* or son) confirms that love of God, or charity, is their primary motivation, and this fear is the result of God's indwelling in them by his Spirit, like charity. The two types of fear thus reflect the difference between a servant's obedience of a master and a child's obedience of a parent whose nature he or she shares. Aquinas's use of these metaphors is a striking reminder of the central place of love in his ethics, even in the treatise on law, and of the way this love is not external to us but is incorporated into and transforms our nature.

Like the interior influence of virtue, moreover, the New Law applies to the full range of interior motions of the will, far beyond the range of enforceable external actions.[42] Aquinas uses Jesus' teachings on anger and

lust in the Gospels to illustrate this point.[43] Aquinas takes these teachings to indicate that in the New Law, the moral precept prohibiting murder found in the Old Law also proscribes any disordered anger or hatred
directed at another, even if it remains hidden in the heart. Jesus' teaching likewise implies that the "eye for an eye" requirement in the Old Law
was designed to keep human revenge within just limits, not to preclude
mercy.[44] The goal of the New Law is not merely just actions but a heart
that loves justice, just as the goal of virtue is not merely good actions but
a good agent.

The New Law, which we saw Aquinas describe as the interior work
of the Holy Spirit in us, centers on the interior formation of the will, by
prompting us to acts of love; it thus serves both as the ally and as the
source of virtue in us. The New Law orders our interior inclinations so
that they not only conform fully to what the law requires but also conform freely. Compared to the New Law, then, Aquinas concludes that
the Old Law was "imperfect."[45] By contrast, "the sermon Our Lord de-
livered on the mountain (Matthew 5–7) includes the whole process of
formation [*informationem*] that is the Christian life," a formation that
Aquinas, in the rest of the *Summa,* proceeds to describe almost exclusively in terms of the virtues.[46]

DEFENDING AN INTEGRATIONIST READING
OF AQUINAS'S ETHICS

Before we turn to the concept of grace, which Aquinas places along-
side virtue and law as a perfecter and director of human action, we must
first address the fact that Aquinas has long been known, both inside and
outside of philosophical circles, as a "natural law ethicist." How does the
view of his ethics that stands behind this label fit with the integrationist
reading of Aquinas's ethics offered here?

The natural law reading of Aquinas makes the topic of the natural
law and the types of actions it prescribes the focus of Aquinas's ethical
project. Advocates of this general position are concerned with how much
of the natural law we can know, what its principles are, and how the various precepts of the natural law can be applied to our lives and used to

evaluate our actions. When discussing Aquinas's ethics, they usually con-
strain their attention to the "treatise on law," especially to the discussion of
the natural law in *ST* IaIIae.94.2, where Aquinas sets out the basic inclinations characteristic of human nature, which the fundamental principles
of the natural law articulate.[47] These principles of the natural law, as we
have already noted, direct us to goods ranging from self-preservation —
based on an inclination we share with all substances — to the acquisition of truth — based on a desire unique to the rational creature. On the
natural law reading of Aquinas, moral theorizing starts from these more
general principles of human nature — the ones we can "read off from"
human nature and its inclinations. Then we must figure out how to derive these more general principles from the "first principle of the natural
law": "Good is to be done and pursued, and evil is to be avoided." From
there, we can further derive more specific moral rules governing human
action.

   This section of the treatise on law is undoubtedly important to
Aquinas's ethics. But a reading of Aquinas that focuses on the natural
law to the near exclusion of any attention to the virtues — a reading that
identifies Aquinas principally as a "natural law ethicist" — is worth challenging on two counts. First, there is evidence that a reading which makes
the virtues — and especially the virtue of charity — the central focus,
rather than the law, is most faithful to Aquinas's own intentions for his
ethics. Second, reading his ethics with the primary attention on the virtues and on Aquinas's theological commitments can still do justice to the
importance of law in Aquinas's thought, and may even do it greater justice than a natural law reading of his ethics.

   What would it mean to put the treatise on law into the context of
Aquinas's ethics as a whole? In *ST* IaIIae, the treatise on law falls between
the treatise on habits (virtues and vices), on one side, and the treatise on
grace on the other. All three together cover the principles of human acts.
In *ST* IIaIIae, Aquinas offers an extensive discussion of the seven principal virtues, which form the structural organizing principle of the rest of
his ethical discussion in this part of the *Summa*. After sketching the most
basic principles of the natural law in *ST* IaIIae, therefore, Aquinas leaves
the task of working out and applying the natural law almost entirely
to the reader.[48] He turns his attention instead to a remarkably detailed

analysis of the virtues. If we follow Aquinas's own emphasis, then, the question seems to be not whether the virtues are important and even central to his conception of the ethical life, but rather what place law might have in a life of virtue.[49]

Even the immediate context of the famous discussion of the natural law indicates that Aquinas is more interested in establishing a theologically informed concept of law than in developing an independent moral system based on a law naturally knowable to us. For example, the single question on natural law is framed by the preceding discussion of eternal law — God's governance of the universe through providence — and natural law is defined as human participation in eternal law.[50] The natural law must be reinforced and supplemented by the divine law, a topic which immediately follows. Finally, the treatise on law closes with a final chapter on the New Law — the Holy Spirit's work of writing the law on our hearts. Aquinas defines the New Law as the supernatural completion and perfection of the natural inclinations on which the principles of natural law are based. It seems closest to what Aquinas had in mind, therefore, to read the natural law discussion within its immediate context — namely, as an account of forms of law designed to direct us, more and more explicitly and directly, to our end in God.

Furthermore, the bulk of the treatise on law is comprised not of the single question on the natural law, but of an extensive section of eight questions on the Old Law (part of divine law), some of them containing eleven objections and detailed replies rather than the usual three objections. Of these eight questions, three argue in detail that the Old Law pointed to Christ, in whom it found fulfillment.[51] Aquinas gives attention to Christ here because he is the exemplar of perfected human nature. Christ's person and his action embody the *telos* of the law and its direction in the moral life. Recall that the purpose of law is to lead to virtue, and virtues, as the perfections of human capacities, perfect both the agent and his actions. Thus, Aquinas's account of the divine law, which completes and corrects for defects in the natural law, points us to virtue and the perfection of human nature.

Aquinas's treatment of law, therefore, integrates virtue and law with each other and with his theological commitments. A reading of the treatise on law in its full ethical context indicates that Aquinas is most concerned with the ways our human nature, its powers, and its actions participate in and reflect the divine nature, because this is how human nature is perfected. This is why Aquinas's attention to the natural law—which can direct us to God only imperfectly—is overshadowed by the divine law, which teaches us about our ultimate end; it is also why grace and charity supplement and perfect our natural inclinations so we can attain that end.

In fairness, it should be noted that historical influences are partly to blame for the common reading of Aquinas as a natural law ethicist, a reading we take to be unbalanced. Historically, the vast section of questions on particular virtues in the *secunda secundae* (*ST* IIaIIae) was often circulated separately from the rest of the *Summa* as a pastoral and practical work.[52] A reading of the *prima secundae* (*ST* IaIIae) alone, with its substantial sections on virtue, law, and grace, could lead one to think that law in general has at least as much importance as virtue in the conceptual underpinning of Aquinas's moral system.[53] We should also take into account the shift in Christian thought away from a Greek ethic of virtue toward a law-based morality, especially in the years following Aquinas's life. As part of this shift, all virtues were relocated in the will as the center of moral agency, and then further reduced to forms of obedience to God's will as the source of moral obligation.[54] Thus law, duty, and obligation gradually replaced virtue, happiness, and love as the focal points of morality and the moral life. This change shaped how Aquinas was read by future scholars.[55] Finally, antireligious pressures in twentieth-century philosophy backed many Christian ethicists into an apologetic mode; a rationalistic, natural law approach may have seemed a promising strategy for winning respectability for Aquinas's ethics in general philosophical circles.

Rather than debating whether Aquinas should be assigned the label of natural law ethicist or of virtue ethicist, however, we maintain that an accurate and rich reading of Aquinas will integrate those two emphases. A holistic and theologically informed reading of Aquinas's ethics has a place—an important one—for the natural law, as well as a place for grace, the New Law, and virtue. The key to this integration is to study Aquinas's ethics, as we attempt to do here, in light of human nature and its capacities, since this background, along with the Christian theology informing it, does much of the work of bringing law and virtue together.

As a study of human capacities makes clear, Aquinas thinks that love (*amor*)—the inclination or attraction of things to the good, as something suitable to their nature—is the most basic inclination of human nature. In its various expressions, love serves as the basic law of movement and orientation of all substances in the world.[56] The much-cited first principle of the natural law found in *ST* IaIIae.94.2—"Good is to be done and pursued"—is, then, really an expression of this "law of the universe" in rational nature. Even in our sinful, fallen state, according to Aquinas, this law is essential to both understanding and evaluating action, as we have seen in part 2 of this book. Because of sin, it also takes on a prescriptive character, for though we seek things as good for us (in some respect), our love is now often directed at things that are not truly perfective of our nature.[57]

Note that this picture of natural law is still teleological and eudaimonistic.[58] Law operates within a natural and moral system of beings oriented to their perfection, not merely under obligation to a superior power or in obedience to a higher authority. Aquinas conceives of God, the maker of the eternal law, as ordering things to their proper ends, to their own good, as determined by their natures and natural capacities. In Aquinas's metaphysical scheme, being is oriented toward its actualization or perfection. The human capacities of intellect and will, perfected by virtue, yield action that not only conforms to law (in its intention as well as its external movement) but also achieves the human good.[59] The natural law expresses our basic inclination toward perfection, and virtue helps fully extend and realize this perfection.[60] *Caritas* is the perfection of *amor* in human nature. Aquinas repeatedly describes the infused theological virtue of charity—or rational love—as the perfected rational expression and fulfillment of the law of human nature.[61] The virtue of charity thus complements the law, for both are grounded in the inclination of human nature to its perfection. But charity, like the divine law and New Law, also constitutes the elevation of that inclination to our ultimate end by grace and the fulfillment of that inclination.

Aquinas explicitly makes the connection between virtue and law when he argues that the divine law clarifies and reiterates the basic moral precepts of the natural law in order to "establish human beings in friendship with God." As he explains: "Now since likeness is a reason [*ratio*] of love . . . it is impossible that there be human friendship with God, Who is supremely good, unless human beings are made good. . . . But the goodness of human beings is virtue, which 'makes those who have it good' (*Nicomachean Ethics* 2.6)."[62] The law's *telos* is virtue, which is why it prescribes acts of virtue, even acts which require grace for their fulfillment.[63] In Aquinas's view, then, the fit of law with the virtues is not strained but seamless.

Furthermore, like charity, law has a "now" and "not yet" structure. As we noted in chapter 7, charity both anticipates and realizes our union with God. Since charity is our participation in the divine nature by grace, our union with God is in one sense already present (realized now). And yet, as a habit, the virtue of charity disposes us to act—for habits are "ordered to action"; that is how they perfect our capacities and powers.[64] It is finally the *activity* of knowing and loving God, not the virtuous habit, in which our beatitude consists. Even though we have a foretaste of union with God through charity now, we still need to act and live in ways consistent with that virtuous habit in order to actualize our nature fully and reach our perfection.

Law, for Aquinas, is thus both an expression of the deepest inclinations of human nature (now) and—given the reality of sin in all of its forms—also an expression of obligations and directives that are no longer "natural" to us. They must, therefore, through practice and action that conforms to law, become "second nature" to us, healing the wounds of sin and perfecting what is (not yet) perfected in the nature with which we were born. The imperfection of the natural law, furthermore, requires the divine law for its completion, a divine law itself further divided into stages of perfection. These are the "imperfect" Old Law, on the one hand—a law that foreshadowed Christ, gave incomplete instruction, and was motivated by fear—and the "perfect" New Law, on the other hand, which constitutes the fulfillment of the law in grace and is motivated internally by love.[65]

Charity, a work of grace initiated by the Holy Spirit, not only compensates for sin by orienting our nature to our ultimate end beyond our own capacities to do so, but also completes and builds upon the natural inclination to the good expressed in the natural law. Charity—our loving union with God, who is *the* ultimate good—constitutes the *telos* of the moral life. Taken as a whole, Aquinas's picture of the moral life begins in love's natural expression (inclination and natural law) and is completed in its supernatural expression (grace, revealed law, and the virtue of charity). This picture reflects the recurring theme that love fulfills the law.[66] What law and inclination point us toward is nothing but what we were originally made for, but are unable to attain on our own. Grace and charity redirect our will to our ultimate end and enable us to attain it.[67]

We can see now why Aquinas integrates virtue and grace into his account of law. He recognizes that the natural law cannot direct and perfect human action without the aid of grace and infused virtue. Thus, it is no accident, but a fitting pedagogical move, that Aquinas ends the treatise on law with a question on the New Law, a fitting transition to the treatise on grace. "The New Law," according to Aquinas, "consists principally in the grace of the Holy Spirit, which is revealed in faith working through love."[68] Notably, he also compares the interior working of the Holy Spirit to a virtue: "Since then the grace of the Holy Spirit is like an interior habit infused [*infusus*] in us inclining us to act rightly, it makes us do freely those things that are becoming to us by grace, and avoid the things opposed to it."[69]

If one stopped with natural law, therefore, the ethics would be incomplete. To operate only under what nature has given—especially now, given the damage of sin, which adds to our original limitations—would be to forfeit human fulfillment.[70] Natural law and its expression in human inclination point us imperfectly toward human fulfillment and thereby expose our need for virtue and grace. Aquinas's account of natural law is completed by divine law, which enlightens us as to the supernatural end of the law. The New Law equips us to cooperate fully and freely with grace and thereby develop and act according to virtue, so that we might attain the perfect good.

GRACE

We have seen how grace is necessary to perfect human nature: it enables us to follow law's ultimate direction and to achieve virtue's perfection of human capacities. Further, we have shown how Aquinas's theological commitments inform his treatment of both virtue and law, and have argued that grace — the third major element in his ethics — is essential to fully understand the other two. Perhaps the most pressing question that remains, then, is how grace enables *human* perfection. That is, how does the infusion of grace and the influence of divine agency on human capacities for action leave room for human agency and human freedom, so that our nature is perfected by genuinely human activity? How do human and divine nature, and human and divine agency, remain distinct if grace perfects human nature?

Interestingly, there is an analogous discussion in Aristotle's ethics. In the *Nicomachean Ethics* 2.1, Aristotle asks whether virtue is natural to us; that is, is it part of our nature as human beings? The answer is yes and no. No, because we are not born with virtue, such that it will automatically develop, say, the way our bodies grow and mature. But yes, because we have the capacity to acquire it — with proper upbringing, instruction, and practice — and acquiring it will perfect our nature. In this sense virtue *is* natural to us, so much so that when we are mature in our development of the virtues, they become, in Aristotle's familiar phrase, like "second nature" to us — yielding acts that accord with our nature, perfect it, and hence give us pleasure.[71]

Aquinas makes a similar move when describing the infusion of grace by the Holy Spirit. Is this grace natural to us? No, in the sense that achievement of our ultimate end "surpasses the capacity of human nature," so that when grace is infused, it is "an accidental quality superadded to human nature" rather than something essential to human nature or an intrinsic quality of the human soul.[72] At the same time, Aquinas also describes the Holy Spirit's operation in us as "like an interior habit" or virtue that is required for human perfection. Compare grace to an antibiotic, which, despite its synthetic (that is, non-natural) composition, is nonetheless fully metabolized and integrated into the system of a human body to enhance its natural operations and achieve health when the body alone would not be able to do so. Likewise, grace, as a supernatural addition to the soul, fits human nature and helps it to become fully perfected beyond its own natural powers. As the antibiotic requires the metabolism of the body and its natural mechanisms to effect health, so too, divine infusion, which prompts and equips us to achieve our ultimate end, nonetheless requires our own acts.[73] Our moral perfection and the activity of loving God perfectly require, therefore, that grace enhance human nature.

The gift of grace thus does not technically count as miraculous; in Aquinas's words, "the soul is naturally capable of grace; since 'from its having been made in the image of God, it is capable of receiving God by grace.'"[74] That is to say, while our nature is not on its own capable of attaining our ultimate end, the addition of grace is not contrary to it. Our ultimate end is something for which human nature was designed, a good that the intellect and will naturally desire.[75] By grace we participate in the divine nature and more completely share in the divine likeness.[76] Even so, this transformation by grace also fulfills human capacities to the utmost, capacities already described in terms of divine likeness (the image of God) in the prologue to *ST* IaIIae. Thus, the movement from nature to grace is one that blends Aristotelian metaphysics with Aquinas's own theologically informed conception of moral perfection.[77] While we may describe our ultimate end in Aristotle's terms as the actualization of human nature, we recognize by reading Aquinas that we can fully grasp what human actualization is and achieve it perfectly only through the supernatural work of grace.[78]

To summarize Aquinas's treatment of the various types of grace, we can speak of two "moments" of grace in the moral life, which he calls "operative grace" and "cooperative grace." These are noteworthy because while both acknowledge that the work of grace is God's action (an exterior principle of human action), both also give due place to the human free will (an interior principle of action). Moral development requires human action, which engages both intellect and will, since both capacities must be perfected if the *telos* achieved is to be a truly human good. Nevertheless, these human capacities will not be perfected if divine force usurps their activities. They are perfected only if the work of grace respects their integrity. Given our nature as rational creatures, we must retain dominion over our own actions.[79]

First, in operative grace, we receive a new orientation and power through God's action of giving us the Holy Spirit. This is sheer gift—that is, we have done nothing to merit it or initiate such infusion; it in no way corresponds to human preparatory actions or capacities we developed in order to receive it.[80] Second, in cooperative grace, through our will and action we must *use* the gifts and habits received to perform acts of virtue. The first moment refers to grace as God's — it is "divine help." The second moment refers to our reception of grace. Once the divine help has been made our own, it is a "habitual gift," usually in the form of the infused virtues, to be acted upon when and how we choose.[81] Further, the freedom which divine action may appear to preempt in operative grace reappears intact under cooperative grace, for we can choose not only to refrain from acting on the infused virtues, but also to act against them. If we act against charity, we in effect reject the gift of divine assistance we need to achieve our end. As a consequence of our rejection we lose the gift altogether — and all the infused forms of the moral virtues with it. Such an act is called a "mortal sin," because by this act of rejection we choose to fall back into a state of mortality, or death, which according to Aquinas's theology is the just punishment for sin.[82]

Aquinas's discussion of grace all but identifies the New Law of the gospel with grace itself, for both involve the interior work of the Holy Spirit. In a similar move he appears to assign grace a role very similar to that of charity. He describes grace as the "principle and root of all the infused virtues" and charity as their "root and mother."[83] Grace is thus, in an important sense, the beginning (or "first principle") of the moral life, as a source of both virtue and law. It is also the final chapter of Aquinas's ethics, the chapter in which the key obstacles to human flourishing — the effects of sin and ignorance — are overcome and the possibility of human nature achieving a state of perfection beyond its own power is confirmed. Each element of his ethics — virtue, law, and grace — is therefore fully comprehended only in light of the whole. Compare a moral life based on acquired virtue and natural law to a life that also incorporates the theological and infused virtues and the eternal and divine law, including the New Law of the gospel. Only the latter sort of life — empowered by grace — would enable human beings to attain their ultimate end, according to Aquinas. Virtue cannot empower and perfect us without grace; and law can only imperfectly direct our way without it. Thus, this last, unavoidably theological element in Aquinas's ethics reveals God's indispensable initiative in human moral formation, even as it leaves room for human freedom. On Aquinas's conception of the moral life, union with

God is our ultimate end, and divine assistance must play an essential role in helping us achieve that end.

Virtue, Law, and Grace as Interior and Exterior Guides to Action

As we have now seen, Aquinas identifies virtue, law, and grace as the three main influences on human motivation and movement, outlining their role as directors and perfecters of human passions and actions via their influence on the intellect and will. He initially divides them into interior and exterior principles — that is, influences from inside and outside of us.[84] Virtues and vices are *interior* principles; as "habits ordered toward action," they are internal dispositions of our capacities toward good or bad actions, respectively. Law and grace are *exterior* principles from God directing us and our acts toward the human good.[85]

Aquinas's initial classification of interior and exterior principles of action quickly becomes complicated by his Christian additions to the Aristotelian elements with which his ethics begins. Take the case of virtues. Virtues count as internal shapers of action because they are dispositions perfecting human powers — capacities that are our own — and because our own actions contribute to their development, through habituation. However, not all moral virtues are acquired by action on our part, as Aristotle taught.[86] Once Aquinas adds grace to the picture, he has to account for infused virtues — virtues caused by the direct action of God's grace through the work of the Holy Spirit.[87] If God perfects and directs our action, through our own powers and capacities, then does that influence now count as internal or external? True, once God infuses the virtue in our intellect or will or sensitive appetite, it is up to us to act on it and thereby strengthen it,[88] so the infused virtue becomes, in a very real sense, our own internal principle of action. Yet the source and cause of virtue is far more external than initially appeared, especially when Aquinas goes so far as to quote Augustine approvingly on the definition of infused virtue: it is "a good quality of the mind, by which we act rightly, of which no one makes bad use, which *God works in us without our help.*"[89]

Similar complications arise when Aquinas discusses law. It turns out that while the eternal law—the providential will of God for all creation—and the divine law—which God discloses through special revelation—are from God alone, natural law refers to our *participation* in God's law as rational creatures. Aquinas believes that our own rational nature (intellect and will) itself bears the mark of God's law: "the rational nature . . . is subject to the eternal law in [two] ways, because each rational creature has some idea of the eternal law ['participating in the eternal law by way of knowledge,' as he puts it earlier in his response] . . . each rational creature also has a natural inclination to that which is in harmony with the eternal law ['participating in the eternal law . . . by way of action and passion, i.e., . . . by way of an *internal* motive principle']."[90] The law, as a natural principle, is a standard feature of our human design plan and a part of our nature—an internalization of providence, as it were.[91]

Beyond this interior character of the natural law, however, the New Law, as we have seen, is nothing other than the Holy Spirit present *in* us *like an interior habit,* making our intellect and will conform more and more to God's.[92] We no longer obey the law commanded by God out of fear of punishment; rather, we obey because we fear, more than any other evil, the separation from God that our sin causes. In this way, love of God, an interior motivation—manifested in the infused virtue of charity—supplants the externally coercive power of law. Paraphrasing both Scripture and Augustine, Aquinas explains that "the New Law is first of all a law that is inscribed [on our hearts]" and only secondarily a written law.[93] Thus law, both human and divine, becomes an internalized external principle, one leaving its indelible mark on human powers of action.

Grace, too, is clearly a divine gift and therefore from an external source, but again, the gift must be internalized to be effective. Aquinas describes some of these gifts as "habitual forms" "added" to the will and other capacities over and above their natural powers.[94] The presence of the Holy Spirit within actually shapes the orientation of the will and empowers it to move in ways beyond its natural capacities; this presence is variously described as "participation" and "indwelling," terms that suggest an internalization of divine assistance. Furthermore, since Aquinas takes seriously the infused virtue of charity—described in Scripture as "the fulfilling of the law"—internal and external sources are finally fused rather than distinguished. Because all infused virtues are created in us by grace alone, grace, too, becomes an *internalized* external principle, while grace-given virtue is identified with fulfilled law.[95]

The point of this discussion is to show how deeply Aquinas integrates virtue, law and grace in his ethics. Separating his account of the three even conceptually requires a measure of artificiality. When we examine the ways that Aquinas interweaves exterior and interior principles of action, we also notice how deeply his theological commitments inform each element of his ethics, and we realize the extent to which human moral action is indebted to divine action as the ground of its perfection. Thus, even when Aquinas is talking about sources of action and motivation *within human beings* and concentrating on *human* capacities (intellect and will), he is not excluding significant divine action and influence. Not only the third main part of the *Summa,* which explicitly considers the work of Christ, but also the second part, which involves the ways human beings return to God, outlines the ways God is acting, enabling human beings to reach their ultimate end. Aquinas's explanations of virtue and law as well as grace depend on taking God as the ultimate end of human beings *and* the ultimate source of the means to achieve that ultimate end. In becoming virtuous and perfecting our capacities; in knowing and ordering our lives according to law; and in receiving grace, human beings evidence their necessary reliance on divine aid to reach their end. This theme of grace and divine agency, running throughout his whole ethics, distinguishes Aquinas's view of the moral life from Aristotle's, which relies on human agency alone.[96]

The internalization of divine agency through grace, however, naturally raises the question of how the role of grace leaves room for human freedom, especially given Aquinas's strong view of grace.[97] Readers are rightly concerned when, for example, they read that the infusion of charity has nothing to do with human beings as an efficient or even dispositional cause: "[S]ince charity surpasses [*superexcedat*] what is proportionate to human nature . . . it depends, not on any natural virtue, but on the sole grace of the Holy Spirit who infuses charity. Therefore the quantity of charity depends neither on the condition of nature nor on the capacity of natural virtue, but only on the will of the Holy Spirit who 'apportions' His gifts 'as He wills'"; and further, "the Holy Spirit forestalls even this disposition or effort"—namely, any "preceding disposition, preparation, or effort of the one receiving grace"—"by moving the human mind either or more or less, according to His will."[98]

Nevertheless, Aquinas insists on preserving a place for human agency and freedom. He holds that we retain the power to act against charity.[99] Despite the workings of divine power in our action, he holds that we do not become robots or puppets: "The movement of charity does not therefore proceed from the Holy Spirit moving the human mind in such a way that the human mind is in no way the principle of this movement, as when a body is moved by some external moving power . . . so that it would follow that to love is not voluntary. This would imply a contradiction, since love by its very definition [*ratione*] implies an act of the will."[100] Our actions are still acts of *will;* once we have a virtue, we can initiate action according to it, or we can refuse to align our actions with it. God's work in us does not subvert the working of our natural capacities but rather completes and enhances them. If grace effaced the will, then it would no longer be a *human* nature that is perfected, according to Aquinas. Our powers are enhanced, not disabled, by God's power working in us.

nine

Theologically Transformed
Virtue and Vice

The ethical part of the Summa theologiae *begins with the treatise*
on happiness but is not complete without the picture of human fulfillment that we find in the treatise on the virtue of charity. Aquinas thinks
that human perfection requires union with God—both the intellectual
vision he calls *"beatitudo"* and also the union of affections in the will,
namely, the friendship he calls charity. Our union with God through
intellect and will is Aquinas's way of spelling out how we participate in
God's divine nature—both as his image-bearers and as his friends. As
Aquinas makes clear, the friendship of charity is possible only because
God communicates something of his nature to us.[1] God's nature as a
person with intellect and will is thus reflected in our rational nature (the
image of God), and these rational capacities make intellectual and loving
union between us and God possible (*beatitudo*). In the previous two chapters we have learned that the dynamic connection between this beginning
point and its supernatural *telos* requires virtue, law, and grace. Human
beings achieve union with God and our capacities reach their perfection
when grace implants the New Law of love in our intellects and shapes
our wills by charity, which enables our actions to conform to the infused
virtues. For Aquinas, *the* moral project is to conform our nature to God's,
and the virtues are his description of this process.

As we emphasized in chapter 7, all the virtues are formed and shaped by charity, their root. All acts of virtue are done, ultimately, for the sake of love of God—the love of friendship that unites us with God and conforms our nature to God's own. To understand the role of charity is to grasp the point or end of the moral project as a whole, for Aquinas. This explains why he devotes so much time and effort to the virtues in his ethics, and why we should look to charity to understand his transformation of them beyond their Aristotelian origins. After discussing virtue, law, and grace in a general and preliminary way, Aquinas spends the rest of the ethical part of the *Summa* (the IIaIIae) considering the particular virtues and their opposing vices. They are at the heart of the process of moral formation, rooted in charity, and directed to fulfillment in God.

In analyzing particular virtues and vices, Aquinas's concern with the many practical details of the moral life is evident in questions such as these:

- How should we pray, and how often? If we fall asleep during our prayers, are they still effective? (the virtue of religion)
- If we steal something from someone and are unable to locate the victim later, how are we to make restitution? (justice)
- If someone does us a favor and we are too poor to repay it, how are we to show our gratitude? (gratitude)
- How do we draw the line between worrying about the future and making careful plans in case things go wrong? (prudence)
- Is it morally better to love our enemies or to love our friends? (charity)
- When it comes to handling money, is it better to be a saver or a spender, and under what conditions? (liberality, magnificence)
- How much of Scripture, if any, does one have to understand to count as believing in God? (faith)
- Is there anything that should regulate our choices of food and drink besides concerns about physical health? (temperance)

In the answers to these questions and in the analysis of all these virtues, the marks of Aquinas's Aristotelianism are also evident. The concept of a virtue as a habit, the psychology of the passions, the basic division of human capacities into intellect and appetites, the general struc-

ture of human action in which the apprehension of the intellect precedes the movement of the will, and even specific moral virtues all have
an Aristotelian pedigree. In contrast to Aristotle, however, for the virtuous character as advocated by Aquinas, love is the source of moral wisdom, humility is a moral virtue, and the greatest expression of courage
is that of self-sacrifice for the sake of love and fidelity to God. How do
we account for the difference between the two?

Our study of virtue, law, and grace has shown that the aim of every
element in Aquinas's ethics is to "establish human beings in friendship
with God."[2] Charity, the virtue of love, *is* this friendship.[3] Grace is chan-
neled through charity, and law finds its *telos* in love. By looking closely
now at two examples, Aquinas's analyses of the vice of sloth and the virtue of courage, we will see how he reshapes the substance of particular
virtues and vices in ways that reflect the centrality of charity in his theory
of the moral life.

THE VICE OF SLOTH

Aquinas, as we have noted already, structures his moral theory
around the virtues. He does, however, include analyses of the traditional
seven capital vices (or seven deadly sins)—a list that includes the vice of
sloth—in his ethics, as well as analyses of the seven virtues—the three
theological virtues and the four cardinal virtues. Especially interesting
about Aquinas's discussion of sloth is that he emphasizes the gravity of
sloth by placing it in direct opposition to the theological virtue of charity.
As we will see, this move demonstrates Aquinas's originality as a moral
thinker and underscores his theological understanding of the moral life.
The psychology of the passions and the eudaimonistic ethical structure that Aquinas adopts from Aristotle help him analyze the vice. But
at the same time, they create a puzzle about sloth that only his appeal to
a Christian understanding of the will and the dynamics of sin and grace
can resolve. A close look at his account of this vice, therefore, gives us a
perfect opportunity to observe Aquinas's theological understanding of the
moral life and the way it moves his ethics beyond that of Aristotle's, even
as it incorporates essential Aristotelian elements.

The tradition of the seven capital vices preceded Aquinas by several centuries; it originates in the work of the fourth-century Christian ascetic Evagrius of Pontus.[4] Sloth began in a place of chief importance in Evagrius's list but was gradually conflated with another vice, usually designated as "sadness."[5] By the thirteenth century, sloth was considered a listless, depressed state, associated with inertia in one's external behavior—a spiritual torpor characteristically matched by physical inactivity.[6] Aquinas's project required integrating a somewhat confused Christian inheritance on this capital vice into an Aristotelian eudaimonistic ethic and its attendant psychology of the passions. How does a vice associated with sadness and inactivity fit into a human life naturally directed toward seeking happiness and actualization?

Contemporary readers might wonder further how and why this peculiar vice came to be counted among the seven capital vices, along with the usual candidates such as lust, avarice, anger, and envy.[7] Its inclusion also seemed to require some defense in Aquinas's time. Aquinas's account is fascinating insofar as he uses tradition in an innovative way to answer this question.

The seven vices were often used independently of the list of virtues as a heuristic device for theology students or for priests instructing the repentant. Aquinas, however, follows the pattern established by Aristotle's ethics of pairing a vice of excess and a vice of deficiency with each virtue. Since he organizes his ethics around the virtues, not the vices, he is faced with the question of how to distribute the seven capital vices among the three theological and four cardinal virtues. Contrary to what we might expect, he does not pair them off one by one, assigning one capital vice for each of the seven virtues. Rather, he puts both sloth and envy in opposition to the virtue of charity. This innovation is one on which the rest of his account of sloth depends.

Charity is the main theological virtue, as we have seen. It is the root of the other virtues, the virtue that directs all others to God as their ultimate end. Charity, for Aquinas, is also an infused virtue, that is, a habit formed by the Holy Spirit's work in the human will so that it is oriented toward God and participates in God's own nature. This likeness of nature forms the basis of our friendship with God—a union of like-natured persons (as in the Aristotelian notion of friendship). To understand sloth, on Aquinas's account, we must recognize that charity brings with it a "now and not yet" state in the human being: we have charity and a share in the divine nature as soon as we receive the gift of the Holy Spirit, and yet we still have to perfect the habit of charity before we are in complete union with God.[8] As an analogy, consider a couple who marry: they *are* married at the moment they say their vows, but living out those vows — *being* married — is also a life-long activity, gradually developing toward perfection. So also with charity, there is both the present reality and the future union yet to be completed or made perfect.[9]

Charity is essentially love, an inclination that has the good as its object and the union of like-natured beings as its natural effect. Recall that what makes charity a theological virtue is its source (or cause) and its end, both of which are God. God infuses charity in us by his action, not ours. Union with God, our ultimate end, is what charity initiates, and the perfection of that union is its goal. Aquinas describes it in terms of "friendship," "communion," and "the fellowship of everlasting happiness."[10]

By placing sloth in opposition to the virtue of charity, Aquinas makes the object of sloth the greatest of goods — namely, our participation in the divine nature itself.[11] Sloth, defined as "sorrow over an interior divine good," is aversion to and dejection about our participation in the divine nature by grace.[12] It turns away from the heart of our divine identity — our communion with God in friendship — and all that that entails. Two things, however, are puzzling about Aquinas's definition. First, a psychological puzzle: how can we feel aversion to or sorrow over something good? And second, a puzzle about human nature and its *telos:* how can we turn away from our own ultimate end as human beings, especially when that end is God, the perfect good? How can we be sorrowful about *happiness?*

In the Aristotelian framework that Aquinas adopts, the inclination toward the good as something desirable — something we want to possess and make our own — is the basis of all the other passions. Aquinas calls it love (*amor*). Sadness or sorrow is the opposite of love's enjoyment of a good that is present and possessed; sorrow expresses aversion from or dislike of some evil. Aquinas distinguishes a movement of aversion in the *will* — one that requires deliberateness or consent, which we will call "sorrow" — from an aversion belonging to the passions, which we will call "sadness."[13] Aquinas elevates this basic aversion or dislike to the will so that sloth is on a par with charity, which is also located in the will.

This only makes sloth harder to explain, however, for reasons an Aristotelian eudaimonist would readily understand. How can we have a fundamental aversion to our own happiness? Usually, in cases in which we act against our own good, reason apprehends the good while the sensory appetite lures us away or sways us from our previous judgment. Sloth, however, consists in a clear-sighted rational apprehension of an object (the perfection of our nature) and the rational appetite's reaction to it (unhappiness or aversion). There does not appear to be a battle here between the rational and sensory appetites, or any confusion in perception. How, then, is it that the divine good infused into our nature through charity can repulse our will?

Even if it is psychologically possible to turn away from some greater goods toward lesser ones — from bodily health, for example, for the pleasure of smoking — Aquinas has to explain how our will could turn against the very perfection of our own nature. According to Aquinas, an inclination toward our ultimate end is a natural orientation of the will, something hardwired into human nature.[14] In both Aristotle's and Aquinas's teleological metaphysics, all things with a nature seek the fulfillment or actualization of their nature. The vice of sloth appears to require nothing less than an explanation of how human beings could act against their hardwired desire for their own fulfillment, and how they could experience distaste and displeasure over possessing their own ultimate end, albeit in a yet-to-be-perfected state.

Aquinas has defined sloth as "sorrow over an interior divine good," by which he means a will-based aversion to human participation in the divine nature through charity.[15] He argues further that this aversion is caused by "the flesh prevailing over the spirit," a phrase he borrows from the apostle Paul.[16] Those of us who normally associate sloth with physical laziness might take Aquinas's reference to Scripture to mean that we resist acts of charity when they become too physically difficult or demanding. In this case our sorrow is not over the divine good itself (a good of the "spirit"), but over the bodily comfort (the good of the "flesh") we must compromise or the energy we must expend in order to attain it or meet its requirements. For example, it takes effort to get up on Sunday morning for worship when we would rather sleep in or watch television. It is easy to see how Aquinas's account might initially mislead one to think of sloth as a standard case of conflict between reason and the sensory appetite. Aquinas, however, denies that our aversion is to bodily exertion or the foregoing of physical pleasures that spiritual pursuits require. That would make sloth a carnal vice like lust and gluttony, he argues, one preoccupied with physical pleasure. He insists, however, that sloth is *not* carnal but spiritual. Vices, like virtues, are classified by their objects; in the case of sloth, its object is a spiritual one: the divine good in us.[17] How, then, does Aquinas explain what causes the slothful person to recoil from his own good?

Sloth, for Aquinas, involves an aversion of the flesh to the spirit, by which—like Paul—he does not mean that the body is opposed to the soul or that reason is opposed to appetite. Rather, he means to distinguish between sinful, corrupted human nature on the one hand, and human nature renewed and reclaimed by grace on the other.[18] Like a sullen child, the slothful person wants to be loved unconditionally, but does not want to have to give herself up for God unconditionally in return. Like a friend after a quarrel, she wants to have the friendship restored without having to apologize or compromise her own ego to reach reconciliation. Sloth is resistance of our selfish, sinful selves to the demands of God's love— demands that require selfless, sacrificial love. The slothful one wants to be counted a friend of God, to be saved and redeemed from sin, and to gain charity, and yet is reluctant to give up the old familiar pleasures and habits of her unredeemed, sinful nature. The friction in a slothful person is *not* between practical reason and unruly passions. It is the full-fledged "identity crisis" of a will divided against itself.[19] To accept God's love in charity is to accept transformation of oneself and to undergo a process of perfection and renewal—namely, the cultivation of virtue that Aquinas has been outlining in his ethics. The slothful one desires the end result, but her will cannot bring itself to embrace and endure the required means to that end, a way that usually involves painful self-renunciation over a long period of time.[20]

Of course, *not* to accept the demands of charity is to be doomed to frustration and restlessness, for only in charity is human nature fulfilled. Hence sloth's easy slide into despair and inaction: it resists the means of human perfection, the only path to happiness and joy, and it thereby refuses, too, the human *telos*. Without an end, the actions aimed toward that end lose their point and purpose. Thus, given his theological definition of sloth, Aquinas can explain the will's resistance to charity and maintain the historical association of sloth with inaction and restlessness. In traditional correlations of vices with virtues, the vice of sloth was often set in opposition to the Sabbath observance.[21] Aquinas associates this Sabbath "rest" with the rest and peace of a will that has attained its ultimate end. Sloth, by its unwillingness to give up its old sinful nature, denies one this rest.

Aquinas's analysis of sloth requires philosophical categories and concepts. The psychology and the eudaimonistic ethics he adopts from Aristotle set up the puzzle, for if the end of human nature were not our own happiness,[22] it would not be difficult to understand the slothful person's resistance and aversion. In addition, Aquinas explains our participation in the divine nature by using the Aristotelian idea of friendship—our union with God in charity. Aquinas's account ultimately transcends strictly philosophical categories, however, by making the definition of sloth depend upon the theological concepts of sin, grace, and regeneration by the Holy Spirit, which in turn rely on conceptions of the will and the virtue of charity that are foreign to ancient Greek philosophy. Sloth, therefore, is not only a spiritual vice—where spiritual is distinguished from bodily or carnal. It is also a theological vice, which finds its home in a moral theory suffused by the idea of divine purposes, goals, and causal agency. Sloth is not fully explicable without an acknowledgment of that theological dimension and context; its viciousness makes sense in Aquinas's ethics because it threatens the goal of a human relationship of friendship with a personal God of love.

In contrast with both the silence of Greek philosophy on the subject and contemporary trivializations of it, Aquinas's conception of the vice of sloth brings it to the center of the moral life. Sloth is a direct threat to one's spiritual identity as a sharer in the divine nature. Aquinas's charity-centered ethics is essential for explaining what the vice is and why it should be taken seriously as one of the capital vices—the ones that spawn all sorts of other sins.[23] It directly threatens the human good itself, understood both philosophically (the actualization of human nature) and theologically (the elevation of human beings from image bearers to friends of God). The "movement of the rational creature toward God"[24] and the renewal and perfection of human nature required for that return are at stake. Sloth is a serious vice because it threatens the very heart of what is, for Aquinas, *the* human moral project—development in virtue, informed by charity and ordered toward perfect union with God.[25]

Aquinas's definition of sloth as resistance to a relationship of love for God is evidence that his Christian theology both frames and informs the details of this specific vice and also highlights the central and defining role of charity in the moral life. We can also see concretely in this vice the ways in which his ethics builds on his account of human nature and his action theory. Sloth resists the inclination of human nature to happiness or perfection, an end that cannot be attained without our own actions— even after the reception of grace and infused virtue.

THE VIRTUE OF COURAGE

Our next case study will be of a virtue rather than a vice, and a cardinal rather than a theological virtue. Courage is a virtue appreciated in ancient Greek philosophy, in Christian theology, and in contemporary secular accounts of virtue—illustrated, for example, in typical American action-adventure films. As in his definition of sloth, Aquinas relies heavily on an Aristotelian theory of the passions in his own account of courage, defining this virtue, as Aristotle does, in terms of fear and daring. Once courage is informed by charity, however, the virtue may be one that Aristotle would no longer recognize as such. Specifically, we argue that Aquinas's transformation of courage can be directly traced to the role of charity as the root of moral character. This transformation, moreover, distinguishes his account from both ancient and modern ideals of bravery.[26]

Essential to Aquinas's definition of courage is that it be directed beyond itself to a good end.[27] Courage (*fortitudo*) involves the exercise of strength (*fortis*) and power, but the question immediately arises, what is this exercise of strength *for*? Courage is firmness in the face of difficulty and danger, most especially the danger of death. This firmness could easily be a vice, however, unless we specify that it is firmness in holding to a good end. The firmness is required because of some danger or threat to the good, some difficulty that arises from our commitment to it, or some obstacle to its realization. To regard courage as merely a stalwart stand in the face of death would be to miss its main point. According to Aquinas, "endurance of death is not praiseworthy in itself, but *only as it is directed to some good consisting in an act of virtue,* such as faith or the love of God. Thus this act of virtue, since it is the end, is better."[28] The goodness of courage thus consists in the "firmness itself, whereby we do not give in to the opposing forces that hinder us *from achieving the good* [that is its end]."[29]

For Aquinas, since the human good is "the good of reason"—that is, our fulfillment as rational creatures, which means the perfection of our intellect and our rational appetite or will—it follows that the concupiscible and irascible passions are meant to serve the ends of those higher, rational capacities. Likewise, the virtues of the concupiscible and irascible powers of the sensitive appetite consist in serving the operation of the virtues of our rational capacities. In the philosophical terminology of chapter 7, prudence and justice are executive virtues, while courage and temperance are enabling virtues. Courage, then, points beyond itself to a good that we can attain only when fear and daring are regulated by reason.

There is another way in which the connection between the firmness of courage and the good end of courage reflects Aristotle's theory of the passions, as it is operative in Aquinas's moral theory. Aquinas quotes Augustine as saying, "Fear is born of love," meaning that the fear against which courage must stand firm arises only because of some presupposed love.[30] Love, as we have noted before, is the most fundamental inclination. Aquinas follows Augustine in making it the condition of all the others: "There is no other passion of the soul that does not presuppose love of some kind."[31] Thus fear arises because something we love is threatened.

Aquinas notes that the more we love a good, the more we are willing to sacrifice and endure for its sake.[32] Here he echoes Augustine's definition of fortitude as an expression of love: "Courage is 'love bearing all things readily for the sake of that which is loved.'"[33] Of course, for Aquinas, the love in question is not merely the natural passion (*amor*).

Rather, love's highest expression in rational nature is the theological virtue of charity. Paralleling the role of *amor* among the passions, charity is the principle of all other virtues. Thus, the loved one for whom a courageous person will be able to make the greatest sacrifice is, on Aquinas's account, none other than God, our ultimate end.

Aquinas locates courage in the irascible power because it involves two passions: fear and daring.[34] These passions (as with the passions in general) arise because of our embodied state: we are not merely rational creatures but also rational *animals*. Courage is about overcoming dangers or difficulties that arise as threats to our bodies, and handling our aversions to bodily pain when they deter us from achieving or preserving some good. While the danger against which the courageous one stands firm is a bodily threat, the firmness itself — the virtue — involves strength of soul, for the virtues are perfections of the soul's capacities and powers, not bodily perfections.

Aquinas thus follows Aristotle exactly in identifying the irascible passions of fear and daring as the ones the courageous person must master. Fear is our reaction of withdrawal or shrinking back when faced with a threat, while daring is the impulse to rush forward and attack and overcome whatever threatens. When fear must be withstood in order to hold fast to some good, the characteristic act of courage is *endurance* — not to give way, which would be the act of cowardice. When daring is called for, the characteristic act of courage is *aggression;* daring, though, must also be moderated by reason so that we exercise caution and avoid acting rashly. Endurance and aggression are the two main expressions of courage.[35]

While contemporary readers might initially think of aggression — rushing forward to fight against evil — as the best expression of courage, Aquinas agrees with Aristotle by naming endurance as its chief act instead. Both thinkers note that humans share the fundamental natural inclination of all beings — rational and otherwise — to value their own lives. Aquinas often calls this the inclination of substance "to preserve its own existence" — a fundamental precept of the natural law.[36] Thus, if something desires or seeks its own destruction, this is an unnatural movement, a deviation from the norm, and a sign of disorder. Further, to receive or enjoy any other goods requires a creature to exist, and death removes that condition. So our resistance to death is part and parcel of our natural inclination to the good, including our own good.

Because of this tendency, Aristotle and Aquinas argue, it is more difficult to withstand fear than to exercise daring. In acting from daring, we rush to defend ourselves from attack, we take action to ward off danger, or we fight for our lives against whatever threatens. This emotion expresses our natural inclination to self-preservation. In withstanding fear, by contrast, we recognize that we cannot keep ourselves out of danger but must face whatever comes. For an act to count as courageous endurance, it must be the case that standing firm and not giving way is the only way to resist the threat and defend the good, even if it costs us our lives. Aquinas explains the difference between the reactions of fear and daring in the treatise on the passions, where he also gives us important clues about how to interpret the act of endurance as he describes it in the treatise on courage.[37]

Perhaps the best way to explain why endurance is more difficult than aggression is to compare the relationship between fear and daring to another set of irascible passions, hope and despair.[38] Hope and despair differ from fear and daring by having as their object a good—something we are inclined toward or take pleasure in—while fear and daring have as their object an evil—something we naturally shun or are pained by.[39] Both sets of passions are alike, however, in having objects that are future (not yet possessed) and that present some difficulty, either to obtain—in the case of a good object—or to avoid—in the case of an evil one.

The key difference between hope and despair is the level of difficulty one perceives in one's attempt to achieve or possess some good thing. When the object seems achievable, although difficulty remains, one presses on in hope; when it seems out of reach, the difficulty is not worth one's effort, and in despair one gives up trying to achieve it. Likewise, fear and daring have a future object in view, but this time it is an evil to be avoided. As in the case of hope and despair, our natural reactions correspond to the possibility and impossibility of that object becoming present or possessed. One strikes out with daring precisely because one perceives that one is in a position of strength—the danger can be overcome, the threat can probably be warded off or diminished with sufficient effort. Fear, on the other hand, is the emotion one feels when the danger is greater than one's strength to keep it away, and when the threat presses in spite of one's best efforts to dispel it. Daring, that is to say, works from a position of strength; fear, from a position of weakness.

This explains Aquinas's conclusion that the act of endurance is more difficult than the act of aggression. The level of danger vis-à-vis our own position is greater, the good is more threatened, and our own vulnerabilities are exposed and inescapable. So, when he argues that in an act of endurance the danger is present and extends longer, Aquinas is not overgeneralizing, but rather extrapolating from the idea that these are the cases in which the threat is from a force stronger than ourselves, such that, by our own efforts, we are unable to keep it at bay and unable to determine when it will end. One's position of weakness or lack of control increases fear and makes the will's resistance more challenging. The more vulnerable and weak we are against an external threat to our bodies, the more inner strength is required to endure it. It would be easier to give up, or give in. Thus, to stand firm against whatever threatens is a greater testimony of courage. This position, Aquinas says, expresses courage at its best. As one commentator observes, "the true 'position' of courage is that extremely perilous situation . . . in which to suffer and endure is objectively the only remaining possibility of resistance, and it is in this situation that courage primarily and ultimately proves its genuine character."[40]

Besides making the theological virtue of charity the source and end of courage, Aquinas also invokes a Christian model for his exemplar of courage and names the Christian act of martyrdom as its chief act. Christ's own endurance of suffering on the cross is Aquinas's paradigm. In martyrdom, a Christian bears faithful witness to the truth of faith, even to the death, for the sake of her love of God. Aquinas thus transcends the Aristotelian foundations of this virtue, not by granting endurance a higher place than aggression, but by recognizing new ways for courageous endurance to be expressed. Courage is not only exemplified by a warrior on the battlefield who defends a just cause or the civic good, as in Aristotle's account; courage is also embodied by a persecuted Christian who refuses to renounce Christ on pain of death. Aquinas deftly names this situation "single combat [*imparticularem impugnationem*]," extending Aristotle's definition of fortitude — standing firm against the dangers of death *in combat*—in ways that Aristotle probably would not even recognize.[41]

How does martyrdom qualify as the principal act of courage?[42] In terms of the definition of courage, it qualifies as an act of endurance, since one must endure death as the only alternative to renouncing the good. The martyr does not seek death either for its own sake or for the martyr's own glory. In fact, early Church Fathers expressly forbade seeking opportunities for martyrdom. For Aquinas, the martyr holds fidelity to the truth of faith higher than her own physical well-being, out of love of God.[43] This act of virtue enables the martyr, in the most perfect way, to hold to the good of the intellect—the highest truth—as well as the good of the will—love of the greatest good.[44]

While the martyr's courage also demonstrates the virtue of faith, Aquinas explains that "charity inclines one to the act of martyrdom, as its first and principal moving principle, by being the virtue commanding it. Fortitude, however, is its proper moving principle, by being the virtue that elicits it."[45] Withstanding the greatest fear, in an act of greatest sacrifice, is made possible only by love for the greatest good. Because the courageous martyr's act of courage stems from charity—Aquinas names it as an act of perfect charity—God is its source and end.[46]

The "superabundance of divine grace" required for this act to be a perfect act of virtue makes explicit the way the concept of grace shapes Aquinas's account of the cardinal virtue of courage.[47] Aquinas notes that it is characteristic of hope to think of possibilities available not only by one's own power but also by the power available to us from another, including God.[48] As in the treatise on charity, Aquinas here capitalizes on the Aristotelian notion of a friend as "another self" to describe how hope counts divine help as a power that is "our own." Thus, through charity, all three theological virtues play a role in the formation of the act of infused courage that is martyrdom.

Aquinas has already focused his account of courage on the act of endurance, an act that works from a position of weakness and vulnerability. Courage is thus not a virtue that highlights human strength and virility, as do the examples of the ancient Greek warrior and the typical contemporary action hero. Instead, Aquinas's conception of courage highlights the way in which human action—especially when weak—is fortified by divine power. The greatest act of courage is primarily an act of love for God, a willingness to trust God for the achievement of the good, and a faithful adherence to God's truth. The martyr's love and strength bear witness to God's grace and God's power, not her own.

We should note that this transformed conception of courage, especially in its exemplary form, is a virtue with much wider accessibility than the Aristotelian philosophical conception. It does not rely on a battlefield context or physical strength, or, finally, on unaided human power at all. If it raises the bar in terms of difficulty (facing death by persecution), by making endurance of suffering for the sake of love of God the main expression of courage, it also makes courage possible — perhaps especially so — for the weak, the vulnerable, and those unable or unwilling to use force. We would not expect this from Aristotle's ethics, which makes virtue possible only for a fortunate few. Aquinas's aim, in contrast, is to show how grace equips any and all for union with God.

The most courageous human action therefore reflects the virtue of faith perfecting the intellect, and hope and love working together to perfect the will. That Aquinas would inform even a cardinal virtue with such theological intent is compelling evidence of the way in which his Christian commitments infuse his moral thought, not only in its structure but in its very substance. When human nature is elevated by grace, love for the ultimate end transforms all human capacities, even the passions of the sensory appetite and the virtues that perfect them. The theological virtues — most notably charity — are the root of the perfection of all human powers and capacities, reorienting our nature and its inclinations to God as our end, and fashioning all our actions in the shape of love.

Epilogue

In this book we have argued that Aquinas's intentions are most accurately reflected by a study that integrates his view of human nature and its capacities, his action theory, and his view of the moral life. For Aquinas, there is no fundamental separation between metaphysics and ethics. Together they form a coherent system. His account of who we are meant to be and the actualization of our human capacities is fundamentally predicated on his theory of human nature.

Aquinas's integrated theory is also best understood as a theological project. Human beings are created by God, and God wants to draw them back to himself in love. Insofar as they are part of a divinely-authored creation, humans are directed toward a particular ultimate end, one unique to them as rational animals and one that involves an intimate relationship with their Creator. Bringing this theological and metaphysical context to bear on Aquinas's ethical theory enables us to understand the substantial role of charity in virtuous character formation and the essential role of grace in perfecting human capacities, as our case studies of courage and sloth have illustrated. The New Law as well as the natural law, infused virtue as well as acquired virtue, and the enhancement by grace of human nature and its capacities of intellect and will are not optional additions to Aquinas's moral project, but are rather its essential elements. Together they give us the holistic picture of human flourishing that he had in mind.

We believe that this rich, comprehensive understanding of Aquinas's thought is worth having in its own right. But further, we think it has rich practical consequences as well. Aquinas's thought helps us understand the flourishing life we are made for, given our nature, but also how and why things can go wrong. It gives us compelling answers to questions that we all ask—What does it mean to be a good human being, and how is that possible for us? How much of our own happiness is under our control? What are the limits of human capacities and how can we best cultivate them? How can we live in a way that honors who we are and fulfills us as human beings?

Our aim, therefore, has been to show that Aquinas's account of human nature and its perfection, the rational capacities of intellect and will, and an ethics that integrates virtue with law and grace is worthy of our attention for both its theoretical and its practical fruitfulness. If this book has set out an engaging framework for the reader's further investigation into Aquinas's thought and the application of Aquinas's ideas, then we will consider it a success.

notes

Introduction

1. Although Aquinas never addresses the question of angels dancing on pins, he was deeply interested in angels (and immaterial substances in general), earning him the unofficial title of Angelic Doctor.

2. This is the conclusion to his famous "function argument" in *Nicomachean Ethics* 1.7.

3. See chapter 3 for a fuller discussion of this point.

4. Note that the term "happiness" thus expresses being a flourishing member of one's kind (an objective condition), not merely feeling happy (a subjective state), as we commonly use the term "happiness" now.

5. Here we use the term "metaphysics" in a general sense that is common in contemporary philosophy; it is worth noting, however, that Aquinas himself used the term more narrowly. In our discussion of metaphysics we include topics that he would have considered part of the philosophy of nature and psychology.

6. As we discuss in chapter 2, Aquinas defines "person" in Boethian terms as "an individual substance with a rational nature." Thus, nonhuman animals—who lack a rational nature—cannot participate in *caritas,* whereas our ability to love in this way is one of our most striking similarities to God.

Chapter One. The Metaphysics of Human Nature

1. See *DEE* 5 and *DSS* 8 for passages in which Aquinas sets up and discusses this hierarchy. *DEE* numbers cited here follow the numbering of the English translation by Armand Maurer, *On Being and Essence* (Toronto: Pontifical Institute of Medieval Studies, 1983), rather than the Latin (Marietti)

edition. *DEE* 4 and 5 (English translation) are numbered *DEE* 5 and 6, respectively, in the Marietti edition.

2. His other summa, the *Summa contra gentiles,* takes a similar approach, moving from a general discussion of God's nature in book 1, to what we can learn of God's nature from examination of his creation in book 2, to God's providence in book 3, to God's special revelation in book 4.

3. *SCG* I.1.

4. Although it might seem odd to say that God is in any sense located on a continuum with creatures, it is important to see that this is a very special case. Among other things, it underscores the radical difference between the uncreated, fully actual God and God's creation.

5. For the origin of this popular description of dividing beings into classes, see Plato's *Phaedrus* 265e.

6. It's important to note here that the picture of the hierarchy of being as a ladder is misleading in a very important respect: Aquinas doesn't believe that there are gaps in the hierarchy. It is a continuous continuum, so to speak. As noted later, this allows for the divisions between classes to be "blurry"; there isn't a neat line between plants and animals, for instance, but rather a range of species that possess attributes of both plants *and* animals.

7. *ST* Ia.75.5.ad 4.

8. One obvious way to explain this would be to hold that an angel's higher place in the hierarchy stems from its being capable of doing things an aardvark is not capable of doing. That is, the greater the number of capacities, the greater the degree of being. An angel seems to have a greater number of capacities in that it can know abstract truths, for example, whereas an aardvark lacks the capacity for rational thought. Aquinas cannot be making such a simple-minded appeal, however. Making the crucial potentiality/actuality split depend quantitatively on the number of a thing's capacities would yield a philosophy of "the more, the better" that would seem to indicate that a human being, for example, would be somehow less in potentiality and more in actuality if it had the ability to fly, or an angel less in potentiality and more in actuality if it could stretch its arms over its head. Furthermore, a cactus can do certain things that the aardvark cannot (such as surviving without water for months on end or growing spines), and an aardvark is capable of things an angel is not (such as curling into a ball or reproducing). If Aquinas were to appeal merely to the raw number of a thing's capacities, this would not yield an orderly ranking of beings. Aquinas's claim makes sense only if the capacities in question are of a relevant *kind.* That is, the sense in which something's

192 Notes to Pages 16–19

capacities limit the extent to which it can participate in divine existence must be understood with respect to the quality or nature of its capacities rather than with respect to the number of those capacities. See chapter 3 for a detailed discussion of human capacities.

9. See, e.g., *ST* Ia.77.3.ad 4: "Compared to a lower capacity, a higher capacity is concerned per se with a characteristic of its object that is more universal. For the higher a capacity is, the more things it extends itself toward."

10. See Augustine's *On Free Choice of the Will*, bk. 2, and Aquinas's *ST* Ia.78.1.

11. See, e.g., *SCG* II.59: "Where the living thing has a higher operation, there is a higher kind [*species*] of life corresponding to that action. For in plants the only action we find pertains to nutrition, whereas in animals we find a higher action, namely sensing and locomotion; and that is why an animal lives by a higher kind of life. Now, in a human being we find a higher operation pertaining to life than we find in the animal, namely, understanding. Therefore, a human being has a higher kind of life."

12. As Aquinas puts it, "There is a distinction of these things one from the other, according to the grade of potentiality and actuality; and so a superior intelligence, which is closer to the first being, has more actuality and less potentiality, and so on with the others" (*DEE* 4.29).

13. *ST* IaIIae.3.2.

14. *DEE* 5.

15. *SCG* II.8.

16. "Anything is perfect in so far as it is actualized [and] imperfect in so far as it is in a state of potentiality, lacking actuality. Therefore, that which is in no way in a state of potentiality but is pure actuality must be most perfect. But that is what God is. Therefore, he is most perfect" (*SCG* I.28). See also *SCG* II.6, where Aquinas comments that "pure actuality [*actus purus*], which God is, is more perfect than actuality mixed together with potentiality, as it is in us."

17. Aquinas's argument for this claim is well known, and it has been addressed in detail elsewhere. See, e.g., Scott MacDonald's "The *Esse/Essentia* Argument in Aquinas's *De ente et essentia*," *Journal of the History of Philosophy* 22 (1984): 157–72.

18. See, e.g., *DEE* 5, where Aquinas writes, "The being that is God is such that no addition can be made to it."

19. "[God] possesses all the perfections of every kind of thing, so that he is called absolutely perfect. . . . In fact, he possesses these perfections in a more

excellent way than other things, because in him they are one, whereas in other things they are diversified" (*DEE* 5).

20. See Norman Kretzmann's *The Metaphysics of Creation* (Oxford: Oxford University Press, 1997) for an extended discussion of Aquinas's view of absolute simplicity.

21. See, e.g., Aquinas's *In Sent* 4.12.1.1.3.ad 3.

22. *DPN* 2.349. See also *DEE* 5, where Aquinas writes, "Form and matter are related in a way that form gives being to matter; for this reason, it is impossible for some matter to exist without form."

23. As Kreztmann puts it in *The Metaphysics of Creation,* "'Prime matter', which is entirely indeterminate, formless, and purely potential, is metaphysical matter considered absolutely—a theoretical terminus of form-matter analysis rather than an actual component of nature, as physical matter is" (212). Prime matter also proves important in Aquinas's discussions of substantial change; he appeals to it, for example, as the principle that remains constant throughout change in substantial form.

24. For a passage in which Aquinas is clear about the conceptual nature of prime matter, see *In Sent* 1.8.5.2: "Insofar as it is considered stripped of every form, [prime matter] does not have any diversity at all."

25. *QDV* 8.6.

26. Part of God's being perfectly intellective, of course, involves his eternally being engaged in active intellection.

27. Interestingly, Aquinas holds that, although our experience is of the material realm, there are far more immaterial than material substances. See, e.g., *ST* Ia.50.3: "[A]ngels, insofar as they are immaterial substances, exist in a certain great multitude, exceeding the whole material multitude. . . . And the reason for this is that, since the perfection of the universe is what God principally intends in the creation of things, to the extent to which some things are more perfect, to that extent does God create them in greater excess. . . . And so it is reasonable to conclude that the number of immaterial substances exceeds that of material substances, almost [*quasi*] incomparably."

28. In Aquinas's own words: "In substances composed of matter and form, there is a twofold composition of act and potentiality: the first, of the substance itself which is composed of matter and form; the second, of the composite substance, and being" (*SCG* II.54).

29. Aquinas explains this in terms of the hierarchy of being as follows: "For form, insofar as it is form, does not depend on matter; but if such forms are found which cannot exist except in matter, this happens because they are

distant from the first principle, which is first and pure act. For this reason, forms which are most close to the first principle are forms subsisting through themselves without matter" (*DEE* 4.24).

30. *QDSC* 1.1.

31. According to Aquinas, each angel constitutes its own species.

32. Since God is the only completely simple being, Aquinas concludes: "It must be the case that in intelligences the *esse* is in addition to form; and for this reason it was said that an intelligence is [a composite of] form and *esse.*"

33. "Some things are of a higher nature because they are nearer to and more like the first [principle], which is God. Now, in God the whole plenitude of intellectual knowledge is contained in one thing, i.e., the divine essence, by which God knows all things. This plenitude of knowledge is found in created intellects in a lower manner, and less simply. Consequently, it is necessary for the lower intellects to know by many forms what God knows by one, and by so many the more according as the intellect is lower. Thus, the higher the angel is, by so much the fewer species will it be able to apprehend the whole mass of intelligible objects" (*ST* Ia.55.3).

34. *SCG* II.68.

35. *DEE* 5. He is here quoting Aristotle's *De historia animalium* 8.1 (588b4–13).

36. Aquinas rules out the possibility of a physical intellect in several places, including *DEE* 4 and *ST* Ia.51.1 and 75.2.

37. *ST* Ia.5.1: "bonum et ens sunt idem secundum rem: sed differunt secundum rationem tantum." We are here using Eleonore Stump and Norman Kretzmann's suggestion for how best to render "sunt idem secundum rem" and "differunt secundum rationem," from their "Being and Goodness," in *Being and Goodness,* ed. Scott MacDonald (Ithaca: Cornell University Press, 1991).

38. One might worry that talking about the natural functions of cacti and tigers makes them sound like cars and can-openers: directed toward ends external to themselves but useful for something (or someone) else. It is important to stress again that Aquinas's use of the term "function" is linked to the essence of a particular thing—living creatures are aimed toward their own, species-specific sort of flourishing, and their function is the characteristic activity that facilitates that flourishing.

39. It is important here to distinguish between the basic goodness of humanity, which any member of the human species has simply insofar as it exists (the same, then, for a newborn infant, rebellious teenager, professional physicist, and person with advanced Alzheimer's), and the goodness particu-

lar to each member of the human species insofar as that person actualizes her human capacities.

40. We tend to think that people who have actualized a potentiality still have the potential to be that way or to perform that activity. Aquinas does not disagree—however, he does tend to reserve the word for cases in which the potentiality has not been actualized. (Once a potentiality has been actualized, he follows Aristotle in distinguishing between first and second actuality: for example, first actuality is when, although I've mastered organic chemistry, I am not currently thinking about it, and second actuality is when I am actually utilizing that knowledge.)

Chapter Two.   Soul and Body

1. Eleonore Stump makes heavy use of this term in her volume on Aquinas. See, e.g., *Aquinas* (New York: Routledge, 2003), 52.

2. Aquinas often describes this unique status in terms of what sets the rational soul off from all other forms. See, e.g., *SCG* II.69, where Aquinas writes that "there is something supreme in the genus of bodies, namely the human body . . . which comes in contact with the lowest thing in the higher genus, namely the human soul, which holds the lowest rank in the genus of intellectual substances, as can be seen from the mode of its understanding. For this reason, the intellectual soul is said to be 'something which is in a way on the horizon or boundary between corporeal and incorporeal things,' insofar as it is both an incorporeal substance and the form of the body."

3. *ST* Ia.50.prol. See also the prologue to Aquinas's treatise on human nature (*ST* Ia.75), where he writes that "having considered spiritual and corporeal creatures, we should consider the human being, who is composed of a spiritual and a corporeal substance."

4. See, e.g., *SCG* II.68, where Aquinas compares the case of human beings to the case of oysters, which he believes bridge the gap between plants and animals.

5. Aquinas devotes *SCG* II.56 to a list of objections making just this point.

6. In *The Philosophical Writings of Descartes,* vol. 2, trans. John Cottingham et al. (Cambridge and New York: Cambridge University Press, 1984), AT 34, added emphasis.

7. *Phaedo* 66b, in *Plato: Five Dialogues,* trans. G. M. A. Grube (Indianapolis: Hackett, 1981).

8. This is, of course, a completely unnuanced reading of both Plato and Descartes on the mind/body relation. Nevertheless, their general lack of regard for the body seems clear from their work.

9. See Richard C. Dales's *The Problem of the Rational Soul in the Thirteenth Century* (Leiden: Brill, 1995) for a detailed overview of the different positions popular in the 1200s in Paris and Oxford, as well as a categorical listing of who held what position.

10. Book I.14 of Robert Grosseteste's *Commentary on the Posterior Analytics,* lines 235–39; line numbers corresponding to Pietro Rossi's 1981 Latin edition, *Commentarius in Posteriorum Analyticorum Libros* (Florence: Leo S. Olschki).

11. As Aquinas makes clear in his discussion of separated souls (souls existing after death and prior to the bodily resurrection), God can aid the soul in cognizing if it is not currently joined to matter.

12. See, e.g., *ST* Ia.84.6–7 for an argument that the soul cannot acquire intellective cognition or actually understand without the body's providing it with sensation and phantasms ("mental pictures" that we form on the basis of sense perception).

13. In his own words: "A person with higher intelligence is ready, from a few principles he has within himself, to proceed to various conclusions which those with a less acute intelligence cannot reach without considerable illustrated explanation and without knowing the proximate principles of these conclusions" (*QDV* 8.10).

14. This is a vastly simplified depiction of Aquinas's extremely complex theory of cognition. In particular, we are here glossing over the crucial role of phantasms; see *ST* Ia.84–89 for an extensive discussion of the way in which human beings cognize and the proper objects of that cognition.

15. The concepts are higher in that they are more universal.

16. As he puts it, our souls involve more potentiality than other intellects; this is one of the reasons they are united to a material body: "[S]ince the human intellect has more potentiality than other intellective substances, it exists in such closeness to material things that a material thing is brought [*trahatur*] to participate in its being, so that from soul and body results one being in the one composite" (*DEE* 5.5).

17. Like all other orthodox Christians who accept the Nicene Creed and Apostles' Creed, Aquinas advocates not just the immortality of the human soul but also the resurrection of the body. On his view, at the final judgment, God will reunite human souls to matter — that is, he will recreate all

the human beings who have ever lived into everlasting bodies. See *SCG*
IV.79 ff. for a detailed discussion of the various issues this raises concerning
the afterlife.

18. Aquinas discusses his reasons for adopting Aristotle's view at length
in *ST* Ia.76.1. See also *QDSC* 2.

19. See, e.g., *QDA* 1.

20. *QDA* 1.ad 3 and 4. Again, in *ST* Ia.75.7.ad 3, Aquinas writes: "Properly, it is not the soul but the composite [of soul and body] that belongs to the
[human] species."

21. As a careful reader will notice, this claim (about which Aquinas is
quite definite) raises a number of problems for Aquinas's account of human
identity. For instance, if the human soul persists in separation from matter
prior to the resurrection of the body, it appears that the human being goes out
of existence for a time — and is then supposed to come back into existence at
the bodily resurrection. A theory that allows for interrupted existence seems
unpalatable, however, and so one might think that Aquinas must be committed either to a view where the human being does not go out of existence at
death (contrary to what he himself says) or to an implausible view of identity.
For a detailed discussion of these issues with reference to the relevant secondary literature, see Christina Van Dyke, "Human Identity, Immanent Causal
Relations, and the Principle of Non-Repeatability: Thomas Aquinas on the
Bodily Resurrection," *Religious Studies* 43 (2007): 373–94, and "The Problem
of the Rich Man and the Rich Man's Soul: Aquinas on Personhood and Disembodied Souls" (forthcoming in *Medieval Philosophy and Theology*).

22. Further, the soul would then seem to require some sort of interme-
diary to join it to the body. In *QDA* 9, Aquinas claims that "diverse and distinct substances cannot be joined together (*colligantur*) unless there is something that unites them." See also *QDSC* 3, *SCG* II.71, and *ST* Ia.76.6.

23. See, e.g., *ST* Ia.118.3 and *SCG* II.69.

24. Aquinas argues that Plato is wrong in holding that the rational soul
is a substance precisely because this would imply that the union of soul and
body is merely accidental. For Aquinas's criticism of Plato's substance dualism, see *QDSC* 2, *QDA* 1, and *QDA* 11.

25. *ST* Ia.76.2.ad 2.

26. *QDA* 1.ad 15. Aquinas follows Aristotle in holding that, properly
speaking, a corpse is called human only homonymously; that is, at death
the human body ceases to be a *human body* and can be called such only in
the same way that the unseeing eye of a painting can be called an eye. See

Christopher Shield's *Order in Multiplicity* (Oxford: Clarendon Press, 1999) for a detailed discussion of the concept of homonymy in Aristotle.

27. See, e.g., *ST* Ia.76.1, where Aquinas argues both that the rational soul is united to the body as its form and that this soul is an intellective principle which can rise above corporeal matter.

28. The intellect also needs to turn back to the phantasms each time it cognizes, at least in this life. For excellent, detailed discussions of Aquinas's theory of cognition, see Scott MacDonald's "Theory of Knowledge" in the *Cambridge Companion to Aquinas,* ed. Norman Kretzmann and Eleonore Stump (Cambridge: Cambridge University Press, 1993), and Robert Pasnau's *Thomas Aquinas on Human Nature: A Philosophical Study of Summa theologiae Ia 75–89* (Cambridge: Cambridge University Press, 2002).

29. *SCG* II.65.

30. For other places where Aquinas draws the same parallel, see *QDA* 8, 10, 11, and 16; also *ST* Ia.75.1.

31. *SCG* II.50.

32. As Aquinas remarks in *QDP* 5.3, "[T]he definition of matter . . . is pure potentiality. Indeed, matter . . . cannot exist without form." In *Quaestiones disputatae* (Rome: Marietti Editori, 1964).

33. Aquinas mentions fluctuation in bits of matter in several places, including *SCG* IV.81 and *ST* Ia.119, in which he writes: "[I]f by 'flesh' we mean the matter of which something is composed, that does not remain, but little by little it is taken away and restored" (*ST* Ia.119.1.ad 2). He makes an analogy with fire to illustrate his point: just as the same fire burns from the beginning of the evening to the end of the evening, although different pieces of wood keep being added to it, so the same human being persists from the beginning of life to the end of it, although different pieces of matter are added to it (through, for instance, the activity of eating). At the same time, it is important to note that Aquinas holds a strong thesis about substantial unity, according to which it is not the case that one particular material particle enters the body, becomes part of it, and later leaves it. When a human being drinks a glass of water, say, and some of those water particles are absorbed into her body, they cease to exist as water. Instead, the water is merely "virtually" present in the animal—that is, its powers are present while it is not. Properly speaking, human beings don't contain water particles; they contain flesh with "watery" powers. This entails that if a water particle later emerges from the human being (in urine, say), such a particle will not be the same in number as the particle that entered in the glass of water. This does not conflict with Aquinas's

claim that bits of matter come and go throughout the life of a living organism, however: it merely describes what happens to those particles while they are part of that organism.

34. See, e.g., *SCG* II.58; *QDA* 9 and 11; *QDSC* 3; *ST* Ia.76.3 and 76.6.ad 1.

35. Fernand Van Steenberghen in *Thomas Aquinas and Radical Aristotelianism* (Washington, D.C.: Catholic University of America Press, 1980) calls this "radical hylomorphism," since it takes Aristotle's general hylomorphism—the belief that physical objects are composites of form and matter—one step further.

36. Indeed, Aquinas explicitly rules out the possibility that the form which makes something a particular kind of body could be something as basic as the substantial form "body" (or *forma corporeitas*). As he says in *SCG* IV.81, "[T]here are not diverse substantial forms in one and the same thing, through one of which the thing is placed in a general genus (say, 'substance'), and through another of which [it is placed] in a proximate genus (say 'body' or 'animal'), and through another in a species (say, 'human being' or 'horse')."

37. Aquinas frequently defends the unicity of substantial form by arguing that since a substantial form is what makes something the very substance that it is, no substance could possess more than one such form. A thing's substantial form vivifies, organizes, structures, and makes something the very thing that it is. Thus, the first substantial form something was understood as possessing would provide its nature—any further forms would be inhering in an already-existing subject, and would thus be accidental rather than substantial forms. If someone claimed that she possessed the substantial form not only of "human being" but also of "body" and "living thing," Aquinas thinks that she would be talking nonsense. The first substantial form that a human being was understood as possessing, say, "body," would make her a substance; the other forms would then have to be understood as nonessential or accidental rather than substantial forms. As he writes in *QDSC* 3, "It is clear that any substantial form, whichever one it is, makes and constitutes a being in actuality; for this reason, it follows that only the first form which comes to matter is a substantial form, and all the forms following after it are accidental forms." In *Quaestiones disputatae* (Marietti edition).

38. Van Steenberghen, *Thomas Aquinas and Radical Aristotelianism*, 73, added emphasis.

39. In his commentary on *De anima*, Aquinas states: "We should not understand the soul's being the actuality of body . . . in such a way that the body is established through one form that makes it be a body while, coming on top

of that, is the soul that makes it be a living body. Soul is, rather, the actuality of body in such a way that from soul comes its being [*qua* being], its being a body, and its being a living body" (II.1.225).

40. Aquinas's commentary on 1 Corinthians 15, lecture 2, added emphasis. In *Super Epistolas S. Pauli Lectura* (Rome: Marietti Editori, 1953).

41. In his *Aquinas on Mind* (New York: Routledge, 1994), Anthony Kenny neatly captures this point when he comments on this passage: "It is remarkable that St. Thomas says [here] not just that the soul is only a part of a human being, but that it is only part of the *body* of a human being. Commonly he uses 'soul' and 'body' as correlatives, and often he writes as if body and soul were related to each other as the form and the matter of the Aristotelian hylomorphism. But the formulation which [Aquinas] uses in this passage is in fact the more correct one from the hylomorphic standpoint: the human being is a body which like other mutable bodies is composed of matter and form; the soul, which is the form of the living body, is one part of the body, and the matter is another part of it, with 'part' used in the very special sense which is appropriate in this context" (138–39).

42. In Descartes's own words: "And, accordingly, it is certain that I am really distinct from my body, and can exist without it" (*Philosophical Writings of Descartes,* vol. 2, trans. Cottingham et al., AT 78). The French edition adds, ". . . I, that is, my soul, by which I am what I am."

43. *SCG* II.50.

44. Aquinas even uses the body's necessary role in human sensation to support his claim that the human being is not merely a soul: "Since sensing is an action of a human being (albeit not the proper action), it is clear that a human being is not only a soul, but is something composed of soul and body" (*ST* Ia.75.4).

45. *ST* Ia.75.2.ad 2.

46. "[S]ince the human soul's act of understanding needs powers—namely, imagination and sense—which function through bodily organs, this itself shows that the soul is naturally united to the body in order to complete the human species" (*SCG* II.68).

47. *QDA* 8.

48. See, e.g., *QDA* 7: "Hence a soul does not possess intelligible perfection in its own nature but is in potency to intelligible objects. . . . Hence in order to perform its essential operations, a soul needs to be actualized by intelligible forms, acquiring them from external things through its sense powers. And since the operation of a sense takes place through a bodily organ, it

is appropriate for the soul, because of the very way its nature is constituted, that it be united to a body and that it be part of the human species, since of itself a soul is not complete in species."

49. The cognition human intellects would possess on the basis of intelligible species received directly from other intellects would be what Aquinas calls "general and confused"; rational souls are joined to bodies, then, in order to have sense perception of individual physical objects, from which they can form phantasms, and eventually abstract to universal concepts that they are able to apply properly to individual beings. See, e.g., *ST* Ia.89.3–4, *QDA* 15, and especially *QDA* 18.

50. For this reason, then, "An intellective soul must act *per se,* as something that has a proper operation apart from union with the body" (*QDA* 1). See also *QDV* 19.1, where Aquinas claims that "if none of the soul's operations is proper to it, in such a way that it can have it without the body, then it is impossible for that soul to be separated from the body."

51. There are serious questions about the plausibility of this line of argumentation. See, e.g., Matthew Kelly's "Aquinas and the Subsistence of the Soul," *Franciscan Studies* 27 (1967): 213–19, and Gerald Kreyche's "The Soul-Body Problem in St. Thomas," *New Scholasticism* 46 (Autumn 1972): 466–84, on the problems of the soul's subsistence; in his *Thomas Aquinas on Human Nature,* however, Pasnau presents an intriguing defense of Aquinas's argument.

52. He presents several arguments to that effect in *SCG* IV.79, where he defends the claim that "through Christ the resurrection of bodies will come." For a closely parallel passage, see the *Scriptum,* IV.43.1.1. Lectures 2–7 of Aquinas's commentary on 1 Corinthians 15 provide his most detailed examination of the doctrine of Christ's resurrection and its consequences for human beings, but they contain little of philosophical interest.

53. Marilyn McCord Adams discusses these arguments in her survey of Aquinas's position on the bodily resurrection in "The Resurrection of the Body According to Three Medieval Aristotelians: Thomas Aquinas, John Duns Scotus, William Ockham," *Philosophical Topics* 20 (1992): 2–8.

54. *SCG* IV.79.

55. The argument also relies on the claim that nothing contrary to nature can exist perpetually. Fortunately, the soundness of Aquinas's argument is not relevant to our purposes—of interest is what this passage says about the nature of the human soul.

56. *SCG* IV.79.

57. *In Sent* 4.43.1.1a.ad 2. He goes on to say, "Other things being equal, the status of the soul in the body is more perfect than the status of the soul outside the body, since it is *part* of the whole composite" (*In Sent* 4.43.1.1a.ad 4).

58. It is also clear that Aquinas realizes this belief raises vexing questions about human identity, questions that he addresses in passages such as *SCG* IV.80–81.

59. In *ST* Ia.29.1, Aquinas discusses each part of this definition in turn, first defending the claim that a person is an *individual substance,* and then explaining the importance of that substance's having a *rational nature.* He makes his case for persons being individual substances with a *rational* nature by arguing that "particularity and individuality are found in a more specific [*specialiori*] and perfect way in rational substances, which have control [*dominium*] over their actions, and are not only moved like other things, but act through themselves." In other words, rationality implies that the substance controls its own actions, and this "self-control" gives that substance a better claim to being an individual than other entities. "Furthermore," Aquinas continues, "actions belong to individuals [*actiones autem in singularibus sunt*]. For this reason, then, even among other substances, individuals with a rational nature have a certain special name. And this name is 'person'. Thus, 'individual substance' is placed in the definition of 'person' which was given above insofar as it signifies an individual [*singulare*] in the genus of substance, and 'with a rational nature' is added insofar as it signifies an individual among rational substances."

60. *ST* Ia.29.3.

61. Lynne Rudder Baker, *Persons and Bodies: A Constitution View* (Cambridge: Cambridge University Press, 2000), 121.

62. See, e.g., *ST* Ia.76.6.ad 2.

63. *ST* Ia.29.4.

64. This leaves Aquinas two responses to the persistent vegetative state case. First, he could claim that the human person is present as long as organic processes continue; second, he could claim that the vegetative physical organism ceases to be a human person and a human being. For a defense of the first claim, see J. P. Moreland and Stan Wallace's "Aquinas versus Locke and Descartes on the Human Person and End-of-Life Ethics," *International Philosophical Quarterly* 35 (1995): 319–30. For a defense of the second possibility, see William Wallace's "Aquinas's Legacy on Individuation, Cogitation, and Hominization," in *Thomas Aquinas and His Legacy,* ed. David Gallagher (Washington, D.C.: Catholic University of America Press, 1994), 173–93.

Chapter Three.   Human Capacities and the Image of God

1. There is some debate among Aristotle scholars as to whether Aristotle holds that the rational soul ceases to exist at death. Nevertheless, in his discussion of happiness, Aristotle certainly never appeals to a life after death in which human beings continue to exist, either as happy or not.

2. In Aquinas's own words, we cognize something's essence "through its surrounding features," or "on the basis of its effects and proper attributes" (*In Sent* 3.35.2.2.1).

3. As Aquinas puts it, "the powers of both [material and immaterial substances] come together in [human beings]" (*ST* Ia.77.2).

4. There is an important disanalogy between God and the chief knitters, however: the knitters have to actualize their capacity to knit in order to make the baby hats. One could imagine the knitters showing up and, although possessing the knowledge and ability to knit, simply talking instead. God, on the other hand, doesn't possess any capacities in this sense — that is, God is fully actual and always participating in divine activity. For the analogy to be complete, the chief knitters would have to knit perpetually, as a manifestation of their essential nature.

5. *ST* Ia.77.2.

6. See, e.g., *ST* Ia.77–83, where Aquinas discusses "the characteristics of the soul's capacities," first generally and then specifically.

7. In contemporary discussions, of course, the claim that intellect and will are nonphysical capacities is hotly contested. Yet Aquinas takes the existence of God and the angels to demonstrate this fact. God and angels are paradigmatically intellective and volitional; they are also paradigmatically immaterial. Thus, the capacities of intellect and will do not depend on matter for their exercise. Although, as we saw in chapter 2, Aquinas does hold that human intellects need to be joined to matter in order to actualize their capacities properly, the capacities themselves are nonphysical.

8. See, e.g., *ST* Ia.89.5.

9. We are referring here to cognition in the ordinary course of things. As discussed in chapter 2, cognition in a separated state is possible — but only when God provides the disembodied soul with the objects of abstract cognition.

10. As Aquinas puts it, the estimative power is the capacity "directed at apprehending intentions that are not grasped through the [external] senses" (*ST* Ia.78.4). Here he is using "intentions" in a technical medieval sense; for a helpful discussion of this issue, see Claude Panaccio's "Aquinas on Intellectual

Representation," in *Ancient and Medieval Theories of Intentionality,* ed. Dominik Perler (Leiden: Brill, 2001), 185–201.

11. Aquinas believes that human beings also possess intellective memory, but this is distinct from sensory memory, in which our sense perceptions ·remain tied to a certain time and place.

12. As he puts it, "Through the first, the soul is inclined simply to pursue what is agreeable to the sense and to flee what is harmful: this is called the concupiscible. Through the second, an animal resists those forces that combat the agreeable and bring harm: this power is called the irascible" (*ST* Ia.81.2).

13. *ST* Ia.77.4. See also *ST* IaIIae.17, especially articles 7 and 8, which detail the ability the will has to command and direct our sensory and vegetative capacities.

14. *ST* Ia.81.3.

15. *ST* Ia.78.1.

16. *ST* Ia.78.1.

17. See, e.g., *ST* Ia.79.8.

18. Although he distinguishes between theoretical and practical reason, however, Aquinas claims that they are not distinct powers. See, e.g., *ST* Ia.79.11.

19. *ST* Ia.79.11.ad 2.

Chapter Four.   Actions and Ends

1. *ST* IaIIae.1.1; see also *SCG* III.2.

2. *ST* IaIIae.1.1. "Thus, those actions that result from a deliberate will are properly called human actions."

3. Aquinas makes this claim in a number of places. See, e.g., *ST* IaIIae.1.1; *ST* IaIIae.1.2.ad 3; *ST* IaIIae.1.3; *ST* IaIIae.8.1–2; *ST* IaIIae.9.1–2; *ST* IaIIae.13.6. See also *SCG* III.2.

4. *ST* IaIIae.10.2; *ST* IaIIae.13.6.

5. This is bound to seem problematic. Obviously there are agents who pursue what is bad and who know it is bad. This worry is addressed in the next chapter.

6. *ST* IaIIae.1.3. See also *SCG* III.2.

7. For Aquinas's arguments, see *ST* IaIIae.1.5.

8. For an interesting discussion of some of these issues, see Scott MacDonald, "Ultimate Ends in Practical Reasoning: Aquinas's Aristotelian Moral Psychology and Anscombe's Fallacy," *Philosophical Review* 100 (1991): 31–66.

9. *ST* IaIIae.1.6.

10. *ST* IaIIae.1.6.

11. The analogy is not perfect since the locomotive is an efficient cause of the train's moving, and in a sequence of actions, the initial cause that sets off the chain of events is a final cause (for a discussion of the difference between efficient and final causation, see chapter 6 in this book, section "Freedom of Action," pp. 115–23). Nevertheless, the example illustrates Aquinas's basic point that there must a first cause in order to get the sequence of events off and running.

12. Thanks to Dan Haybron for his help in characterizing our ordinary concept of happiness.

13. *ST* IaIIae.2.1–8. See also *SCG* III.26–36. Although Aquinas believes that all human beings have the same ultimate end, he also recognizes that this is a controversial issue. He argues that if we consider the ultimate end from the standpoint of its general concept, then all human beings have the same ultimate end. For the concept of an ultimate end is the complete fulfillment of all of our desires, which Aquinas thinks all human beings naturally desire (*ST* IaIIae.5.8). However, if we consider the ultimate end from the standpoint of its instantiation, then he agrees that not all human beings have the same ultimate end because there is no agreement over what constitutes the ultimate end (*ST* IaIIae.1.7).

14. *ST* IaIIae.2.7.

15. *ST* IaIIae.3.8. Aquinas builds up to this conclusion throughout question 3. See also *SCG* III.37 and III.51.

16. *ST* IaIIae.10.2.

17. *ST* IaIIae.3.1.

18. The beatific vision cannot be a sensory apprehension because the vision of the divine essence is a type of union with an uncreated good that is not material. The senses can perceive only what is material. Aquinas is willing to concede that sensory apprehension makes a contribution to whatever happiness we are able to achieve in this life. This is because this happiness consists in contemplation, which is a cognitive operation, and in the absence of an intervention of God, sensory apprehension is a necessary condition for the intellect's activity. Sensory apprehension also plays a role in happiness after the bodily resurrection insofar as there is a body present into which the joy generated by the beatific vision is able to flow; see *ST* IaIIae.3.3.

19. *ST* IaIIae.3.4.

20. *ST* IaIIae.4.4.

21. *ST* IaIIae.4.1.

22. Aquinas does think that in some sense, God is the ultimate end for other creatures as well. However, the sense in which nonrational animals have God as their end is very different from the human case. See *ST* IaIIae.1.8.

23. *ST* IaIIae.4.3.

24. *ST* IaIIae.3.2–3; *ST* IaIIae.3.5–6.

25. *ST* IaIIae.4.7.

26. *ST* IaIIae.4.5.

27. *ST* IaIIae.4.7.

28. *ST* IaIIae.5.5; *ST* IaIIae.5.7.

29. *ST* IaIIae.5.5. See also *SCG* III.52–54.

30. See *ST* IaIIae.109. The idea that human beings cannot attain happiness by their own efforts and are dependent upon God's grace raises problems over whether aiming at the ultimate end in fact involves human actions at all. Furthermore it raises problems for Aquinas's theory of free will. We address these concerns in chapter 6.

31. *ST* IaIIae.1.6.ad 3.

32. See *ST* IaIIae.56.

33. Aquinas organizes his discussion of the mechanics of action around the activities of the will; see the prologue to *ST* IaIIae.8.1. He divides the activities of the will into two groups: those that are elicited by the will and those that are commanded by the will. Elicited acts result directly from the activities of the will. The will's act of willing, say, to study philosophy is an example of an elicited act. Commanded acts are those in virtue of which the will moves the other powers of the human being to their characteristic activities. When an agent raises her arm, Aquinas thinks that the will has stimulated the muscles in her arm to move. In a sense, the will has commanded the muscles in her arm to contract, thereby sending her arm up into the air. As we shall see, Aquinas modifies this idea a bit. Command turns out to be an act of the intellect by which it commands the will to move the other powers of the body to execute the action. Nevertheless, as an organizing principle for his account of action, Aquinas associates command with the will. The discussion in this book is organized around a different principle. We consider the sequence of steps involved in the production of an individual action. This seems to be the most natural way to understand what is going on in the production of an action.

34. See *ST* Ia.75.2.ad 2.

35. *ST* IaIIae.12.1–2. "Action" in this discussion refers to what we might call an "external action," that is, the action that is visible to a third-party

observer. Aquinas also recognizes what we might call "internal actions"—actions such as thinking and willing that are observable only from a first-person perspective, that is, by the one doing the thinking or willing.

36. *ST* IaIIae.12.1.ad 3.

37. *ST* IaIIae.14.2. Although deliberation is an activity of the intellect, Aquinas argues that the intellect is moved to deliberate by the will; see *ST* IaIIae.16.4.

38. *ST* IaIIae.14.1 and 14.4.

39. *ST* IaIIae.14.2.

40. See *ST* IaIIae.14.2.

41. *ST* IaIIae.15.4.

42. See *ST* IaIIae.15.1 and 15.4.

43. *ST* IaIIae.15.3.

44. *ST* Iaiae.15.3.ad 3.

45. *ST* IaIIae.13.1.

46. See *QDV* 24.2.

47. *ST* IaIIae.13.1.

48. *ST* Ia.83.3. "With respect to choice, something on the part of the cognitive power concurs with something on the part of the appetitive power. On the side of the cognitive power, deliberation is required on the basis of which it is judged what is to be preferred to another, while on the side of the appetitive power, an act of inclination is required toward that which has been judged on the basis of deliberation." As we shall see later when we consider the freedom of human action, this position and this interpretation are quite controversial. But for now we simply focus on the mechanics of choice.

49. *ST* IaIIae.17.5 and 17.9.

50. *ST* IaIIae.16.1; see also *ST* IaIIae.16.4.

51. The activity of use can arise in another, earlier part of the sequence. Insofar as the will is able to move the intellect to its activities, the will is able to move the intellect to its act of deliberation. Thus, first the will intends a particular end; then it moves the intellect to deliberate over the means to that end. The will's action upon the intellect at this point is also an act of use; see *ST* IaIIae.16.4.

52. Alan Donagan, *Choice, the Essential Element in Human Action* (London: Routledge and Kegan Paul, 1987).

53. *ST* IaIIae.11.1.

54. *ST* IaIIae.11.3.

55. *ST* IaIIae.11.4.

56. This claim might seem too strong. After all, there are lots of actions that we do, the performance of which do not bring us pleasure. The student does not enjoy taking the difficult calculus exam. The athlete does not enjoy stretching out her painful hamstring. Aquinas would argue that what we enjoy is the achievement of the end, not necessarily the performance of the action that is the means to that end. The student takes the difficult exam in order to pass the class, and passing will give her a feeling of satisfaction. The athlete stretches in order to engage in her sport, which she enjoys.

57. We might also be acting on the basis of habit, which makes explicit deliberation unnecessary. For a discussion of the role of habits in action and ethics, see chapter 6.

58. *ST* IaIIae.14.1.

59. *ST* IaIIae.13.1.

60. *ST* IaIIae.14.1.

61. *ST* IaIIae.22.3; see also *ST* IaIIae.23.4. Aquinas's discussion of the passions is found in *ST* IaIIae.22–48. For more information on the passions, see Peter King, "Aquinas on the Passions," in *Aquinas's Moral Theory,* ed. Scott MacDonald and Eleonore Stump (Ithaca: Cornell University Press, 1999), 101–32; and Kevin White, "The Passions of the Soul," in *The Ethics of Aquinas,* ed. Stephen J. Pope (Washington, D.C.: Georgetown University Press, 2002), 103–15.

62. *ST* IaIIae.22.2; *ST* IaIIae.22.3; see also *ST* IaIIae.23.2.

63. *ST* IaIIae.23.4.

64. *ST* IaIIae.23.1. See also *ST* IaIIae.23.2.

65. *ST* IaIIae.23.1.

66. *ST* IaIIae.23.3.

67. *ST* IaIIae.24.3.

68. *ST* IaIIae.9.2.

69. *ST* IaIIae.77.1.

70. *ST* IaIIae.33.3.

71. See *ST* IaIIae.45.1.

72. *ST* IaIIae.24.1.

73. *ST* IaIIae.10.3; *ST* IaIIae.77.7.

74. *ST* IaIIae.77.7. Aquinas argues that the resulting action will be involuntary and hence not culpable. These issues will be discussed in chapter 6.

75. This also implies that strictly speaking, for Aquinas, there is no weakness of will—that is, situations where agents recognize and desire a greater good yet pursue a lesser good, often trying to explain their behavior in terms of being overwhelmed by strong passion.

Chapter Five.   The Moral Appraisal of Actions

1. *ST* IaIIae.18.8; *ST* IaIIae.18.3.

2. For this reason, only human actions (as opposed to acts of a human being) are subject to moral appraisal. In his discussion of sin, Aquinas identifies a third principle of human acts, namely, the passions. The passions, however, move human beings to act only through the permission of the intellect and will. Thus, there is a sense in which although passions move us to act (and hence must be considered a principle of human acts), still, they are a lesser principle.

3. Rationality in this sense also has to do with Aquinas's notions of natural and eternal law, discussed in part 3.

4. It is of course a difficult matter to determine whether or not a particular action promotes human flourishing, or even how to differentiate between various instantiations of the same physical manifestation. For example, causing the death of another can be viewed as an act of murder, an act of fulfilling one's military duty, an act of self-defense, or an act of justice (in Aquinas's eyes). While this is an important point, it will not be addressed here. This discussion presupposes that we can make these kinds of distinctions, difficult as it may be. For further discussion of these matters, see Steven A. Long, "A Brief Disquisition Regarding the Nature of the Object of the Moral Act," *The Thomist* 67 (2003): 45–71; Stephen L. Brock, *Action and Conduct* (Edinburgh: T & T Clark, 1998); Tobias Hoffman, "Moral Action as Human Action: End and Object in Aquinas in Comparison with Abelard, Lombard, Albert, and Duns Scotus," *The Thomist* 67 (2003): 73–94; Kevin L. Flannery, S.J., "The Multifarious Moral Object of Thomas Aquinas," *The Thomist* 67 (2003): 95–118; Joseph Pilsner, *The Specification of Human Actions in Thomas Aquinas* (Oxford: Oxford University Press, 2006); James F. Keenan, S.J., *Goodness and Rightness in Thomas Aquinas's Summa Theologiae* (Washington, D.C.: Georgetown University Press, 1992); Daniel Westberg, "Good and Evil in Human Acts (IaIIae, qq. 18–21)," in *The Ethics of Aquinas,* ed. Stephen J. Pope (Washington, D.C.: Georgetown University Press, 2002), 90–102; Ralph McInerny, *Aquinas on Human Action* (Washington, D.C.: Catholic University of America Press, 1992); Ralph McInerny, *Ethica Thomistica* (Washington, D.C.: Catholic University of America Press, 1982).

5. See *ST* IIaIIae.64.7.

6. Aquinas describes the species of an action in terms of the action's object; see *ST* IaIIae.18.2. This language of object will not be used here because, as we have seen, Aquinas uses object language in a number of other instances

(e.g., the good as the object of the will; the intellect's act of presenting the will with its object), thus avoiding any potential confusion.

7. *ST* IaIIae.18.9.

8. There are of course all kinds of purported counterexamples to this position: stealing food in case of dire need, lying in order to protect a friend from a murderer, the case of Abraham and Isaac in the Hebrew scriptures. For a discussion of these and other cases, see John Boler, "Aquinas on Exceptions in Natural Law," in *Aquinas's Moral Theory,* ed. Scott MacDonald and Eleonore Stump (Ithaca: Cornell University Press, 1999), 161–204.

9. *ST* IaIIae.18.3.

10. See *ST* IaIIae.18.4.

11. Actually, Aquinas argues for four conditions, but one of them essentially drops out of moral appraisal because it is a condition that is met by all action, whether good, bad, or neutral. This is a condition that follows from Aquinas's commitment to the convertibility relationship between being and goodness, namely, the idea that being and goodness are the same in reality although they differ in concept. Since all actions exist insofar as they are actually performed, it will follow that all particular actions have at least some minimal amount of goodness insofar as they exist. There are of course some worrisome issues that arise from this view, in particular the worry that it surely would have been better had certain events or actions, such as the Holocaust or the rape of Lucretia, never existed. Aquinas needs to address these concerns, but because this claim about goodness is true of all action, this condition essentially drops out.

12. *ST* IaIIae.20.5.

13. Aquinas does not specifically address the case where the agent foresees good consequences; his example is one where the agent foresees bad consequences yet performs the action anyway. However, he does state that foreseen consequences contribute to the goodness or badness of an action and so would surely agree that recognizing the potential goodness of an action's consequences makes that action a better action.

14. This example is not original though its source is unknown.

15. Of course it also has some bad consequences—the death of the victim.

16. This case involves what Aquinas calls "invincible ignorance"; see chapter 6.

17. A further factor in moral appraisal is the influence of one's conscience. Conscience is a very complex notion in medieval philosophy and lies outside the scope of our purposes in this book. For Aquinas's views on the

nature, function, and influence of conscience, see *ST* Ia.79.12 and 79.13; *ST* IaIIae.19.5 and 19.6. For a discussion of the notion of conscience in the Middle Ages, see Timothy C. Potts, *Conscience in Medieval Philosophy* (Cambridge: Cambridge University Press, 1980).

18. *ST* IaIIae.71.1.

19. *ST* IaIIae.49.1; *ST* IaIIae.49.3.

20. See *ST* IaIIae.47.4.

21. See *ST* IIaIIae.112.1.

22. See *ST* IaIIae.78.2.

23. See *ST* IaIIae.71.2.

24. *ST* IaIIae.73.1; see also *ST* IaIIae.72.2.

25. See *ST* IaIIae.78.1.

26. If an action is the result of a nonculpable defect, then the action is involuntary.

27. See *ST* IaIIae.75.3.

28. See *ST* IaIIae.6.8; *ST* IaIIae.76.3 and 76.4.

29. *ST* IaIIae.76.4.

30. See *ST* IaIIae.76.2.

31. See *ST* IaIIae.76.1.

32. *ST* IaIIae.76.3.

33. This is in fact Aquinas's example in *ST* IaIIae.76.1 in all but name.

34. The claim that sins of passion have their origin in the sensory appetite is not meant to be a causal claim or to suggest that the sensory appetite is somehow able to cause the sin independently of the intellect's control. It is merely to say that the sin has its source in the sensory appetite in the same way in which a river has its source in a spring or a lake. The sin first arises in the sensory appetite by the stimulation of passion, which is compatible with the idea that intellect still retains control over the sensory appetite.

35. See *ST* IaIIae.77.1.

36. Aquinas also concedes that there might be physical ailments that affect one's ability to cognize and so enable the passions to gain a foothold over the intellect. If the illness is strong enough, the intellect might not be able to control the passions. The ability of the passions to influence the action is directly correlated to the extent to which the illness interferes with the ability to cognize: the stronger the illness's effect on reason, the greater the influence of the passions. If the effect upon reason is strong enough to incapacitate reason, then the agent is no longer responsible for her actions, for she has lost the ability to control her behavior. See *ST* IaIIae.77.2.

37. *ST* IaIIae.77.6 and 77.7.

38. In arguing that agents ought to pursue what is in their own interests, Aquinas does not mean to hold an egoistic account of ethics in any objectionable sense. To pursue what is in fact in our own best interests is to pursue a flourishing life, which on Aquinas's account ultimately has to do with promoting the common good; see *ST* IaIIae.90.2; *ST* IaIIae.94.2. On Aquinas's account, supporting the conditions that will in fact bring about the flourishing of everyone never requires an individual to sacrifice her own flourishing and in fact will bring her genuine happiness, which she desires above all. For further discussion, see Scott MacDonald, "Egoistic Rationalism: Aquinas's Basis for Christian Morality," in *Christian Theism and the Problems of Philosophy,* ed. Michael Beaty (Notre Dame: University of Notre Dame Press, 1990), 327–54.

39. *ST* IaIIae.78.1.

40. *ST* IaIIae.78.1.ad 2.

41. This is a very common reference; see, for example, S. I. Benn, "Wickedness," *Ethics* 95 (1985): 795–810. The passage from *Paradise Lost* is found in book IV, line 110.

42. The latter is Anselm of Canterbury's explanation of the devil's motivation in *On the Fall of the Devil.* In Anselm's eyes, of course, Satan is mistaken, since even the disobedient Satan is not able to be truly independent of God's will.

43. *ST* IaIIae.78.1.ad 2. It seems likely that the pleasure Aquinas has in mind is fornication or adultery, although here he leaves it an open question, unlike *QDM* 3.12, where he raises the same idea using adultery as his example.

44. One might wonder why this is a sin of passion, given that it involves daydreaming about the beach, which one might consider to be an activity of the intellect. Although the sin would not have occurred without an act of intellect (i.e., the sudden thought of the beach), the thought itself is not the sin; rather, the thought stimulates the passion, which inclines the agent (with the acquiescence of the intellect) to the daydream. Thus, the sin itself originates from passion, even though the occasion for the passion is located in the intellect.

45. See *ST* IaIIae.78.4.

46. See *ST* IaIIae.78.4.ad 3.

47. *ST* IaIIae.78.2–4.

48. Whether Aquinas can in fact explain this satisfactorily is an open question. Ultimately he might have to say that it is a mystery.

49. *ST* IaIIae.78.3.

50. The example is taken from the 1962 John Frankenheimer movie *The Manchurian Candidate.*

51. For a classic discussion of this issue, see P. F. Strawson, "Freedom and Resentment," in *Freedom and Resentment and Other Essays* (London: Methuen, 1974), 1–25.

Chapter Six.   Habits and Freedom

1. *ST* IaIIae.49.4.

2. *ST* IaIIae.54.4.

3. *ST* IaIIae.49.4.

4. *ST* IaIIae.49.4.

5. *ST* IaIIae.50.3.

6. *ST* IaIIae.50.4 (on the intellect); *ST* IaIIae.50.5 (on will).

7. *ST* IaIIae.58.1.

8. Aquinas also thinks of such bodily states as health and beauty as habits, since these states are subject to change (*ST* IaIIae.49.1; *ST* IaIIae.50.1). However, these states are habits only in a qualified sense. These habits are not terribly important for our purposes.

9. *ST* IaIIae.51.2 and 51.3.

10. *ST* IaIIae.49.2.

11. *ST* IaIIae.54.3.

12. *ST* IaIIae.51.4.

13. For further discussion of Aquinas's notion of grace, see chapter 8. Aquinas also argues that some virtues are available only in an infused form— most notably, the theological virtues of faith, hope, and charity; see *ST* IaIIae.62 for a general discussion of the theological virtues. Aquinas treats each of the theological virtues in turn later in *Summa theologiae.* In addition, Aquinas argues for an infused form for each of the so-called cardinal virtues (prudence, justice, fortitude, and temperance); see *ST* IaIIae.65.3. The infused virtues are especially important in obtaining the ultimate end. For further discussion of both the acquired and infused virtues and their relationship and functions, see chapter 7. See also Jeffrey Hause, "Aquinas on the Function of Moral Virtue," *American Catholic Philosophical Quarterly* 81 (2007): 1–20.

14. See *ST* IaIIae.51.4.ad 3.

15. For Aquinas's discussion of the details of habit reinforcement, see *ST* IaIIae.52.

16. *ST* IaIIae.53.1.

17. See *ST* IaIIae.53.1.

18. *ST* IaIIae.53.1.

19. See *ST* IaIIae.60.4; *ST* IIaIIae.157.1.

20. *ST* IaIIae.53.2; *ST* IaIIae.53.3.

21. See *QDM* 6; *QDV* 24.1.

22. *ST* IaIIae.6.prol. One might think that this way of describing voluntariness implies a commitment to the Principle of Alternative Possibilities (PAP)—roughly, the principle that agents act freely (i.e., voluntarily) or are morally responsible for their actions if and only if it is possible for them to act otherwise. Traditionally it has been argued that God lacks alternative possibilities. Thus, if it were necessary to understand voluntariness in terms of PAP, it would follow that God does not act freely, which contradicts another traditional theistic commitment. Aquinas's understanding of voluntariness in terms of reasons for acting does not rely on PAP. An agent's reasons for acting in a particular way can be so compelling that she has no other feasible alternative. Yet she acts freely, for it is always open to her to consider other reasons or to reexamine the reasons she has. For an argument that Aquinas's view does not depend upon PAP, see Eleonore Stump, "Intellect, Will, and the Principle of Alternate Possibilities," in *Christian Theism and the Problems of Philosophy,* ed. Michael D. Beaty (Notre Dame: University of Notre Dame Press, 1990), 254–85.

23. *ST* IaIIae.6.2.

24. *ST* IaIIae.6.1.

25. *ST* IaIIae.6.2.

26. See also Aquinas's discussion in *QDV* 24.1. For a discussion of this idea in Aquinas, see Scott MacDonald, "Ultimate Ends in Practical Reasoning: Aquinas's Aristotelian Moral Psychology and Anscombe's Fallacy," *Philosophical Review* 100 (1991): 31–66.

27. Part of Aquinas's claim also has to do with what is going on in the Latin. The Latin word for voluntariness is *voluntarius.* The Latin word for will is *voluntas.* The connection between these two notions is obvious in the Latin while it is obscured in the English translation. Nevertheless, the explanation is deeper than simply a matter of etymology.

28. Thus, Aquinas's view of freedom is an intellectualist account as opposed to a voluntarist account. This is a controversial interpretation. For some competing views, see Eleonore Stump, "Aquinas's Account of Freedom: Intellect and Will," *The Monist* 80 (1997): 576–97; and David M. Gallagher, "Free Choice and Free Judgment in Thomas Aquinas," *Archiv für Geschichte der Philosophie* 76 (1994): 247–77. For an interpretation similar to the one argued here,

see Scott MacDonald, "Aquinas's Libertarian Account of Free Choice," *Revue Internationale de Philosophie* 52 (1998): 309–28.

29. *QDV* 24.2.

30. This is in contrast to a number of medieval thinkers who argued that the intellect is determined by the world around us and thus cannot be the source of human freedom of action. See, for example, John Duns Scotus, *Quaestiones super libros metaphysicorum Aristoteles* IX, q.15, ed. Robert Andrews et al. (St. Bonaventure, N.Y.: Franciscan Institute Publications, 1997).

31. *QDV* 24.2.

32. *ST* IaIIae.17.1.ad 2.

33. *QDV* 24.4 and 24.5.

34. See *ST* Ia.83.3.ad 2.

35. *QDV* 24.6; see also *ST* Ia.83.3.

36. See *ST* Ia.83.3.

37. *ST* Ia.83.3 and 83.4.

38. *ST* Ia.82.4.

39. For Aquinas's discussion of this distinction and its implications for his theory of freedom, see *ST* IaIIae.10.2 and 13.6; and *QDM* 6.

40. Aquinas thinks that, as a matter of fact, only one thing is perfectly good, and that is happiness, which just is what satisfies completely all of our desires. So if we encounter that which satisfies completely all of our desires, we cannot help but pursue it, Aquinas says, *if* we pursue anything at all. Aquinas thinks that only one thing actually instantiates this idea of happiness; that is, only one thing can in fact satisfy completely all of our desires, and that is God. Since we do not encounter God directly in this life under ordinary circumstances, nothing we encounter in our ordinary lives necessitates our choices. One other complication to keep in mind is that human beings are structured in such a way that they naturally desire happiness. As a result, human beings cannot will misery for its own sake. This is an additional way in which happiness necessitates our choices, but Aquinas would argue that it does so only in an innocuous way. This was a controversial matter in the Middle Ages; for a discussion of this controversy, see Colleen McCluskey, "Happiness and Freedom in Aquinas's Theory of Action," *Medieval Philosophy and Theology* 9 (2000): 69–90.

41. *ST* IaIIae.10.2.

42. *ST* IaIIae.13.6.

43. *ST* IaIIae.10.2.

44. This example is a variation of one given by Eleonore Stump; see "Intellect, Will, and the Principle of Alternate Possibilities," especially 269.

45. *ST* Ia.82.4.ad 3.

46. For example, Augustine in the fifth century, Anselm of Canterbury in the tenth century, Philip the Chancellor in the thirteenth century, and John Duns Scotus and William Ockham in the late thirteenth and early fourteenth centuries all argue for a voluntarist account of freedom. In the early modern period, René Descartes argues for freedom in the will. Immanual Kant also discusses freedom in terms of the will.

47. For philosophers who argue that Aquinas is a compatibilist, see Thomas J. Loughran, "Aquinas, Compatibilist," in *Human and Divine Agency: Anglican, Catholic, and Lutheran Perspectives,* ed. F. Michael McLain and W. Mark Richardson (Lanham, Md.: University Press of America, 1999), 1–39; Robert Pasnau and Christopher Shields, *The Philosophy of Aquinas* (Boulder, Colo.: Westview Press, 2004), 149; and Thomas Williams, "The Libertarian Foundations of Scotus's Moral Philosophy," *The Thomist* 62 (1998): 193–215. For philosophers who argue that Aquinas is a libertarian, see John H. Wright, S.J., "Human Freedom and Divine Action: Libertarianism in St. Thomas Aquinas," in *Human and Divine Agency: Anglican, Catholic, and Lutheran Perspectives,* 41–47; Scott MacDonald, "Aquinas's Libertarian Account of Free Choice," *Revue Internationale de Philosophie* 52 (1998): 309–28; Stump, "Aquinas's Account of Freedom: Intellect and Will"; Colleen McCluskey, "Intellective Appetite and the Freedom of Human Action," *The Thomist* 66 (2002): 421–56.

48. Another important issue in the current discussion of free will is whether libertarian free will is required for moral responsibility. It is clear that, for Aquinas, some kind of free will is required for moral responsibility; see *QDM* 6. Whether on Aquinas's view we need libertarian or compatibilist free will for moral responsibility will depend upon which theory of free will he ends up holding.

49. At least one important philosopher in the history of philosophy would say no: Immanuel Kant. See his *Groundwork for the Metaphysic of Morals.*

Chapter Seven. The Virtues

1. "Since therefore we reach happiness [*beatitudinem*] through certain acts, we must next consider human acts, in order to know by what acts we may reach happiness, and by which acts impede our way to it" (*ST* IaIIae.6.prol). Happiness or beatitude is defined as the vision of God, the perfect activity of

the intellect. Love for God is the perfected activity of the will which accompanies this knowledge. See *ST* IaIIae.3.8, *ST* IIaIIae.23.1. Aquinas links the two when describing charity (love of God): "Vision is the cause of love, as stated in *EN* ix.5 [Aristotle's *Nicomachean Ethics* 9.5], and the more perfectly we know God, the more perfectly we love him" (*ST* IaIIae.67.6.ad 3).

2. *ST* IaIIae.49, 55 prologues.

3. *ST* IaIIae.90.

4. Later in the *Summa theologiae* Aquinas concentrates more heavily on *divine* agency and the way it makes human achievement of union with God possible, for example, in Christ's redemptive work and the sacraments.

5. *ST* IaIIae.49–70 and *ST* IIaIIae.1–170, respectively.

6. There are a few additional questions on law and grace in *ST* IIaIIae. The IIaIIae itself is structured around the seven principal virtues, with the ten precepts of the Decalogue (the two main tables of the law) and the seven gifts of the Holy Spirit each considered within a discussion of the virtue with which they are associated. Thus there is typically a single question on law and on the gifts at the end of each treatise on virtue.

7. Especially since the publication of John Rawls's *A Theory of Justice* (Cambridge, Mass.: Belknap/Harvard University Press, 1971), debates in contemporary ethics have tended to oppose theories that make the concept of goodness central (and derive all other concepts from it) and theories that make the concept of rightness central. As the following chapters will make clear, Aquinas is engaged in a quite different, nonreductive moral project. To frame his theory in terms privileging law (right) over against virtue (good), or vice versa, is to misunderstand Aquinas's use of these terms and his conception of the moral landscape. Thus Aquinas presents an attractive alternative for those who find contemporary reductivism in ethics unsatisfying.

8. See *ST* IaIIae.55.1–3; *ST* IaIIae.55.2.ad 1.

9. Recall that, for Aquinas, perfection is a process that comes in stages — so a capacity can be more or less perfected. In Aristotelian terms, the natural capacity is a potentiality, the virtue a first actuality, and the virtuous action a second actuality.

10. *ST* IaIIae.55.4; Aristotle, *Nicomachean Ethics* 2.6, quoted in *ST* IaIIae.55.2 sed contra.

11. What Aquinas means by *prudentia* is roughly the equivalent of Aristotle's *phronesis* or practical wisdom.

12. *ST* IaIIae.71.1.ad 2: "'Virtue' conveys not only the perfection of a capacity [*potentiae*] which is a principle of action, but also the due disposition

of the agent who has the virtue, because a thing operates according as it is in act. This requires that something needs to be well disposed itself if it has to operate well."

13. *ST* Ia.78.prol.

14. *ST* IaIIae.55.1. Vegetative functions, like breathing, aren't sufficiently under our control to count as part of the moral life, even if they do contribute to our bodily good. As we will see shortly, the passions of the sensory appetite—which are linked much more closely to the body than even intellect and will—have a substantial role to play in Aquinas's ethics. This is because they are subject to the direction of reason.

15. We will return to this idea in our discussion of the natural law in chapter 8. By way of summary now, we can say that virtues perfect and direct the natural inclinations expressed in the precepts of the natural law.

16. See *ST* IaIIae.2.8; *ST* Ia.77.3, 78.1, and 80.2.ad 2.

17. For Aquinas's own examples of honoring divine goods over human goods, see *ST* IIaIIae.125.4 and 124.5.ad 3. From the agent's point of view, these "objects" and "goods" are things under certain descriptions. Agents can get descriptions wrong and can misperceive goods.

18. *ST* IIaIIae.26.

19. *ST* IaIIae.54.2 reply and ad 3.

20. As we will note later, Aquinas describes the virtue of charity in terms of the love of friendship and names joy and peace as some of its effects.

21. Notice that it is not required that the college student neglect her physical good for the sake of the spiritual goods of justice and friendship or the divine good of charity. Suppose that by foregoing her purchase of an oversized bucket of popcorn and a super-sized soft drink at the movies, she is able to pay her rent, thereby meeting her basic physical need for shelter as well as honoring her commitments and strengthening her friendships. Respecting the ordering of goods enables her to flourish on every level. In a more extreme case, Aquinas also believes this works for the act of martyrdom: the martyr gives up her mortal, physical life for the sake of the divine good, but her act of faith and charity, enabled by grace, merits for her eternal life with an imperishable, resurrected body. Aquinas is obviously concerned there, as elsewhere in his ethics, with the good of all of human nature.

22. *ST* IaIIae.28.6: "Every agent acts for an end, as we said above (q. 1, a. 2). Now an end is a good desired and loved by the one acting. Thus it is clear that all agents, whoever they be, perform every action from love of some kind."

23. Aquinas marks this distinction by using *amor* to describe natural inclination, and *dilectio* or *caritas* to describe rational love.

24. See, for example, *ST* IaIIae.71.2.ad 3.

25. *ST* IaIIae.55.1.ad 4.

26. *ST* IaIIae.71.2: "Now human beings have their species through having a rational soul. So anything that is contrary to the order of reason is, properly speaking, contrary to the nature of human beings, as human, while whatever is in accord with reason, is in accord with the nature of human beings. Now 'the human good is to be in accord with reason, and human evil is to be against reason,' as Dionysius states (*On the Divine Names*, ch. 4). Therefore, human virtue, which 'makes a person good, and that person's work good,' is in accord with human nature, insofar as it accords with human reason; while vice is contrary to human nature, insofar as it is contrary to the order of reason." Aquinas will later make a parallel argument for divine reason being the rule of human virtue and action, insofar as human beings also participate in the divine nature by charity in order to achieve their ultimate end.

27. Recall that the human good involves loving God for his own sake, so Aquinas's view is not egoistic. In fact, the egoism/altruism distinction is another dichotomy (like the distinction between the right and the good) that does not fit Aquinas's ethics. See, for example, the case made by Thomas Osborne, Jr., in *Love of God and Love of Self in Thirteenth-Century Ethics* (Notre Dame: University of Notre Dame Press, 2005).

28. This describes the internal case, in which lower appetites refuse to be subordinate to reason. Aquinas is also acutely aware of external cases, in which our reason refuses to submit to God's will, as in the vice of pride.

29. *ST* Ia.77.4.

30. See the examples in note 21 above.

31. *ST* IaIIae.24.3: "Therefore just as it is better that human beings should both will the good and do it in their external act; so also does it belong to the perfection of the moral good that they should be moved to good not only according to wills, but also according to their sensory appetites."

32. Because the proper operation of the sensitive appetite necessarily involves a bodily organ, the perfection of the person includes the body as well (*ST* Ia.77.5).

33. *ST* IaIIae.56.4.

34. *ST* IaIIae.40–48. See also R. K. DeYoung, "Power Made Perfect in Weakness: Aquinas's Transformation of Courage," *Medieval Philosophy and Theology* 11.2 (2003): 147–80.

35. *ST* IIaIIae.53.6, 55.8.

36. *ST* IIaIIae.45.

37. See *ST* IaIIae.58.3.

38. See *ST* IaIIae.66.3 reply and ad 1 and 2. Another intellectual virtue, called "art" (in Greek, *poesis*), is also in the practical intellect but directs the production of things (making) rather than human actions (doing). It does not engage the will morally like prudence does, so we will not comment further on it here. The vision of the divine essence — which is possible only in the next life — is an activity of the speculative intellect, and the virtue of faith, the precursor of that vision, is likewise located there. Because that vision is unavailable to us now, ethical action in this life concerns the work of the practical intellect directing action (albeit enlightened by faith); hence the focus of this book on the means to happiness, not the activity of happiness itself.

39. *ST* IIaIIae.47.8.

40. *ST* IaIIae.58.

41. There are exceptions: some moral virtues like magnanimity have up to three vices of excess (*ST* IIaIIae.130), and others don't fit the schema neatly at all: prudence has vices opposed by way of resemblance and opposition, rather than by way of excess and deficiency (*ST* IIaIIae.53). See also *ST* IaIIae.64.4 on the mean of the theological virtues.

42. Aristotle treats all four cardinal virtues in *Nicomachean Ethics* but does not privilege the four over other moral virtues he discusses. Courage is also known as fortitude (from the Latin *fortis,* or "strong").

43. The cardinal virtues function something like archetypes for the other moral virtues. Included under temperance are other virtues that involve the moderation of desire, such as abstinence and fasting, chastity and purity, modesty and *studiositas* (the temperate use of the intellect), and even humility. Aquinas makes further distinctions among the virtues classified under a given cardinal virtue, dividing them into integral parts (elemental virtues without which the main virtue cannot operate), subjective parts (species of the main virtue), and potential parts (virtues whose definition is similar in formal structure to the main virtue but not fully identical). For prudence, for example, its integral parts are counsel, judgment, and command; its subjective parts include prudence about an individual life (monastic prudence, from the Greek word *monos-* for "one") and prudence about the community (regnative and legislative prudence); and its potential parts include things like the ability to reason well from principles to conclusions and to exercise due caution when attending to circumstances.

44. *ST* IaIIae.61; *ST* IIaIIae.47–170.

45. Note that this comment and the chart that follows include only the capacities relevant to the cardinal virtues. The practical intellect is not a distinct power from the speculative intellect (*ST* Ia.79.11). The intellect is the

subject of *all* the intellectual virtues, not just practical wisdom; the practical work of the intellect is distinguished from the intellect's speculative functions by directing the truth it considers to operation.

46. Recall from part 1 of this book that on Aquinas's account of human rational nature and its capacities in the treatise on happiness, the goods of the intellect and will are universal truth and the universal, perfect good (*ST* IaIIae.2.8).

47. Aquinas often provides summaries of the relationships among the four cardinal virtues in his treatises on particular virtues, hence this text from the treatise on fortitude: "Now the good of reason is the human good, according to Dionysius (*On the Divine Names*, ch. 4). Prudence, since it is a perfection of reason, has that good essentially; while justice is this good enacted, since it belongs to justice to establish the order of reason in all human affairs. The other virtues safeguard this good, insofar as they moderate the passions, so that they do not draw us away from the good of reason. In the order of this last kind [of virtue], fortitude holds first place" (*ST* IIaIIae.123.12).

48. See *ST* IIaIIae.47.6.

49. Aristotle, *Nicomachean Ethics* 6.5; *ST* IIaIIae.50.3.obj 1; see also *ST* IIaIIae.47.2.

50. *ST* IaIIae.62; *ST* IIaIIae.1–46. This is the famous Pauline trio from 1 Corinthians 13, a source Aquinas averts to in *ST* IIaIIae.23.4. *Caritas* (charity) corresponds in Aquinas's Latin to the Greek *agape* (love) in the New Testament reference.

51. *ST* IaIIae.62.2; *ST* IIaIIae.17.6 and 23.4.

52. *ST* IaIIae.62.1, *ST* IaIIae.65.3.

53. *ST* IaIIae.62.2.

54. *ST* IaIIae.62.1 reply and ad 3. This distinction between the "good of reason" as the rule of human acts, and the "Divine Rule" (or divine reason) will be echoed in the treatise on law, where Aquinas distinguishes natural law, which is available to us by our nature as rational beings, from divine law, which is available to us only through revelation. "Moral and intellectual virtues perfect our intellect and appetite properly in relation to a created rule or measure; whereas the theological virtues perfect them properly in relation to an uncreated rule or measure" (*ST* IaIIae.64.4.ad 2). Also, the use of "supernatural" in this book indicates something not attainable by human nature on its own. As we will see later, what is above human nature, for Aquinas, includes things that may also be consonant with it and perfective of it.

55. *ST* IaIIae.63.3.

56. *ST* IaIIae.62.1 reply and ad 3.

57. *ST* IaIIae.62.1 and 62.2; *ST* IaIIae.63.3 reply and ad 1.

58. *ST* IaIIae.61.5.

59. Aquinas takes charity to be a commanding virtue, and the cardinal virtue to be the eliciting virtue for a given act, while Augustine takes the cardinal virtues to be forms of love itself (Augustine, *On the Morals of the Catholic Church* 15.25, Patrologiae Cursus Completus, Series Latina, ed. J. P. Migne, vol. 32:1322).

60. *ST* IaIIae.65.3. See also *ST* IIaIIae.23.4.ad 2.

61. *ST* IaIIae 63.3.ad 2.

62. See Aquinas's defense of otherwise "extreme" actions as lying in the mean of the moral virtues (*ST* IaIIae.64.1.ad 2 and ad 3). The theological virtues do not follow the Aristotelian schema of a mean between two extremes, since it is impossible, for example, to love God too much (*ST* IaIIae.64.4).

63. *ST* IaIIae.62.1, quoting 2 Peter 1:4.

64. *Nicomachean Ethics* 8.3 (1156b5–10); *ST* IIaIIae.23.1.

65. *ST* IaIIae.61.1.ad 2; *ST* IaIIae.62.1.

66. Alasdair MacIntyre memorably illustrates the process of habituation in his analogy of the chess-playing child in *After Virtue,* 2nd ed. (Notre Dame: University of Notre Dame Press, 1984), 188. The child initially plays only for the sake of the candy he is offered, but with the practice that comes from playing repeatedly, he gradually comes to love the game for its own sake.

67. *ST* IaIIae.63.2, emphasis added; see also *ST* IaIIae.63.2–4.

68. *ST* IaIIae.55.4, 63.2. All virtues, infused or acquired, meet the first three necessary conditions in the definition—each is a *habitus* of the soul, ordered to operation, by which we act rightly (as opposed to vices, which dispose us to disordered, or evil, acts). The two types of virtues differ, then, as to their source (divine infusion vs. habituation) and their end (natural or supernatural happiness).

69. *ST* IaIIae.65.2; see also *ST* IaIIae.61.5 and *ST* IIaIIae.23.7.

70. *ST* IaIIae.55.4.ad 6.

71. *ST* IaIIae.51.4.ad 3.

72. *ST* IaIIae.63.4.

73. This is not surprising, as Aquinas was commenting on the *Nicomachean Ethics* at roughly the same time he was writing the ethical part of the *Summa theologiae.*

74. Aquinas defines patience as the ability to endure the sorrow that comes with the loss of some good. While it may be possible, absent grace, to bear the loss of some goods without being overcome by sorrow, this sort of patience does not extend to the loss of all temporal and created goods. Aquinas

thinks true patience must be able to meet this final test, since he has defined virtue as the "limit" or "perfection" (*ultimum*) of a capacity. In this way, his definition of patience is like his characterization of courage, which is defined by its ability to stand firm against the greatest danger—the danger of death. Thus, of patience he writes, "Now the fact that we prefer the good of grace to all natural goods, the loss of which can cause sorrow, is due to charity, by which we love God above all things. Thus it is clear that patience, as a virtue, is caused by charity. . . . But it is also clear that it is impossible to have charity except by grace, according to Romans 5:5, 'The charity of God is poured forth in our hearts by the Holy Spirit Who is given to us.' Therefore it is clear that we cannot have patience without the help of grace" (*ST* IIaIIae.136.3; for perseverance, see *ST* IIaIIae.137.4).

75. Most likely, his fellow Dominicans.

76. It may be helpful here to note that Aquinas's usual pattern in a treatise or series of questions on a given topic is to introduce an idea as simply as possible, often beginning with philosophical or Aristotelian terms, and then to build gradually on that account, complicating it, adding subtle but important distinctions, and incorporating theological concepts and sources. By the time he is done with a topic, his considered and fully developed view may look surprising when compared to what he said first (and even seem to stand in tension with it). Thus he first introduces virtue without the distinctions between infused and acquired forms; mentions later that his discussion so far (the definition of habits and virtues in general) has been about humanly acquired virtues; and proceeds to defend the view that acquired and infused forms of the virtues in fact have different causes and species—a direction one never would have guessed from his first introduction of the topic. Similarly, he begins the treatise on law by defining law as an exterior principle of human action, distinct from a habit or virtue as such, and ends it by declaring the New Law to be the Holy Spirit working in us like an interior habit. For this reason, it is especially important to read Aquinas's texts holistically, to catch the way the first categories or definitions have to be read later, with greater nuance.

77. Given the religious vows of his audience, this also explains the attention he gives to virtues such as fasting and virginity (or celibacy). While it is possible that these virtues might also have an acquired form, they are most naturally understood in their theological form. For more on the reach of acquired virtue, see Bonnie Kent, *Virtues of the Will* (Washington, D.C.: Catholic University of America Press, 1995): 19–34, and Brian Shanley, "Pagan Virtue," *The Thomist* 63 (1999): 553–77.

78. Augustine, *On the Morals of the Catholic Church* XV, quoted in *ST* IIaIIae.123.4.obj 1.

79. *ST* IaIIae.28.6 reply and ad 1. See the further discussion of infused courage in chapter 9.

80. *ST* IIaIIae.23.7; *ST* IaIIae.65.2.

81. *ST* IaIIae.109.2.

82. It is probably best to think of the infused virtues as subjects of the same human capacity as the acquired virtues, but with the capacity enhanced and directed toward an extended and more inclusive end in view. If this life is all that one has in view, for example, temperance would seem to prescribe moderate, healthy eating; but if one's eternal spiritual well-being is in view, then at certain times fasting is more appropriate than eating moderately. It is not that each type of virtue operates independently in a given person, but rather that the acquired virtue gets taken up into the operation of the infused virtue—as nature becomes perfected, not obliterated, by grace. When operating in different persons, however, the two types of virtue could issue in incompatible acts (eating and not eating), which is why Aquinas designates them as different species.

83. *ST* IaIIae.63.2, 68.1.

84. *QDVC* 10.ad 14.

85. See *Nicomachean Ethics* 7.10 (1152a30–35).

86. See, for example, *ST* IaIIae.62.4. For the same reason, Aquinas treats prudence, located in the practical intellect, before the other cardinal virtues, which are located in the rational and sensory appetites.

87. *ST* IIaIIae.4.2.ad 3.

88. Since faith engages the will, why isn't faith, like prudence, in the practical intellect? Aquinas locates it in the theoretical intellect because the truth that faith believes is truth about the person of God—truth sought for its own sake, not for the sake of acting or directing action. Aquinas thinks that knowing the truth about God is itself enough to perfect the intellect, even if this knowledge indirectly shapes our action as well. Theological virtues such as faith are directly concerned with the end, whereas prudence is concerned with directing well that which is for the sake of the end. The *gift* of wisdom, associated with charity (not to be confused with the intellectual virtue, which is not related to the will), also directs our actions well in light of our knowledge of God, and informs both the speculative and practical intellect (*ST* IIaIIae.45.3).

89. *ST* IIaIIae.4.4. Aquinas actually has a rather complicated account of faith. In their incipient forms, faith and hope precede charity, for the good must be apprehended and desired before the will is moved to possess it, but

faith and hope must in turn be informed by charity once one possesses charity. They reach their full form only in that latter state. Note, too, that charity is the only one of the three theological virtues that is not superseded in the next life. Faith gives way to full vision, and hope's desire gives way to the complete and final possession of the good.

90. *ST* IaIIae.3.8.

91. He discusses the antecedent and consequent acts of will involved in happiness in *ST* IaIIae.3–4, but the account overall in the treatise on happiness comes across as highly intellectual (more Aristotelian than Augustinian, to put it another way).

92. *ST* IaIIae.3 and 23.

93. See *ST* IaIIae.28.2.

94. ST IaIIae.67.6.ad 3; quoting *Nicomachean Ethics* 9.5.

95. For a more extended look at this issue, see Michael Sherwin, *By Knowledge and by Love* (Washington, D.C.: Catholic University of America Press, 2005).

96. We refer here only to the state of the present life.

97. *ST* IIaIIae.17.1 and 17.7; *ST* IaIIae.40; *ST* IIaIIae.23.6.ad 3.

98. *ST* IIaIIae.17.1, 4, and 6.ad 3; *ST* IIaIIae.17.7.

99. *Nicomachean Ethics* 3.3; *ST* IaIIae.5.5.ad 1–2. In what sense is God's grace still an exterior principle of human acts, rather than an interior principle? This question is likewise prompted by Aquinas's discussion of the theological virtues in *ST* IaIIae.62.1: "Now we are able to reach the other happiness, which exceeds human nature, only through divine power, according to a certain participation in the divine nature [*divinitatis participationem*], about which it is written (2 Peter 1:4) that by Christ we are made 'partakers [*consortes*] in the divine nature.'" For similar language, see *ST* IIaIIae.23.3.ad 3. This point, as well as the relationships between virtue, law, and grace, will be addressed at the end of chapter 8.

100. *ST* IIaIIae.23.2.ad 3 and 35.2; see also ST IIaIIae.23.1. For descriptions of participated charity, see *ST* IIaIIae.24 and 28.2. The passion of love is treated at *ST* IaIIae.26–28; in question 28 especially, love's effects are described as union, friendship, and mutual indwelling between lovers. (Aquinas takes himself to be following 1 John 4 in this characterization of love, at least in its rational form.)

101. *ST* IIaIIae.24.2.

102. *ST* IaIIae.65.3.

103. *ST* IaIIae.64.4.

104. *ST* IaIIae.65.3.

105. See especially *ST* IaIIae.25 and *ST* IIaIIae.27.4. The most obvious counterevidence against the "unity [or reciprocity] of the virtues" thesis is the phenomenon, well known to most by experience, of otherwise good people with moral blind spots or character flaws: the nurturing mother with an acute anger problem, the devoted pastor with a secret sex addiction. Aquinas acknowledges that our development in various virtues may be uneven; they grow, he says, like the fingers on your hand, not in equal quantities but in proportion to each other (*ST* IaIIae.66.2). (Whether any proportion is possible, he does not say.) We might be better at patience than generosity, but growth in one area will typically be accompanied by growth in others. Our ability to endure suffering and hardship (fortitude and hope), for instance, may enable us to be pained by the sufferings of others and recognize, in that pain, a call to action (mercy and practical wisdom). It may augment our willingness to help those in need, even when that means foregoing our own pursuit of pleasure (justice, charity, and temperance). Progress in virtue is therefore supposed to be a package deal. The flip side of this tenet, for practical purposes, is that our character flaws also have the power to hold us back in areas in which we might otherwise make progress. For example, Aquinas warns of the deleterious effects of pride, laziness, and worry on the operation of prudence. When our ability to see our situation clearly is clouded by fear, or our willingness to take counsel is corrupted by pride, our ability to direct, lead, and act well is compromised in a host of ways. Whatever the plausibility of his case, however, the unity thesis remains an area of controversy.

106. *ST* IaIIae.62.4, *ST* IIaIIae.4.7; see also *ST* IaIIae.17.7–8.

107. *ST* IaIIae.65.3, *ST* IIaIIae.23.8. Like *ST* IaIIae, *ST* IIaIIae begins with questions concerning the ultimate end—in the latter case, the theological virtues, which are directly ordered to God—and then treats the means to it—the virtues indirectly ordered to that end by faith, hope, and charity.

108. *ST* IIaIIae.45.2–3, including the replies to objections.

109. *ST* IaIIae.68.1.

110. *ST* IIaIIae.45.2.

Chapter Eight.   Law and Grace

1. As we will see later, Aquinas's discussion of law also ends with God, since he holds that God the Holy Spirit writes the New Law on our hearts and gives us the grace to act in accordance with that law.

2. *SCG* I.1.1, *ST* IaIIae.91.1.ad 3.

3. *ST* IaIIae.91.1.

4. *ST* IaIIae.prol, *ST* IaIIae.91.2.ad 3.

5. *ST* IaIIae.90.3.

6. *ST* IaIIae.90.4.

7. *ST* IaIIae.91.3.

8. *ST* IaIIae.90.prol.

9. *ST* IaIIae.91.

10. When we speak of "ordering" in this context, we mean to imply the teleological sense of "putting things in their proper order" by "directing them to their ends," in contrast with merely "giving orders."

11. *ST* IaIIae.93.3.ad 2.

12. *ST* IaIIae.91.2, 96.2.

13. *ST* IaIIae.17, *ST* IIaeIIae.47.8. One difference between law and prudential reasoning is the generality of the enterprise. Law is meant to cover what holds generally, while prudence, working from the universal to the particular, applies general principles and precepts to individual cases and situations. There are several special virtues of the intellect and rational appetite devoted to just this task — namely, equity, *synesis,* and *gnome* (see *ST* IIaIIae.120; *ST* IIaIIae.51.3, 4; and *ST* IIaIIae.120).

14. *ST* IaIIae.91.2.

15. The notion is first introduced in Plantinga's *Warrant and Proper Function* (Oxford: Oxford University Press, 1993), chapter 2.

16. *ST* IaIIae.94.2.

17. Aquinas's articulation of the precepts of the natural law is probably the result of his extensive theoretical study, perhaps enhanced further by the light of faith. We need not therefore assume that everything he tells us about the natural law is automatically, innately, or explicitly available to every human being.

18. *ST* IaIIae.91.6, 94.6, 99.2.ad 2.

19. Virtues are therefore necessary for two reasons: not only to perfect and direct our natural inclinations to the good, but also to correct them when our inclinations are disordered.

20. *ST* IaIIae.10.1.

21. *ST* IaIIae.95.2.

22. *ST* IaIIae.96.1.ad 3.

23. *ST* IIaIIae.94.4.

24. *ST* IIaIIae.47.3.ad 2.

25. *ST* IaIIae.96.6; *ST* IIaIIae.51 and 120.

26. *ST* IaIIae.92.1, 96.2–3. Aquinas thinks that the virtue of individuals is partly constitutive of the common good, so the two will not conflict in a case of genuine law.

27. *ST* IaIIae.92.1.ad 2.

28. *ST* IaIIae.92.1.ad 1. Law can only command what virtuous people do (their exterior actions) rather than how they do it (from the right interior disposition or motivation). Nevertheless, Aquinas, like Aristotle, thinks that practicing the right sort of acts can develop and strengthen virtuous habits in us, the way a child learns to be fair and unselfish by being made to share her toys with her playmates. Virtue entails acting not only in a way that conforms to law, but also in a way that integrates our interior sources of motivations, so that our actions are done with wholehearted integrity rather than mere external conformity. Aquinas follows Aristotle in singling out three marks of this sort of action: it is chosen because it is good, done with pleasure, and done reliably because the habit is anchored firmly in one's character. A child who has internalized the virtue of generosity takes pleasure in giving to others, rather than doing so merely out of duty or fear of punishment. This explains Aquinas's concern with the delight attaching to acts of virtue in the *Summa* (e.g., the fruits of the Holy Spirit in *ST* IaIIae.70, charity's effect on the soul in *ST* IIaIIae23.2, and the effect of grace on the operation of courage in *ST* IIaIIae.123.8).

29. *ST* IaIIae.91.4.

30. *ST* IaIIae.109.1, 110.3.

31. *ST* IaIIae.99.2.ad 2.

32. *QDM* 15.2.ad 2–3.

33. This is another example where law commands a minimum of action, while virtue (in this case, chastity) concerns the perfection of action. For a related discussion of the thresholds required by law and virtue, see *ST* IIaIIae.80.

34. *ST* IaIIae.99.2.

35. *ST* IaIIae.107.1.ad 2.

36. See especially *ST* IaIIae.99.2, 99.1.ad 2.

37. In addition to its general moral precepts, the Old Law contains both judicial and ceremonial precepts. The ceremonial precepts regulated worship practices (e.g., sacrifices, ritual purifications) and were meant to prefigure "the mystery of Christ." (Thus the Passover was a sign of Christ's redemptive work on the cross, and is now replaced by the Eucharist.) Since their only function was to point symbolically to Jesus Christ, who is their fulfillment, they no longer apply. (In fact, Aquinas argues that observance of them shows either

ignorance or denial of Christ's identity and work, and as such they *ought* to be avoided.) The judicial precepts regulated human actions with respect to community life and neighbor-to-neighbor relations. As Aquinas notes, these precepts were designed to prepare God's people for the coming of Christ. Thus, they too are no longer binding in their specific determinations, although the general moral precepts they embody still hold. For example, benevolence toward widows, orphans, and the poor is still a moral obligation, although the categories must be widened to cover peoples outside of the Israelite nation and implemented in ways that fit different economies.

38. *ST* IaIIae.108.1.

39. *ST* IaIIae.106: in article 1, Aquinas makes the most explicit connections between law, virtue, and grace. See also *ST* IaIIae.107.1.

40. *ST* IaIIae.108.1.ad 2.

41. *ST* IIaIIae.19.

42. *ST* IaIIae.108.3.

43. Found in the Sermon on the Mount (Matt. 5–7). In taking Jesus' teachings here as the *locus classicus* of the new law, Aquinas is following Augustine.

44. *ST* IaIIae.107.2, 108.3.

45. *ST* IaIIae.98.1.

46. *ST* IaIIae.108.3.

47. The treatise on law is found at *ST* IaIIae.91–108.

48. This contrasts with the extensive and detailed effort he devotes, for example, to explaining the significance of the ceremonial precepts of the Old Law as prefiguring the mystery of Christ's life and work. Aquinas's own emphasis, then, would lead us to focus attention on the divine law.

49. Certain considerations may explain the tendency to treat the natural law as the center of Aquinas's ethics and deliberately separate law from its theological and ethical context. For example, one might want to consider Aquinas's work from a strictly philosophical point of view—one available to "all rational persons" irrespective of religious persuasion—for the sake of gaining a hearing in certain professional circles. Or one has an apologetic intention and must address audiences who do not share Aquinas's theological commitments. Our contention here is that this approach, given that it must artificially set aside the relationship between natural law and the other types of law—eternal and divine and New—is less fruitful *for understanding Aquinas* than the one we take.

50. Similarly, Aquinas describes prudence as an imitation of divine providence (*ST* IIaIIae.49.6.ad 1). This does not imply that all knowledge of the natural law or its application through prudence requires divine revelation.

51. See *ST* IaIIae.101–3.

52. See Leonard E. Boyle, O.P., "The Setting of the Summa Theologiae of St. Thomas—Revisited," in *The Ethics of Aquinas,* ed. Stephen J. Pope (Washington, D.C.: Georgetown University Press, 2002), 10–11.

53. That does not yet explain the near complete neglect of virtue by twentieth-century philosophical readers of Aquinas, nor an emphasis on natural over divine law, however.

54. For a more detailed and nuanced account, see Bonnie Kent, *Virtues of the Will: The Transformation of Ethics in the Late Thirteenth Century* (Washington, D.C.: Catholic University of America Press, 1995).

55. For one account of this shift, see Servais Pinckaers, *The Sources of Christian Ethics* (Washington, D.C.: Catholic University of America Press, 1995).

56. *ST* IaIIae.28.6.

57. See *ST* IaIIae.28.5. The literature on Aquinas's famous list of inclinations and the prescriptions of law that express them in rational nature is voluminous. Its most famous recent proponents are Germain Grisez (*Christian Moral Principles* [Notre Dame: University of Notre Dame Press, 1983]) and John Finnis (*Natural Law and Natural Rights* [Oxford: Clarendon Press, 1980]). See also Ralph McInerny, *Ethica Thomistica: The Moral Philosophy of Thomas Aquinas* (Washington, D.C.: Catholic University of America Press, 1982), and Kevin Flannery, S.J., *Acts Amid Precepts: The Aristotelian Logical Structure of Thomas Aquinas's Moral Theory* (Washington, D.C.: Catholic University of America Press, 2001), for representative treatments of Aquinas's ethics that center attention almost exclusively on law and individual actions. A notable exception to this interpretation of Aquinas is the anthology of essays on the virtues edited by Stephen Pope, *The Ethics of Aquinas,* already cited.

How optimistic is Aquinas himself about our ability to know what the law commands and to read this off of human nature? One might reasonably wonder how much of what is "written on our nature" in the natural law is discernible, to Aquinas, without the correcting and illuminating "light of faith," informed by a thorough study of Scripture. That is, how much of what Aquinas says about the substance of the natural law is informed by his position as a theologian, a member of a contemplative religious order, and a Scripture scholar, and how much would be available to unbelievers or those unacquainted with special revelation?

58. See *ST* IaIIae.99.1 reply and ad 2.

59. The whole structure of the *Summa,* tracing the movement of created things back to God, and in particular the rational creature's return to

God via the perfection of its capacities of intellect and will, is a reflection of that theme.

60. Aquinas describes the theological virtues as parallel "first principles" or fundamental inclinations of our graced nature, directing us to our supernatural end. See *ST* IaIIae.62.3. But even in the realm of natural acts, the virtues perfect our natural inclinations into stable and enduring dispositions that reliably lead to virtuous action.

61. *ST* IaIIae.65.3, *ST* IaIIae.99.1.ad 2, *ST* IIaIIae.44.1.

62. *ST* IaIIae.99.2. This quotation is found within the treatise on law— further evidence in favor of our integrationist interpretation.

63. *ST* IaIIae 99.2.ad 3.

64. *ST* IaIIae.55.2.

65. *ST* IaIIae.98.1.

66. See, for example, *ST* IaIIae.99.2.ad 2.

67. *ST* IIaIIae.23.2.

68. *ST* IaIIae.108.1.

69. *ST* IaIIae.108.1.ad 2.

70. Analogously, to stop with the Old Law would be to fail to recognize that its entire purpose was to prepare us for and prefigure the person and work of Christ.

71. *Nicomachean Ethics* 7.10 (1152a30–35).

72. *ST* IaIIae.62.1, *ST* IaIIae.110.2 reply and ad 2; see also *ST* IIaIIae.23.2 and 24.2–3.

73. *ST* IaIIae.108.1.ad 2.

74. *ST* IaIIae 113.10, quoting Augustine.

75. *ST* IaIIae.2.8, 5.1.

76. See, for example, *ST* IaIIae.112.

77. To put it even more starkly, Aquinas's conception of moral formation and its goal is Trinitarian: The grace that perfects human nature is given through the saving work of Jesus Christ, who is not only divine but also a perfect human being (see prologue to *ST* IIIa), and the interior work of the Holy Spirit (in charity and the other infused virtues, the New Law, and the gifts), in order to bring us into union with God the Father.

78. See, for example, the explanation of how we can attain the happiness we are made for in *ST* IaIIae.5.5.ad 1. Like Aquinas's definition of the virtue of charity, this is an interesting integration of Aristotelian friendship with an Augustinian notion of grace.

79. Aquinas also makes this point when discussing the infusion of charity in the will: *ST* IIaIIae.23.2.

80. *ST* IaIIae.111.2 and 112.2, *ST* IIaIIae.24.3.

81. Interestingly, Aquinas uses the Aristotelian distinction between habit and act to add divine agency to the moral life while leaving room for human agency.

In addition to the infused virtues, Aquinas also thinks that grace comes in the form of gifts (which are superadded to the virtues as dispositions making us amenable to being immediately moved by God, beyond what we are capable of through infused virtue); the beatitudes (the most perfect acts associated with the gifts); and fruits of the Holy Spirit (the delight in these perfect acts as means to our last end) (*ST* IaIIae.68–70).

We should note, however, that it would be misleading to think of the relationship of divine and human agency as breaking too cleanly into two separate moments or activities. In fact, the blend of the two is much more intimate, since nothing happens (including human action) without God's conservation.

82. *ST* IIaIIae.24.12.

83. *ST* IaIIae.110.3.ad 3.

84. *ST* IaIIae.49.prol and 90.prol.

85. Aquinas says that the devil is a rival exterior principle, prompting evil acts that thwart that good (*ST* IaIIae.90.prol, cf. *ST* Ia.114).

86. *ST* IaIIae.61.5.

87. *ST* IaIIae.51.4, *ST* IaIIae.55.4, *ST* IIaIIae.23.2–3, *ST* IaIIae.108.2.ad 2, *ST* IaIIae.110.3 reply and ad 3.

88. In most cases. See *ST* IIaIIae.24.4–7.

89. *ST* IaIIae.55.4.obj 1, emphasis added.

90. *ST* IaIIae.93.6.

91. *ST* IaIIae.109.1. Like the first principle of the natural law, there are parts of our nature that are not and indeed cannot be lost, even in the face of original sin (*QDV* 15.1–2).

92. *ST* IaIIae.108.1.ad 2.

93. *ST* IaIIae.106.2.

94. *ST* IIaIIae.23.2 and 45.5.ad 3; see also *ST* IaIIae.68.3 and 110.2.

95. *ST* IIaIIae.23.3, *ST* IaIIae.109.

96. While Aristotle makes formation in virtue a community rather than an individual effort, he still keeps it firmly in the realm of human effort (and natural contingency).

97. Aquinas is concerned to safeguard human freedom even in the face of grace. A first-time reader might find his assertions about the way divine

and human action coincide puzzling (see for example, *ST* IaIIae.113.3 and *ST* IIaIIae.23.2). Aquinas's views on this difficult topic cannot be explored in detail here. The reader should note that Aquinas takes God's causal agency to be compatible with human free action, whether grace is an additional complicating factor or not.

98. *ST* IIaIIae.24.3 reply and ad 1.

99. *ST* IIaIIae.24.11–12.

100. *ST* IIaIIae.23.2.

Chapter Nine.   Theologically Transformed Virtue and Vice

1. *ST* IIaIIae.23.1.

2. *ST* IaIIae.99.2.

3. *ST* IIaIIae.23.1.

4. From Evagrius in Egypt, the idea of the capital vices made its way into monastic circles in Europe through the *Institutes* of John Cassian (360–430 A.D.), Evagrius's disciple. The traditional seven were taken up and given weighty authority by Pope Gregory the Great (540–604 A.D.) in his *Moralia on Job,* a source on which Aquinas relies heavily in his discussion of the vices. For more on the capital vices, see chapter 1 in Rebecca Konyndyk De-Young, *Glittering Vices* (Grand Rapids, Mich.: Brazos Press, 2009); for more on the history of sloth, see DeYoung, "The Vice of Sloth: Some Historical Reflections on Laziness, Effort, and Resistance to the Demands of Love," *The Other Journal* 10 (Fall 2007), www.theotherjournal.com.

5. Or *tristitia; QDM* 11.1.resp.

6. *ST* IIaIIae.35.1.

7. It is fascinating in our own day to observe the puzzlement that attends the inclusion of sloth in the list of the seven deadly sins. Not only has the description "deadly" lost its theological meaning—it originally indicated the distinction between mortal and venial sin—but it has come to mean something like "really serious" or "especially evil." But also, in the absence of a theologically informed account of sloth, this vice has been reduced to mere laziness at best, and at worst, apathetic neglect of one's work. For laziness to count as one of the "really serious" sins presupposes that work itself has become glorified or of quasi-sacred value. This view, however, seems to fit a secular view of life that has little or no use for the concept of sin. See DeYoung, "The Vice of Sloth" and the chapter on sloth in *Glittering Vices.*

8. After we receive charity, it can still increase. When this happens, "God increases charity: that is, he makes charity inhere more greatly in us, and the soul more perfectly participate in the likeness of the Holy Spirit" (*ST* IIaIIae.24.5.ad 3).

9. *ST* IaIIae.65.6. "Charity signifies not only the love of God, but also a certain friendship with God, which also adds to love a certain mutual return of love, together with mutual communion [*communicatione*]. . . . Now this fellowship [*societas*] of human beings with God . . . begins in this present life, by grace, but will be perfected in the future life, through glory."

10. *ST* IIaIIae.23–24. In the next section on the virtue of courage we observe what happens to moral virtues when they are informed by charity.

11. *ST* IIaIIae.35. For a further defense of this interpretation, see DeYoung, "Resistance to the Demands of Love: Aquinas on *Acedia*," *The Thomist* 68:2 (April 2004): 173–204.

12. *QDM* 11.4. He also refers to it as sorrow over a "spiritual and divine good" in *ST* IIaIIae.35 and elsewhere in *QDM* 9.

13. He makes this distinction explicitly in *QDM* 11.1.resp. We use "sorrow" to translate *tristitia* in order to track Aquinas's acknowledgment of the traditional use of *tristitia* to name a capital vice. He uses *dolor* and *tristitia* interchangeably in the treatise on the passions.

14. *ST* IaIIae.10.2.

15. *QDM* 11.2. ·

16. *ST* IIaIIae.35.3, *QDM* 9.2; the Scripture Aquinas quotes is Galatians 5:17.

17. *ST* IIaIIae.35.2.

18. See Aquinas's commentary on the book of Ephesians (also authored by the apostle Paul), chapter 4, lecture 7.

19. This is the sort of struggle found in Augustine's account of his conversion in *Confessions,* bk. 8. The struggle with sloth, however, plagues those who already have charity—and in Augustine's case, it is not clear he was yet in possession of charity, since this episode precedes both his final conversion and baptism.

20. This is strong evidence that the eudaimonistic structure of Aquinas's ethics does not mean that the moral life consists in seeking the perfection of one's nature in a selfish or egotistical manner.

21. *ST* IIaIIae.35.3.ad 1.

22. *Beatitudo* is the Latin equivalent in Aquinas of Aristotelian *eudaimonia*.

23. Aquinas uses the term "capital vices" for the seven instead of "deadly sins" because he argues that not all of the capital vices ensue in mortal (i.e., deadly) sins. Sometimes they produce acts that are venial sins. He takes the Latin root *caput* (meaning "head") not to indicate that these vices earn us "capital" punishment (death) as mortal sins, but rather to define them as a prolific source, principle, or "fountainhead" of other vices. Thus he accepts Gregory the Great's list of offspring vices for each of the principal seven. See his treatment of the topic in *QDM* 8–15.

24. *ST* Ia.2.prol.

25. Aquinas, as a Dominican, would have understood moral formation and spiritual growth in virtue in terms of the imitation of Christ's character. He describes Christ in the third main part of the *Summa* as the one in whom human nature was perfected and perfectly united to God. The Pauline injunction to put off the sinful nature and put on the new self is also often explicitly cast in terms of the imitation of Christ (Eph. 5:1). See Nicholas M. Healy, *Thomas Aquinas: Theologian of the Christian Life* (Aldershot, U.K.: Ashgate, 2003), chapter 2.

26. For an extended discussion of Aquinas's transformation of Aristotelian courage, see Rebecca Konyndyk DeYoung, "Power Made Perfect in Weakness: Aquinas's Transformation of the Virtue of Courage," *Medieval Philosophy and Theology* 11:2 (2003): 147–80.

27. *ST* IIaIIae.123–24.

28. *ST* IIaIae.124.3, emphasis added. His mention here of faith and charity as virtues to which courage is directed is not accidental, as we will see later.

29. *ST* IIaIIae.124.2.ad 1, emphasis added.

30. *ST* IIaIIae.123.4.ad 2.

31. *ST* IaIIae.27.4. "The reason is that every other passion of the soul implies either movement towards something or rest in something. Now every movement . . . arises from some suitability [*connaturalitate*] or aptness to that thing; and this belongs to the definition [*rationem*] of love."

32. *ST* IIaIIae.124.3.

33. Quoted in *ST* IIaIIae.123.4.obj 1.

34. *ST* IIaIIae.123.3.

35. *ST* IIaIIae.123.6.

36. *ST* IaIIae.94.2.

37. The relevant passage in the treatise on the passion is found at *ST* IaIIae.22–28.

38. See *ST* IaIIae.40–45.

39. Passions are defined as inclinations in the sensory appetite *toward* good or *away from* evil.

40. Josef Pieper, *The Four Cardinal Virtues* (Notre Dame: University of Notre Dame Press, 1980), 128. Aquinas probably has a scriptural example in mind, too. Paul shows this kind of courage in the New Testament when he tells of his own unsuccessful struggle to overcome his "thorn in the flesh" and of Christ's answer to his pleas to free Paul from this difficulty: "My grace is sufficient for you, for power is made perfect in weakness" (1 Cor. 12:7–10 NRSV).

41. Aristotle adds "in combat" to the definition of fortitude to exclude cases in which one is accidentally imperiled. This fits his definition of virtue as being deliberately chosen and willed for its own sake.

42. *ST* IIaIIae.124.

43. *ST* IIaIIae.124.5 reply and ad 2.

44. Aquinas quotes John 15:13 in *ST* IIaIIae.124.3—"Greater love has no one than this, that one lay down one's life for one's friends"—to make the point that Christ is the premier example of courage rooted in love. So the martyr's imitation of Christ enables her to bear witness not only to the truth of faith but also to the Truth who is Christ (John 14:9).

45. *ST* IIaIIae.124.2.ad 2. This quote is evidence of Aquinas's more general claim in *ST* IIaIIae.23.8 reply and ad 3 that charity is the form and final cause of all the other virtues, and thus the *sine qua non* of the ethical life.

46. Reading the treatise on courage and especially the case of martyrdom in light of what Aquinas says about the theological virtue of hope and its relation to the gift of filial fear (*ST* IIaIIae.19.9) further reinforces the connections between this cardinal virtue, the gifts of the Holy Spirit (grace), and charity.

47. *ST* IIaIIae.123.8; see also *ST* IIaIIae.23.2.

48. *ST* IaIIa.45.3, *ST* IIaIIae.17.1 reply and ad 5.

index

abilities
  to act, 6, 119–20
  rational, 5, 88
actions, 206n.33
  bad, 70, 90–190
  deliberate, 71
  freedom of, 115–23, 214n.22
  good, 9, 90–93, 115
  human, 5–9, 13, 15, 36, 39, 62, 69–110,
    130, 136, 154–55, 166, 169–72, 175
  morally neutral, 88, 90–93
  rational, 25–26, 96, 132
actuality, 8, 15–28, 44, 47, 50, 63, 132
  pure, 8, 15–20, 50, 59, 192n.16
actualizing, 6, 25–26, 32, 48, 50–51, 57,
  65–66, 132, 140, 167, 178
agency
  divine, 9, 112, 130, 141–49, 153,
    166–72, 177
  human, 84–89, 92–123, 130, 144–49,
    166–72
animals, rational, 4–6, 8, 13, 16, 26, 48,
  64, 135, 154, 183, 187
appetites, 133, 138. *See also* powers
  rational, 28, 62, 71, 115, 117, 133, 138,
    140, 148, 178, 182
  sensory, 62, 86, 102–4, 133, 135–36,
    178–79, 182, 187

Aristotle
  agreement with, 3–7, 16, 24, 34, 41, 46,
    52, 86, 129, 140, 174–75, 177, 180–84
  concept of happiness, 3, 6, 47, 149
  contrast to, 3–4, 6–7, 47–48, 144–46,
    149–50, 169, 171, 175, 180–81, 187
  definition of courage, 185–87
  definition of virtue, 132
  eudaimonistic ethical structure,
    175–76, 178, 180
  friendship, 9, 143, 148, 176, 180, 186
  function argument for human
    happiness, 4–7
  habituation, 143
  happiness, 3–4, 6
  human function, 5–6, 47
  metaphysics, 5, 33, 167, 178
  model of form and matter, 82
  moral life, 4, 171
  Nichomachean Ethics, 3–6, 145, 164,
    166
  organizing virtues and vices, 138,
    149–50, 176, 185
  passions, 146, 175–77, 181–83
  reason, 4
  "second nature," 166
  species, 16
  virtue, 5–6

Augustine
    definition of courage, 145
    definition of fortitude, 182
    definition of virtue, 132, 142, 144, 169
    New Law, 170

beatific vision, 75–76, 147–48, 157,
        205n.18
being, 22, 59, 61–66, 163. *See also*
        existence
    God's, 19, 22
    hierarchy of, 13–27, 29, 31, 46–47, 134,
        191n.6
beings
    created, 6, 15
    human, 13, 28–29, 33–38, 43–45,
        50–54, 171, 187–89
    immaterial, 13–14, 20–24, 29, 42, 46,
        50, 193n.27
    intellective, 17, 21, 28–29, 50–51
    material, 13–14, 20–29, 35, 46, 50
    rational, 7, 15, 117, 135, 167, 170,
        181–83
    teleological, 6, 132
body, 29–45, 70
Boethius, 43

capacities, 16–17. *See also* powers
    appetitive, 55, 65, 71, 98, 113, 138
    human, 7–9, 40, 48, 51, 53, 60–69, 91,
        133, 163–67, 171–72, 187–89
    of intellect, 48, 117–23, 133, 137
    natural, 16, 25, 63–64, 73, 112, 132
    ordering of, 16–21, 38, 57–59
    rational, 5–6, 13, 28, 36, 45, 55–63, 70,
        76, 83, 88, 103, 112, 115–23, 129,
        131–39, 173, 182, 189
    sets of, 17, 53
    of the soul, 40–45, 47–49, 51, 63–66

causation
    causal determinism, 123–24
    efficient, 120
    final, 120
charity, 9, 76, 134, 141–51, 157, 160–64,
        168–81, 186, 234n.9
    definition of, 149
choice, 6, 74, 77–85, 91, 107, 118–23,
        215n.40
circumstances, 92–93
cognition, 7, 17, 31–41, 53, 57, 60, 70, 82,
        91, 108, 115–17
composite, 19–20, 26, 33, 36, 38–39
consent, 80–81, 177
consequences, 93–95
contemplation, 3, 76–77, 150
Convertibility Thesis, 24
courage, 136, 144–45, 181–87
Creator, 6–7, 14–15, 20, 26, 48

deliberate wrongdoing. *See* sin, of will
deliberation. *See* choice; intellect, process
        of deliberation
Descartes, 30, 39
determinists, 123–24
devil/Satan, 98, 105
Dominican Order, 2–3

ends, 92, 115–16, 119, 132–34, 140, 142,
        148, 151, 174, 180
    practical, 2–3, 140
    ultimate, 3–4, 7, 9, 15, 50, 57, 73–89,
        91, 95–97, 112, 132–34, 140–46,
        149–50, 162–64, 166–68, 171,
        177–78, 187, 205.n.13
essence, 22–25, 49, 64, 78
ethics, practical goal of, 3
evil, 64, 105, 135–36
excellence, 5–7, 132

existence, 23–26, 44, 59, 61–63
  actualized, 19
  participated, 16

first cause, 14, 60, 63
first mover, 74
fittingness, 77
flourishing, 142
  failure of, 7, 65
  human, 2, 4, 8–9, 13, 15, 46, 48, 57,
    62–63, 91, 124, 132–35, 140–41, 145,
    149, 168, 188–89
form, 8, 21–27, 33–37, 45–47, 82, 129,
  142
  substantial form, 27–28, 33–34,
    36–40, 42, 44, 49, 52, 199n.37
  unicity of substantial form, 38–39
formation
  habit, 106–8
  intellectual, 2
  moral, 3–4, 9, 135–37, 159, 168, 174,
    231n.77
free will. See will, free
freedom, 9, 109, 115–24, 166–68,
  171–72
friendship with God, 143, 148–49, 157,
  163–64, 175–77, 179–81
function, 5–6, 25, 49, 64, 133, 194n.38
  human, 5–6, 28, 32, 46–47, 64, 111
  of wisdom, 15
function argument, 4–7

good/goodness, 24–26, 48, 60–66,
  70–72, 86–87, 121, 132–40, 146,
  152, 156, 163–64, 182, 184
  definition of, 66
  moral, 93–94
  ordering of, 134–36, 140
  rational, 139

grace, 9, 15, 51, 77, 112, 125, 130–31,
  142–57, 162–72, 186–88
  cooperative and operative, 167–68

habits, 78, 89–90, 96, 106–15, 124,
  131–32, 144, 146, 152, 164–65, 177
  appetitive, 113
  infused, 112–13, 131–32, 158, 165–66,
    168–70, 174, 177
  intellectual, 113
habituation, 156
happiness, 1–4, 6–8, 13, 43, 47, 50, 59,
  74–77, 132, 143, 147–49, 173–78,
  180–81, 189, 190n.4, 216n.1
  definition of, 75
hierarchy of being. See being,
  hierarchy of

ignorance, 7, 98–103, 113, 168. See also
  sin, of intellect
image of God, 4, 6–8, 15, 28, 43, 45,
  47–48, 166–67, 173
immortality, 35, 42
intellect, 6–9, 22–23, 28–29, 31–32, 34,
  40–41, 45, 48, 52, 57–66, 70–72,
  75–91
  freedom of, 117–23
  immaterial, 8, 13, 23, 41
  intellective powers. See powers,
    intellective
  intellective virtues. See virtues,
    intellective
  interaction with the will, 8, 57–63,
    70–85, 97–103, 106–8, 111, 117–24,
    147
  nature of, 60
  object of, 61
  process of deliberation, 76–85, 88,
    118–23, 140

knowledge, 30, 59–60, 98–102, 147,
194n.33

law, 9, 130, 152–65, 170–75, 187
definition of, 153
divine, 157–65
—New, 158–59, 161, 168, 170, 173, 188
—Old, 158–59, 161, 228n.37
eternal, 151, 153
natural, 15, 125, 130–31, 153–65, 168,
170, 183, 188
libertarians, 124
love, 7, 17, 59–60, 135, 137, 142, 145–50,
158, 163–65, 177, 182–83, 187

matter, 8, 19–29, 33–36, 38–47, 82, 129
compositional, 37
ensouled, 37, 39
functional, 37
prime, 8, 15, 18–21, 36–37, 39,
193n.23
metaphysical parts, 27
moral
appraisal, 9, 85, 90–112, 124, 140
failure, 64–66
life, 26, 28, 48, 60, 133, 136, 138, 162–65
responsibility, 66, 88–89
motivation, 69–89

nature, 154
divine, 15, 143, 149, 162, 167, 177, 180
human, 2–6, 13, 15, 26–45, 50–66,
132–33, 149, 154–55, 161–67, 172,
177–81, 187–89
rational, 43–45, 163, 170, 173
Nichomachean Ethics. See Aristotle,
Nichomachean Ethics

order, 15, 17–18

passions, 85–89, 102–6, 113, 118, 135–36,
146–47, 174–77, 181–84, 187,
236n.39
effects of, 85–89
perfection, 7, 9, 17–19, 63, 73–76, 121,
132, 136–37, 141–48, 161–64, 171,
173, 182, 217n.9
of a power (capacity), 110, 131, 134–35,
137
phantasms, 34–35, 40
physicality, 8
Plato, 30, 40
potentiality, 8, 15–28, 31, 34, 36, 63, 132
powers
to act, 6
appetitive, 49, 55, 85–86
— concupiscible, and irascible, 55–56,
58, 86, 138–40, 182–84
cogitative, 54, 61
cognitive, 122
estimative, 54, 91
intellective, 17, 20–23, 27, 40, 49–51,
60, 118, 122–23, 137, 153–54
locomotive, 49, 55
nutritive (vegetative), 17–18, 21, 38,
40–41, 49, 53, 55–56, 58, 64–65,
111, 218n.14
rational, 7, 178
sensory, 17–18, 21, 31–35, 49, 53–56,
59, 64–65, 70, 97–98, 102, 104, 107,
111, 133, 135–39, 178
preferences, disordered, 106–9, 114
prime matter. *See* matter, prime
principles, exterior and interior, 169–71
prudence, 137–41, 148, 154

rational
actions. *See* actions, rational
animals. *See* animals, rational

appetites. *See* appetites, rational
capacities. *See* capacities, rational
nature. *See* nature, rational
powers. *See* powers, rational
soul. *See* soul, rational
rationality, 4, 36, 38, 44–45, 91, 97, 115, 129
reason, 91, 112–13, 118, 136, 139–40, 153
  divine, 142
  inadequacy of, 156–57
  order of, 135
  particular, 54
  practical, 61, 70, 132, 137
  theoretical, 61, 70, 137
relationship to God, 47–49. *See also*
  friendship with God
resurrection of the body, 32, 40–43,
  196n.17, 197n.21

senses, external and internal, 53–55
sensory
  appetites. *See* appetites, sensory; sin, of
    passions
  memory, 54–55
  powers. *See* powers, sensory
simplicity, 19, 23
sin, 96–114, 135–36, 155, 164, 168, 175, 180
  of intellect (ignorance), 97–103. *See*
    also ignorance
  origin of, 104, 108
  of passions (sensory appetite), 96–98,
    102–4, 211n.34, 212n.44
  of will (deliberate wrongdoing),
    97–98, 104–9, 114
sloth, 175–81, 233n.7
soul, 27–43, 49, 70, 75, 116, 166–67,
  182–83, 199n.39
  activity of, 32, 34
  rational, 19, 27, 30–42, 45, 49, 51–52
  structure of, 139

species, 14, 16, 21, 26, 33, 35, 37–39, 45,
  63, 92, 144, 150
style of argumentation, 1
substance dualism, 28, 32, 40, 42
substances. *See* beings
Supreme Good, 77
synthesis of Aristotle with Christian
  belief, 4–7

teleological beings. *See* beings,
  teleological
truth, 133, 137–38, 147–48, 186

ultimate end. *See* ends, ultimate
unhappiness, 7–8
union with God, 9, 50, 112, 141, 147–48,
  150, 164, 168–69, 173, 177, 180–81

Van Steenberghen, Fernand, 39
vices, 96, 112–13, 175–81
  capital, 176, 180, 235n.23
  organization of, 138, 176, 179
virtues, 9, 15, 112–13, 130–51, 166–75,
  181–87, 224n.82, 228n.28
  acquired, 143–47, 157
  cardinal, 138–42, 145, 148, 150,
    175–76, 181, 186–87, 220n.43
  definition of, 131–37
  function (goal) of, 133, 159
  infused, 143–47, 149–51, 157, 168–76.
    See also grace
  intellective, 137, 147
  moral, 137–51, 169
  organization of, 138, 142, 147, 149–51
  theological, 141–43, 145–51, 158, 175,
    177, 181, 186–87
  unity of, 149–50, 226n.105
voluntariness. *See* actions, freedom of;
  freedom; will, free

will, 6–9, 22, 28, 45, 48, 52, 57–66,
    104–8, 111, 115, 117–23. *See also*
    appetites, rational
  deliberate, 71, 78–88, 104–9, 114,
    118–20, 177–78
  free, 26, 117–23, 167, 171–72
  goal of, 72

  interaction with the intellect, 8, 57–63,
    70–85, 97–103, 106–8, 111, 117–24,
    147
  nature of, 62
  rectitude of, 76
wisdom, 132, 137–38, 142, 147, 150–52, 175
  function of, 15

Rebecca Konyndyk DeYoung
is associate professor of philosophy at Calvin College.

Colleen McCluskey
is associate professor of philosophy at Saint Louis University.

Christina Van Dyke
is assistant professor of philosophy at Calvin College.